Civil Rights Chronicle

Civil Rights Chronicle

Letters from the South

by Clarice T. Campbell

Foreword by John Dittmer

University Press of Mississippi *Jackson*

Manufactured in the United States of America
00 99 98 97 4 3 2 1
The paper in this book meets the guidelines for permanence and durability of the Committee on Production Guidelines for Book Longevity of the Council on Library Resources.

Library of Congress Cataloging-in-Publication Data

Campbell, Clarice T.
Civil rights chronicle : letters from the South / by Clarice T. Campbell : foreword by John Dittmer.
p. cm.
Includes index.
ISBN 0-87805-952-0 (alk. paper). — ISBN 0-87805-953-9 (pbk. : alk. paper)
1. Campbell, Clarice T.—Correspondence. 2. Afro-American women civil rights workers—Southern States—Correspondence. 3. Civil rights workers—Southern States—Correspondence. 4. Civil rights movements—Southern States—History—20th century—Sources. 5. Universities and colleges, Black—Southern States—History—20th century—Sources. 6. Southern States—Politics and government—1951– —Sources. I. Title.
E.185.615.C29 1997
323.1'196073—dc20 96-17995
CIP

British Library Cataloging-in-Publication data available

To those who passed on the torch of learning during years when teaching an African American was either illegal or starved of funds

Contents

Foreword

I first met Clarice Campbell in 1968, when I was a first-year history professor at Tougaloo College. Clarice was attending the University of Mississippi, completing work on her doctoral dissertation, later published as *Mississippi: The View from Tougaloo.* She had taught history at Tougaloo for two years in the mid-1960s, and of course I had heard of her. In many ways Clarice seemed to fit the stereotype of the northern white "missionaries" who came south to teach in schools like Tougaloo after the Civil War. Older than most of us on the faculty (she was now past 60!), Clarice had been a life-long Republican, and upon first glance she struck you (to use her words) as "a sweet little grandmother."

Well, not exactly! The same person who could support Richard Nixon in the 1960 election would also become an active board member of the Southern Conference Educational Fund (SCEF), one of the most militant (and red-baited) human rights organizations in the 1950s and 1960s. Wherever she taught in the South, Clarice brought with her strong religious principles, which she acted out daily in a variety of settings, many of them uncomfortable, to say the least.

Clarice was no newcomer to the South. A native of California, she spent the summer of 1956 at Ole Miss, where she took an American history course from Jim Silver and discussed the racial politics of ping-pong with Will Campbell. (Her own struggle to establish coeducational ping-pong at Rust College is a hilarious story that also illustrates her tenaciousness and sense of purpose. Her adversary, the business manager at Rust, was simply out of his league!)

The bulk of the correspondence in this magnificent book deals with Clarice Campbell's years as a history professor at three historically black Southern colleges: Rust, Claflin, and Tougaloo. Here she gives the reader a participant's view of the rewards and frustrations of teaching students who came from underfunded, overcrowded segregated public schools. A caring yet no-nonsense teacher, she chronicles her failures with students as well as the success stories, and provides valuable insights into the precarious position of Southern black colleges, especially when a school's students and faculty became active in the civil rights movement.

That struggle is at the heart of Clarice Campbell's journey through the South in the late 1950s and 1960s. As her letters indicate, she was an active participant in the black freedom movement, challenging Jim Crow wherever she went, often to the discomfort of her friends and colleagues as well as her segregationist opponents. As a professor at Rust College in 1960–1961, she was working in the state when the sit-ins and freedom rides created the cadre of young "outside agitators" who, working with local people in communities across the state, would change the face of Mississippi—and the nation.

Tougaloo College was a center of civil rights activities in the mid-1960s. *Civil Rights Chronicle* provides us with an insider's view of the campaign waged by students and faculty to desegregate white churches, restaurants, theaters, and other places of public accommodations before and after passage of the Civil Rights Act of 1964. Professor Campbell was clearly in her element at Tougaloo and was exhilarated by the experience ("What have I ever done to deserve this delightful place?"). She also gives us a glimpse of the political machinations surrounding the forced retirement of Tougaloo president Dan Beittel, whose civil rights advocacy alienated several of the school's influential constituencies.

Civil Rights Chronicle is an extraordinarily valuable book for both scholars and general readers. Professor Campbell's prose is a joy to read. She writes beautifully, and with insight. Given the serious nature of the subject, this is at times a funny book. Clarice has a marvelous sense of humor, which she often directs at herself. For example, in 1962 she took a trip with an integrated group, which attempted to desegregate restaurants along the way: "For the noon meal we stopped at the best hotel. . . . We feel safer always in a place of quality where they are likely to have good manners. If we are to be thrown out, we want it to be done with dignity."

Her sharp eye for detail is matched by her insatiable curiosity. When she and her mother were in Montgomery, Alabama, in 1957, they stopped by Dexter Avenue Baptist Church to hear the young Dr. Martin Luther King, Jr., preach, then introduced themselves afterward and visited at the Kings' home. Throughout the book we run across men and women who were key figures in the civil rights movement. Clarice is no name dropper, but she does tell us about her encounters and work with movement people more visible than she.

We are fortunate that Clarice Campbell was an inveterate letter writer, that she preserved her correspondence, and that she combines the best qualities of both journalist and historian. More than that, we are inspired by her example, a person acting on moral principle at a time when acts of quiet courage usually went unnoticed. Although this book ends in 1965, Clarice has continued to be active in the battle for human rights for the past three decades. As she approaches her ninetieth birthday, may we look forward to a sequel?

John Dittmer

Preface

"Nothing has changed!" In the past, I heard this refrain from young African American students. I attributed such ignorance to their having been born too late to know what life, especially in the South, was like during the pre-1960s. But now I hear this refrain from some who were themselves involved in the Civil Rights Movement of the '60s. And I ask, does it mean nothing that today African Americans have access to education, public accommodations, and the ballot, the same as do European Americans? These are powerful tools which every American today can use to bring about continued advancement.

Anyone who says "nothing has changed" must have forgotten or never have known the daily indignities, not to mention the powerless position of blacks in our Southern culture before the 1960s. It may be that many did not realize how circumscribed their lives were, having expected no more. But an outsider could be shocked at just the indignities, let alone actual deprivations endured by African Americans.

Unable to give you a videotape of "This is your life in the pre-1960s," I offer you *Civil Rights Chronicle: Letters from the South*, which registers my reactions as an outsider to what I saw and experienced as I lived four school years with African Americans in Mississippi and South Carolina colleges.

"Why did you come to Mississippi?" How many times I have been asked that question!

I spent my early adult life as the mother of three children and as a bookkeeper. At forty-five I completed my college education, which had been interrupted by marriage, and became a school teacher. For ten years I taught school in Pasadena, California, and initiated efforts to end busing of white students to primarily white schools.

In California people from the South derided us, saying, "You Californians don't know how to deal with Negroes. We understand them, and they are much happier with us." This puzzled me. But I was really intrigued after reading the following article that appeared in *Time* on February 27, 1956:

> Religious Emphasis Week at the University of Mississippi was rapidly approaching, and the committee on arrangements thought it had a solid list of guest speakers. Among them was the Rev. Alvin Kershaw of Oxford, Ohio, the Episcopal rector who won $32,000 on TV's *The $64,000 Question* a few months ago by answering questions on jazz. A mild-mannered man, he seemed anything but controversial. No one could have suspected that he would set off the weird chain reaction of resignations and denunciations that hit Mississippi last week.
>
> The reaction began when James Morrow Jr. of the state legislature wrote Chancellor J. D. Williams of the university that Kershaw had said he would give some of his winnings to the National Association for the Advancement of Colored People. Morrow suggested that Williams "revoke the Reverend's invitation ever to appear in Mississippi." Later Kershaw wrote a letter to the student *Mississippian* conceding that he had indeed supported the N.A.A.C.P. because "I am convinced that the core of religious faith is love of God and neighbor." Though Kershaw's scheduled topic ("Religion and Drama") sounded innocent enough, Chancellor Williams told the rector that he had better stay home.
>
> When the news broke, another out-of-state guest speaker announced that he too would stay home. Then, Professor Morton B. King Jr., chairman of the university's sociology department, resigned from the faculty. The university administration, he charged, is "no longer able to defend the freedom of thought, inquiry and speech which are essential for higher education to flourish." Two days later, at Mississippi State College, Political Scientist William Buchanan decided to resign too. The state house of representatives denounced the two professors as "misguided reformers," urged the heads of all state-supported colleges to "use every effort to prevent subversive influences from infiltrating into our institutions." Governor James P. Coleman agreed. "If a man feels a team is unworthy," he said of the professors, "he ought to get off the team." Other men were also getting off the team. By last week, all five out-of-state speakers had said they would not show up for the university's Religious Emphasis Week.
>
> With their speakers' slate wiped clean, the committee on arrangements decided to replace its guests with five Oxford, Miss. clergymen. After all, wrote Negro-baiting Editor Fred Sullens of the Jackson *Daily News*, "we may feel reasonably sure that [local clergymen] will not be spewing poison into the minds of our young people." The five untainted ones, however, respectfully declined. At week's end the committee on arrangements decided to turn Religious Emphasis Week into three days of meditation and prayer—without any clergymen around who might have dangerous ideas.

I knew then that, sooner or later, I must see this strange land.

After my husband's death in 1959, I volunteered my services as a teacher (in exchange for room and board) at Rust College in Holly Springs, Mississippi, followed by a year at Claflin College, South Carolina. In 1963 I moved to Mississippi where I taught at Tougaloo College until 1965.

In 1965 I began work on a doctorate in history at the University of Mississippi. Upon completion of the degree I returned to Rust College, from where I retired in 1978.

As history, these letters are primary sources—usually written within hours or days of the events and attitudes they describe—not recalled at some later date when faulty memories can cloud a picture.

Actually, the Civil Rights Movement brought us no new rights. The Fourteenth Amendment to the Constitution had granted equal rights to all Americans in 1868. But by the 1890s and continuing into the 1960s, many of those rights, for all practical purposes, had been lost through state laws, intimidation, indifference, and sheer greed by some persons or corporate entities. This was especially, but not exclusively, true in the Southern states. It is an obvious law of nature that *not to use is to lose.* The genius of the Civil Rights Movement of the '60s was that it turned this dictum on its head and acted on the basis that *to use is to restore.*

These letters give vivid pictures of ordinary people who risked the loss of jobs, homes, and, at times, life itself, to *use* the rights which had been entombed in heavy and dusty law books for years. While the Movement was breathing life into these laws, Congress passed two important statutes: the Civil Rights Act of 1964 and the Voting Rights Act of 1965.

Who says nothing has changed? I would say we are light years ahead of where we were in 1960. To acknowledge that *change*—even dramatic change—occurred in the past thirty or so years is not to say that all is perfect now. The playing field is not yet level. More needs to be done. That is our challenge today. Mississippians are working together, black and white, to bring about such improvements as I might have thought impossible at one time. They did not do it alone. Sympathetic Americans from coast to coast—particularly in the Freedom Summer of 1964—helped. Perfection has not arrived yet nor will it ever. But I elected to retire here that I might watch the state continue to improve. Using tools which those before the Civil Rights Movement did not always have, especially access to education, public accommodations, and the ballot, the present generation should make even greater advances than any generation before.

Gen. Colin Powell, former chairman of the Joint Chiefs of Staff, says,

"The young must never forget the battles their elders fought." While we are remembering the recognized great leaders, we should not forget the many persons, black and white, who were determined to use the laws on the books, come what may.

We must not again lose any victories our elders have given us because we fail to use them.

Clarice T. Campbell

Acknowledgments

It would be impossible to name all to whom I am indebted, but any list would begin with the presidents of Rust, Claflin, and Tougaloo colleges, who accepted me, an outsider unacquainted with the difficulties of administering schools within the constraints of Southern culture in the 1960s. Though, at times, each may have questioned his judgment, they were gracious enough to continue the relationship to the end of the contracts.

My experience in race relations activities in Pasadena, California, was not the asset which I, and possibly they, anticipated. As the letters reveal, those things I thought could be done with impunity were likely to be frowned upon in the South if for no other reason than that I was an "outside agitator." I never quite adjusted to Southern state laws and mores where race was at issue. If I seemed arrogant, in retrospect I think I was. My apologies, herewith.

I want to acknowledge my indebtedness to faculty colleagues and my students, as well as those members of the college communities who had the courage to extend a hand of friendship in spite of the problems which that could cause them. Their acceptance of me deepened my understanding and broadened my knowledge of the South.

Yet, for all this encouragement and help, the letters might never have found publication had it not been for my good friend Jan Hillegas, who came to Mississippi from Syracuse University in the Freedom Summer of 1964. It was she who collected extant copies, most of which were on onionskin made difficult to read by age and the blurring from carbon paper. (Not even the primitive photocopy machines of the day were available, and I only occasionally had access to ditto [purple print] or mimeograph equipment.)

Together we edited the letters in an attempt to avoid duplications caused by my writing to my family as events happened, then several weeks later writing a summary of events to a wide circle of friends. Purely family content was mostly deleted. In a few instances, material was merged from more than one letter or rearranged to provide continuity. Throughout my letters, I used the racial terms which at that time seemed most appropriate to the incidents described. We tried to be true to the letters as written.

The original letters, presided over by an efficient and accommodating staff, may be found at the Mississippi Department of Archives and History in Jackson.

The office staff at Traceway Retirement Center ran off countless photocopies, mailed packages, even came to my apartment to oust the pesky gremlins that all too often invaded my typewriter, putting me temporarily out of business! I am indeed thankful to all the Traceway personnel.

I found the suggestions of the many friends who read the manuscript of real value. To them a big thanks.

For their faith in the manuscript, their advice on publication, and their loyal friendship, I am grateful to Ann Abadie and Joanne Hawks of the University of Mississippi.

Of course, I am delighted that the University Press of Mississippi is publishing *Civil Rights Chronicle*, giving me the experience and advice of its associate director and editor-in-chief, Seetha A-Srinivasan.

And I want to express here my deep appreciation for the continued support and help from my children—Florence (Camie), Charlotte, Don and Jean.

Civil Rights Chronicle

Mississippi 1956

[University of Mississippi, Summer 1956]

In El Paso, I saw my first "COLORED" signs. I stepped up to the clerk and in as calm a manner as I could muster I said, "This is my first experience in the South. I am rather surprised to see these 'COLORED' signs as I thought that due to the interstate nature of travel they had been discarded in all depots and stations."

The clerk said, "This is Texas and we have to abide by Texas law."

"Oh," I said, "Then Texas law takes precedence over federal law."

"I know it is right or Greyhound wouldn't do it," she replied, and I thought I detected a bit of emotion.

At another station I asked the same question. "We have a number of passengers who travel just within the state," she said.

"I see. You leave it up to the individual to decide whether or not the signs apply to him. If he is traveling between states he disregards the signs; if within the state he observes the signs."

"*They* know where to go," she answered.

In Dallas I repeated my query and was told, "You're right. We can't enforce these signs but tradition is so strong we don't have to enforce them."

Over in the corner of the Dallas station I saw three of my fellow travelers, Negro teachers who were returning from the National Education Association convention in Portland. One of them had been my seat companion all day. One of the others was writing in a little black book as I had noticed her doing several times during the day. I stepped over to her and said, "What is it you are writing? Notes, perhaps, for your convention report?"

Without a word she handed me the little book. I read in it of the treatment afforded her at each stop, where she had to eat, what the "COLORED" restrooms were like, etc. I said, "If this is your feeling, why don't we go into the cafeteria together for dinner?"

So we did. I had just put a salad on my tray and my Negro friend had just picked up her tray when the manager approached her. "You will have to go to the colored room next door," she said.

I spoke up, "We are traveling together. I understood from the agent that these signs were not enforceable."

"He has nothing to do with the cafeteria," she informed me.

"Then may I go with my friend to the other dining room?"

"If you like."

Just off the kitchen was the small colored dining room which would accommodate about 10 persons, maybe 12. It had a counter and stools with a few sandwiches and drinks advertised on the wall. The two other Negro teachers came out while we were still standing in line waiting our turn.

"What do you suppose that manager said to our waitress? She said, 'A white woman is coming in here to eat. Be sure she has a clean plate.' "

By the time we were seated at the counter, it was nearly time for bus departure; besides I had lost my appetite. I said to my friend, who had ordered just a carton of milk, "Won't you eat some of my sandwich?" She did.

Back in the bus she wrote again in her book describing our experience, ending "and so Mrs. Campbell and I ate together in the colored dining room. We ate off the same clean plate."

University, Mississippi
July 19, 1956

Life in Mississippi is not at all as I imagined. Sitting in air-conditioned classrooms, studying in the beautiful air-conditioned library, and eating in an air-conditioned cafeteria, I haven't yet felt the heat. Our dorm is not air-conditioned but it is quite comfortable due to several large fans circulating air through the halls.

Of course if I were picking cotton in the noonday sun, I'd tell a different story.

The campus is as beautiful as any I've seen. Large and spacious with fine buildings of brick construction. A few were built pre-[Civil]war and the dean tells me are only here now because a Confederate general who was a West Point classmate of Union General Ulysses S. Grant persuaded him not to burn them. The university was being used as a hospital and the Southern women were nursing the Union men as well as the Confederate. It came to me as a shock that Mississippi was interested in higher education in antebellum[1] days. Somehow I always imagined Mississippi as down-river with large plantations con-

1. Meaning "before the war." "The war" always means the Civil War, or "War Between the States," as white Southerners prefer to call it.

trolled by overseers whose sole interest was making a big profit for their absentee owners who in turn would reward them well. How wrong can one be!

Oxford is an interesting little town about a mile away. My first two visits impressed me because of the bustling of it. Then I went down on Saturday afternoon and it was completely transformed. All the Negroes from miles around must have come in. It seemed more like a big church picnic. People visiting, strolling along, sitting around, standing against buildings, or playing dominoes at card tables set up on the lawn around the courthouse. Surrounding stores were open, with a glorified variety store doing the best business.

The churches surprised me, too. Quite large—at least the main five are. Went to Sunday School and church service at the Baptist last Sunday. The average age was much younger than at our church. Good attendance; thirty-one in choir.

[Upon arrival at the University of Mississippi, I enrolled in two classes: Dr. James Silver's American History and Dr. Huey B. Howerton's Constitutional Law.]

The question asked by everyone almost without exception was, "Why did you come HERE?" The first day in Constitutional Law Dr. Howerton asked me, "How did you happen to come here?" I answered him as I had everyone else, "I have found summer work more interesting if I take it in different parts of the country. One summer I went to Michigan, another to Oregon, and since I have always wanted to see the South, I decided to come here this year."

The prof turned to the class and said, "I think she's here to see what makes us tick!"

Three weeks later this same Dr. Howerton stopped in the middle of a discourse and said, "Mrs. Campbell, I still can't understand how you happened to light here."

This time I said, "With this beautiful state and your outstanding university, why shouldn't you expect out-of-staters to be attracted?"

He answered, "Well, ma'am, if that isn't an evasive answer, I never heard one."

Right from the start I gathered I was suspect.

Before going, I determined I would not fly under false colors; I would not be silent when to be silent would indicate acquiescence or approval. I would not become involved in arguments. I would use a question technique. I was going to learn, not to preach. I would be bold in seeking out persons whose opinions I wanted to hear.

One day Dr. Howerton could not meet with us. He asked one of the boys to carry on. At the conclusion of my report on a civil rights case, Charles Bobo said, "May I ask you a question, Mrs. Campbell? Why is it you folks are always criticizing us? I've been up North and I was in California while in the service. You are segregated even though you don't call it that. You live in different neighborhoods, your children go to different schools, your churches are segregated. So why do you criticize us?"

I really felt on the spot. My answer to him was, "In the first place, I'm sorry you think I am here to criticize. I do admit to being very interested in the whole problem which I think is bigger than the South or any one section. What you say is true about California. And we have no excuse. Tradition is not against us as it is with you, and our state laws are not on the side of segregation. Thus when we segregate it's purely our own cussedness that is showing. All I can say in our defense is that we are working at it. We have many organized groups working to bring about a change. I myself live in a thoroughly integrated neighborhood, but it is the exception, not the rule. Our church has about a dozen Negro members or regular attendants, but that in a church of 3,000 is only a token number. I can assure you I will be kept plenty busy working in Pasadena for a good many years."

[Though the atmosphere was tense for a while, by the end of the hour we were on friendlier terms than ever before. Two of the boys even offered to drive me to Holly Springs, 30 miles away, to visit Rust College, a Methodist school for blacks. There I had a long visit with Dr. Lee Marcus McCoy, president of the school, and his wife.]

[My husband] Harold wrote me that our own Bishop [Gerald] Kennedy had preached a wonderful sermon on "I saw the Lord"; I wrote back that I, too, saw the Lord in Dr. McCoy. Such a beautiful Christian spirit, entirely devoid of any bitterness, yet not submissive in the unattractive meaning of the word. Dr. McCoy named some of the Rust alumni, two of whom I recognized as outstanding Angelenos, Judge Jefferson and his brother, who is an attorney. This Methodist college is doing a great work, sending out Christian graduates, many of whom become teachers, but the thing that depressed me was the inadequacy of the buildings. There was one good administration building on the naturally beautiful grounds but the others would not make any Methodist proud. This is not the fault of the South—this is the responsibility of our entire

Methodist Church. I hope that next February when my Methodist readers are asked on Race Relations Sunday for an offering for the Negro Methodist colleges, they will remember the need and give generously.

The White Citizens Council is very strong in Mississippi, and more dangerous than the old Ku Klux Klan because it is made up of the so-called better citizens—the judges, lawyers, doctors, church leaders, etc. If anyone says anything in favor of integration he is likely to be socially ostracized or lose his job, or find his credit cut off or, if in business, he may not be able to buy supplies. In some instances he is "encouraged" to leave the state. White Citizens Council members are constantly on the lookout, as are the men whom the governor employs to keep an eye and ear open for any signs of sympathy with the idea of desegregation.

The Director of Religious Life at the university, a minister, told me he had a Negro Baptist friend with whom he played ping-pong at the campus Y. No one was around when the game began, but a White Citizens Council member happened to walk by and saw through the open door this awful sight—a white man and a colored man playing together.

The next day the Director of Religious Life was visited by an official of the university. It was not the first time the minister had done something indiscreet and in exasperation the official said, "*Why*, why did you do it?"

"I like to play ping-pong."

"You know what I mean. WHY DID YOU PLAY WITH THIS MAN?"

"Well," thought the minister out loud, "I suppose you might say it is an accumulation of years of Southern guilt, but every morning when I read my paper, I feel like going out and finding the dirtiest, most ragged little cotton-picking boy, throwing my arms around him and saying, 'I love you.' If you can't understand that, then I can't explain to you why I played ping-pong."

The week after I left, this minister's case was brought before a university board to determine whether he should be retained on the staff.[2]

One of the most hopeful things about Mississippi is the accelerated school building program. As far as they can, they are building good schools which are equal to or better than the white schools, admitting that they hope, thereby, to

2. Later, I received a Mississippi paper announcing his resignation to take a position with the Council of Churches in Tennessee. Will Campbell is known today throughout the country as a fine author, philosopher, and preacher.

persuade the courts to release the pressure for integration. Also the teachers are on a single salary scale—equal pay for equal qualifications. It would seem to me that this building program might satisfy the courts as a first step toward integration, for, after all, you can't integrate in a one-room shack, but one county superintendent said absolutely not. That would be to admit they were expecting to integrate eventually, which they will not concede. Nevertheless with the improving quality of education, whether they like it or not, they are nearing an era of enlightenment which I feel sure brings them closer to desegregation.

Alabama 1957

Tuscaloosa, Alabama, Summer 1957

Last summer, I went by myself to the University of Mississippi and traveled on Greyhound. This summer, Mother and I drove her car to the University of Alabama. We both are taking courses here, living in the dormitory, eating in the school cafeteria. The fact that we are a mother/daughter team of rather ancient vintage, from California, makes us unusual enough to be written up and pictured in a state newspaper and interviewed on the university's TV program.

By way of conversation, people in the cafeteria frequently ask, "And what courses are you taking, Mrs. Campbell?" When I answered one student that I was taking two courses from Miss Elizabeth Coleman, all who heard me intimated that they thought I was a glutton for punishment. One little girl, a college senior from Connecticut, said, "I'd quit school before I'd take another course from her. The first day I was in her class, she asked, 'Are there any Yankees in this class?' Timidly, I raised my hand and she said, 'They were the scuttle of the earth in 1860 and I have no reason to think they have changed since!' I'm an English major and I worked like a dog in her class but I got a D for my effort." (So far, I've found her a wonderful teacher, albeit prejudiced.)

Being a Methodist I wanted to know how a Methodist minister working on the campus felt about these racial problems. I sought a conference with the minister of Wesley Foundation, a campus church. This man was eager to explain his position: "You recall this was the campus setting for the Authorine Lucy incident.[1] When Authorine Lucy was here, there were about a dozen of our Wesley Foundation members who wanted to do something to help her. They came to me and asked what I would think of their surrounding her as she passed from one class to another, in a friendly, informal manner. I, of course, had to tell them it was not a good idea. 'That would be forcing your way on

1. Authorine Lucy, admitted to the University of Alabama in February 1956 by court order, was suspended "for her own safety" after whites rioted. Though reinstated by court order, she was expelled on a technicality. Some whites said the riots had "worked," restoring segregation.

other people which would be fully as wrong as for others to force their way on you.' You see my point don't you?" he asked me.

"Not clearly," I answered. "Will you explain how such action on the part of those boys would differ from the act of the Good Samaritan, for instance?"

"No comparison at all," he answered. "We have police today to protect people. Citizens have no right to take the law in their own hands."

"How did you feel, then, about Rev. Paul Turner's escorting those students to school in Clinton [Tennessee]?"

"I felt it was absolutely wrong, of course! What right has a minister to usurp the duties of the law? Next door to our church is a restaurant that was forever letting its dirty dishwater flow onto our church property. Did I take it upon myself to stop it from this? Of course not, I called the police. The same should be done in these other cases."

This minister, as proof of his kindness and fondness for the Negro people, told me of his son-in-law, a judge in Mobile. At the close of court he noticed an old Negro "Uncle" still sitting in the room. He asked one of the lawyers to talk with him and learn his problem. The lawyer did and came back to the judge. They settled the case right then, which meant the Negro was not cheated out of his property as was threatened. The minister said, "I asked my son-in-law how much the lawyer charged the old uncle for his service. 'Nothing; he wouldn't think of charging the old man.' Where but in the South would you find such concern on the part of a lawyer for an unknown Negro uncle!"

Then the minister called in his maid, who had been with the family for 25 years. "Rosy is a very intelligent woman, Mrs. Campbell, even though she can neither read nor write. Rosy, tell Mrs. Campbell, who is from California, how the white people here treat you."

"Very nice, they do."

"Rosy, how did the boys on campus treat you that afternoon of the excitement over Authorine Lucy?"

"Yes, ma'am, they told me not to go near there or I might get hurt. They warned me to stay away. They were good to me."

"Now maybe you would like to ask Rosy some questions, Mrs. Campbell."

I asked her several questions about schools but she didn't know any answers. "I don't know, ma'am," was all I could get out of her, and the minister said, "She doesn't know about schools. I said she was unlettered."

In relating this to Dr. [Jim] Dombrowski, executive secretary of the

Southern Conference Educational Fund,[2] he said this minister was unusual for ministers of Wesley Foundations, on campuses. Usually they are in the forefront of progressive movements. This minister, having been there for over 20 years, is probably a product of the older school of thought.

By contrast we visited Dr. and Mrs. Hays. Dr. Hays is the [white] president of Stillman College, a Presbyterian school for Negroes on the outskirts of Tuscaloosa. When Mr. Jagears, a [white] junior high principal [also enrolled in University of Alabama summer school], asked us where we would like to go for a drive, I suggested this college. That morning at breakfast, Mr. Jagears had mentioned that if I should try to teach in a Negro school in Alabama, I'd be run out of town.

On the way to the college he remarked that if Mrs. Campbell were to enter a school room with 30 colored children in it, the odor would be so great she couldn't remain. "What would you do in such a case?" he asked me. "I think I'd give them baths," I replied. "It won't wash off," said he. "Have you ever been in a room with 30 Negroes?" "Yes," I answered. "Have you?"

We were met at the door by a white woman who said she would call her son, Dr. Hays. Mr. Jagears said in a whisper, "Did she say her son?" This was a very worthwhile evening, I felt, for Mr. Jagears posed question after question and Dr. Hays answered them—every time—just as I would want to hear them answered. Mr. Jagears would take him more seriously because he was a Southerner and because of his fine quality so evident in every word and movement.

Such questions as: Suppose our colored schools were comparable in every respect to our white schools; do you not think a separate school system would still be better? Dr. Hays answered in his quiet unemotional way, "I have not found the Negroes particularly desirous of being with white people. For the most part they would prefer to be with their own. I think what they resent is being told they CAN'T associate with white. Free choice just might be our answer."

Even if integration should finally occur in the student body, do you think colored teachers would ever be accepted as teachers of white children? Answered Dr. Hays, Why should we object to Negro teachers for our children? We have always used Negro nurses who have a much more intimate association with our children than teachers and have that influence during their most formative years.

2. SCEF (pronounced 'skeff'), an interracial civil rights organization founded in 1946.

Again, Mr. Jagears asked, "Do you find the Negro students coming to you adequately prepared for college work?"

Why should we expect them to be? Many of these young people come from homes having not a single book in them. They are mostly first-generation students. Added to this, you and I know their schools have been very inadequate and their labors in the cotton fields often interrupted even that inadequate schooling. Then, too, we often forget the number of white students who drop out of college because of inadequate preparation. We take our colored students as they come. Our freshman English is very intensive. Before they graduate they have to pass a proficiency test to be sure they haven't forgotten what they learned as freshmen. English is their hardest subject, usually.

The highlight of our trip was attendance at the Dexter Avenue Baptist Church in Montgomery to hear Dr. Martin Luther King, Jr., preach. His sermon was at the level of the people's need. It was both intellectual and powerful. It had dignity. His topic was "Factors that Determine Character." The fatalist says man is the victim of cosmic, social and economic forces beyond his control; man cannot alter his fate. Others feel with the poet that man is in complete control—"I am the master of my fate, the captain of my soul." Dr. King accepted neither of these philosophies. He discussed factors that determine character in three steps:

Heredity: the color of the skin, the texture of the hair, the shape of the head, the mental capacity, the physical stamina, the glands—all have a part in shaping our lives.

Environment: geographical, cultural, friends, church, books, TV.

Of greater importance is the third factor of individual response to one's environment and heredity. It is first necessary that you feel you are important; you *are* somebody and want to *be* somebody. Our environment as a race is often tragic. Your environment says you are less than, not equal to. But, though there is need for a better environment, you still can be somebody.

Marian Anderson, Roland Hayes, Langston Hughes, Mary Bethune, Howard Thurman, Booker T. Washington, Charles Drew, George Washington Carver, Ralph Bunche—all rose above their environments. Being a Negro cannot keep you from being one of the great.

And of course we have the noblest example of all in our Jesus. Born in an oxen stable, working at a carpenter's bench, one of a subject people, he became the spiritual leader of millions. We have it from our Jesus we can rise above our environment. We can rise above our heredity. When you think of it, those three men who died on the cross that day, died for the same reason: they all rebelled against their environment. Two rebelled in weakness; one rebelled in strength to transform his environment.

After the service I asked Rev. King if there were any place in the city where he and his wife and little daughter could be our guests for dinner so we could visit. He said there was no such place. We would be allowed in a Negro restaurant but there was none conducive to conversation. He conferred with his wife and they asked us to go to their home. We refused the dinner as Mother insisted she knew all too well the many calls on a minister's wife, but we did go to his home for a short talk. As we were ready to leave, we asked how to get to Alabama State College, and he insisted on taking us. Just before we returned to the parsonage, the rain came down in torrents. So we talked some more while waiting in the car for the rain to let up a bit.

Dr. King says the greatest good that came from the bus protest was the increased dignity and solidarity of the Negroes, themselves. I mentioned we had taken a bus ride the night before and were happy to find Negroes sitting in front of us but I wondered about a COLORED-WHITE sign now separating the races at the bus stop in the center of town. He said that and a recently imposed sign at the airport were, he supposed, a last-ditch effort. At the airport *he* does not abide by the sign and neither do some others. Nothing has been said to him about it. (In our newspapers, however, we have read of several in Montgomery who were hauled before the court for being in wrong areas of a park, and another arrest in Bessemer near Birmingham for violation of segregation rules in a Bessemer park.)

The cloudburst continued in its full magnitude, so finally we were embarrassed to keep Dr. King from his dinner any longer and made a dash for our car after he drove us as close to it as he could. We were drenched. Our car windows were open so we sat on a thoroughly wet seat. Dr. King had told us that Tuskegee was a good place to eat if we could hold out that long, so we headed toward the Institute.[3] The storm continued the entire way. We saw no country between Montgomery and Tuskegee; at times not even the white line was visible. At 4:30 we arrived for dinner.

The dining room was beautiful, the dinner good and well served. This service is a feature of the home economics training program. We decided it was too late to go back to Tuscaloosa though the rain was just a drizzle by the time

3. Tuskegee Institute, a black school and college founded by Booker T. Washington in 1881, is 42 miles east of Montgomery.

we finished eating. We would have liked to stay at the Institute, but the only room left (a convention was in progress there) was a suite for [a then expensive] $15.00. Thus we went on toward Auburn, where the state college [now Auburn University] is located (larger than the university at Tuscaloosa) and found a motel. Next morning we saw the college and drove home by way of Birmingham, arriving at school just as the last class was getting out. Couldn't have timed it more perfectly if our object was to get out of classes.

The next Sunday we were in the little town of Fayette where we had gone to hibernate in an air-conditioned motel to study. We did go to church and were surprised to find the young man who sat next to me in American Literature ushering. In the tradition of Southern hospitality he insisted on taking us out to dinner after church. I casually mentioned by way of conversation our pleasure at being in his church—that we found visiting churches a very rewarding experience. Last Sunday we were at Dr. King's church in Montgomery. Immediately, his interest was aroused. "You mean you heard Dr. Martin Luther King preach?" Continuing in my calmest manner I said, "Yes. He gave a powerful sermon."

"Weren't you afraid?"

Mother said, "Afraid? In church, afraid?"

"Were there any other white people?"

"Yes, I don't know how many, but I saw two others and they were not together, either."

After we answered many more questions for him, he said, "You know, I'd like to hear him myself. But of course, I wouldn't dare."

A young man entered the dining room about then. Our host motioned to him to join us. After introductions he said, "These people heard Dr. King in Montgomery last Sunday." The friend said nothing. Our host said, "Did you hear what I said? They heard Dr. King. They attended his church."

We found the reaction was always pregnant with this kind of surprise and interest. So we used our visit to Dr. King's church to advantage, we felt, many times.

The reason I say "to advantage" is that I feel very definitely that much of their trouble is getting over the hurdle of the idea that certain things just aren't done. "Don't ask me why" is their attitude. "One just doesn't do these things if one wants to be held in respect by his peers." If our presence did any good at all I believe it was just to demonstrate quietly that nothing terrible happens when one steps over the lines—in fact there are people who do it quite naturally—as for instance the other white people in the Dexter Avenue Baptist Church—also to encourage them to reason out some of their accepted behavior. This, I felt, was done by asking questions—never saying, "That is not right," but turning the matter in question back to them to defend.

An attorney said to me, "The Supreme Court decision was merely a political one." To which I answered, "Justice [Hugo] Black is from your own state of Alabama. Do you believe he concurred in that decision for political reasons?"

Or I could use the "as I understand it" technique. This same lawyer said, "For years every decision handed down by the court on this subject upheld the principle of separate but equal. Then why should this court change what had been upheld by many courts over many years?"[4]

"As I understand it, new light has been shed on what constitutes equal. The findings of sociologists and psychologists are conclusive now that [enforced] separation can never be equal—it is inherently unequal."

A man eavesdropping from behind my lawyer, and who I could see was getting very emotionally involved, spoke up and said, "But the Constitution says separate but equal schools are right."

"I don't think it does, but this man is a lawyer, ask him."

"That's right, isn't it?" our emotional eavesdropper asked in a fraught voice as though the fate of the world depended on that one answer.

"No," the lawyer answered. "The Constitution says nothing about schools."

In the little town of Greensboro we went to see Hobson Home. Richmond Hobson was an admiral in the Spanish American War. After hearing from Mr. Joseph Hobson, who now lives there with his sister, about how the house was built by 200 slaves, etc., we moved the conversation into racial matters. This man, obviously very intelligent for all his 80-some years, said, "We haven't always done right by the Negro in the South. But now we are doing better. Now we have new schools equal to any white schools."

"We have just come from your schools in Greensboro. We saw both the colored and the white," I said.

"Then you saw they were equal?"

"No, we were very disappointed," I answered. "The white school was a

4. The *Brown* v. *Board of Education* (of Topeka, Kansas) decision of the U.S. Supreme Court in 1954 overruled *Plessy* v. *Ferguson* of 1896, which had said separate facilities were okay if they were equal.

beautiful new building. The colored school was old and we were told it was very much overcrowded."

Miss Hobson, sister of Joseph, came in at about this point. She insisted the schools were equal. She knew because someone in authority had told her just recently. A new school had just been built. "I know that is so," she said quite vehemently.

"But sister, these folks have just seen it. You and I have never seen the colored school."

"Perhaps there is another school that we didn't see," I said. "I'd like to know where it is, for we really are interested in seeing the new colored schools."

She left the room to call the man who had told her. Returning, she said, with a little less enthusiasm, "Well, I knew we had built a new colored school, but it is in the other end of the county."

Well, it is easy to talk about Alabama and Mississippi. What is harder is facing up to our own shortcomings. This, of course, was thrown up to me many times: You don't allow Negroes in your better residential areas. Your schools are for all practical purposes segregated. Your churches are segregated. To most of this I readily agreed, adding that we were doing our best to change the situation. We have active groups in our churches, our clubs, our cities working to create better relationships, adding that I myself live in an integrated neighborhood and attend a church that has at least made a beginning toward integration.

When our neighborhood first began to change, there was considerable skepticism on the part of many of us. Would they keep their property up, etc.? I like to tell the story of Miss [Dorothea] Fry, a junior college teacher and one of our neighbors. A young man called to solicit her membership in a protective organization to keep Negroes out. She listened politely to his arguments, then said, "I'm sorry, but I can't join your organization. You see, I believe in democracy."

"But you wouldn't want a Negro living next door to you, would you?"

"I think I would want a family of good character next to me and I would hope that family would keep its yard up. Other than that I don't think I would care who the family might be."

"But your property values," he hastened to explain, "would go down."

"Statistics I have seen leave me in doubt as to that point, but IF you should be right, if the value of my property goes down because of the color of some of my neighbors, then I am prepared to pay that price for my belief in democracy."

She says he left a very puzzled young man. She doesn't know his name but she hopes he can see our neighborhood as it is today with its Negroes and Japanese-Americans all living harmoniously together with the original Caucasian owners who are left. She hopes he knows of the increase of property values in our area. She hopes he drives around and sees the well-cared-for yards. Indeed, the Negro and Japanese-American yards put us to shame at times.

We have been happily surprised that they do keep their places up so well. Harold, my husband, does our gardening and he does a good job of it, too. But he doesn't like geraniums and I do. Tired of hearing me complain because we had no ivy geraniums, he finally gave me a strip between our house and the Taylors next door to plant geraniums. Those geraniums for some reason never grew well. They always looked ratty. One day Harold came in after making the place look as spic and span as possible, and sinking in the nearest chair, said, "You know, if it weren't for your little strip of geraniums, no one would ever guess white people live here."

[From 1957–1960, I taught at Washington Junior High School in Pasadena.]

Rust College, MS, 1960–61

[Rust College, Holly Springs, MS], September 1, 1960

Here I am at last, in a new state, on a new job!

Yesterday driving southeast from Memphis I found myself wondering—as one always wonders on the verge of that last irrevocable leap into a new experience—whether this year would not be a good deal more exciting and difficult than I had imagined.

Mississippi might not be the easiest state to live in. Half-remembered passages from books I had read kept coming to mind, tales that had sounded strangely fiction-like to my California-bred concepts. Mississippi was not known for its receptivity to new things, and I was undoubtedly new.

Furthermore Mississippi had been second to secede from the Union, and some maintained it had never quite returned. Stars and Bars[1] are still featured prominently in its flag.

From the beginning, Mississippi had been conservative. The first Anglo-Saxons there were mostly Tory sympathizers so friendly to Britain during the Revolution that they had been forced to flee their neighbors' wrath.

I was heading for the small town of Holly Springs, population 3,200. Once Holly Springs was the site of Civil War battles; now it is to be the site of my life for a year as a teacher at Rust College.

I am the first faculty member to arrive, and my room in Foster Hall is still being painted. It is lonely in the empty three-story building, but I am told there is a night watchman and the thought is reassuring.

I am to be the only white person living on the Rust campus.

September 2, 1960

I am taking my meals with President [Earnest A.] Smith and his wife until the cafeteria is ready to serve more than the football squad. Mrs. [Milverta] Smith is a gracious hostess and a splendid cook, and I enjoy getting acquainted with her.

1. The symbols on the Confederate battle flag.

The President's home is new and beautifully built, at the start of the curving drive which leads to the main part of the campus. Crowning the hill is the fine red brick administration building, where most of the classes are held. With its white belfry [resembling Independence Hall], this two-story structure has rooms for five hundred students.

Rust, which is the oldest Methodist Negro college in the South, was founded in 1866, and the buildings have burned several times. The present administration building which dominates the campus was built in 1947.

Originally, Rust had been taught by teachers from some of the best Northern schools, including Harvard and Yale; more recently, it has been through some difficult years.

[September 1960]

These are the finest of young people here, but I'm not too happy with the first week of teaching. I haven't quite geared it to reach them. They seem to want and need a definite job to do each day.

At present I have just 12 hours of teaching during the week—a very light load compared to the regular teachers here. I didn't ask for any more, for I am quite apprehensive over my approach and ability in this situation so new to me.

The benefit to me scholastically, here, is that I have time and feel I must do some real studying. I am learning more than I would learn in any regular history course in which I might enroll. It's a bit hard on the students to be guinea pigs for me, but there is nothing like teaching to learn.

Did I tell you I caught a mouse in my room? The conventional way—not by closing the car door on him as I did in Colorado.

September 17, 1960

One of the fascinating features of this college is the singing. It may be a group in the cafeteria waiting for the line to move or a group off in some remote corner of this beautiful campus; it may be a young man mowing the lawn and singing above the clack of the motor. I wish you could have been in the chapel service last Wednesday. The student body, the congregation, that is, sang "All Hail the Power of Jesus' Name" using the third tune in the Methodist Hymnal.

It has some exciting bass and tenor which was not lost on this group. The vitality of their singing lifted one up as on wings.

Miss [Natalie] Doxey, Director of the Music Department, who has been here 51 years, is given credit for capturing this spirit of song and directing it. There are some really good instructors here; they are dedicated to the college.

I have just three classes. Two classes are in American History, but one of them meets three times a week and the other six times a week (for five weeks), making it necessary to have two preparations for the same subject. The daily group is made up of in-service teachers. Many Negro schools begin in July or August then close for the cotton-picking season. During that time the teachers return to college in pursuit of those elusive credentials. Then I have a small class of only ten in Recent American History. Altogether, I have about 70 students. Several teachers have more than that in a single class, but I'm grateful they are easy on me to begin with for I'm still feeling my way.

In a few weeks I will get another Saturday class of in-service teachers, again for those needing to work toward full credentials. Eventually, when enough teachers are trained before starting to teach, there will be less need for this in-service program.

This, of course, is one reason why the preparation of the college students is no better; they have not had qualified teachers from the beginning. Another reason *just might* be that the classes are too often overcrowded. Some of these teachers have primary grades numbering in the fifties and sixties.

President Smith always has just the right word for the students. That man can really communicate—and always with a winning and contagious smile. Wednesday in chapel we had a guest minister from Iowa who had dropped in just to see and "feel the pulse" of Rust College. After this guest had given the message, President Smith said, peering over the audience, "I'm looking for the president of a certain campus organization. I don't see him. I'm going to write him a letter and tell him he can't lead where he doesn't go!" Then he continued, "We often have guests here at Rust College. We don't ever send word around campus that a guest is here. Our guests want to know you as you really are. Now if you're good, that is the way our guests see you, and that is fine. If you're bad—well, that's the way it is. And isn't that just the way it will be at Judgment? Nobody is going to send you up, or send you down. No! Your body will just fall away from your spirit, and there you will be—just as you really are. And do you want me to tell you where you're going? You're going right where you've been *trying* to go all along. Won't that be wonderful? At last you can go where you want to!"

The First Methodist [white] members have been most cordial to me. One of the W.S.C.S. [Women's Society of Christian Service] women called for me and took me to the meeting. She came in to see my room, too. I was invited to Sunday School.

Of course, one reason for their immediate hospitality may be that Olive Sainz [white] paved the way for me by writing some of her friends that I was coming.[2] Everyone, without exception, thinks so very highly of Olive. She taught seven years here at Rust and is now teaching in Los Angeles.

Don't know that I should mention this to you who have been suffering through weather of 102 degrees, but for the past ten days we have had BEAUTIFUL weather. So, if California gets unbearable, why not try Mississippi? No smog, either.

But if you come here, you must behave yourself, for everyone knows when a stranger is in town, especially a foreigner from California. I bought a few groceries and the young man asked if I'd like him to carry my packages out. He said, "It's the white car with the green top, isn't it?" Surprised, because my car was one of a hundred in the court square on a Saturday afternoon, I asked, "How did you know?" He answered, "I saw the California license and you speak with an accent."

Or take the time I failed to put "California" on a card I addressed to Mother in Winchester. The card was mailed in a box on the court square so no postal clerk saw me mail it; it was signed merely "Clarice" and had no return address on it. Mother's name being different from mine would give no clue. But that card was returned to me at Rust College for a better address!

[September 28, 1960]

Some of my relatives would like to know what to give me for my birthday, and I have written them to send a dollar toward a ping-pong table. It occurs to me that one need around here is constructive leisure time activities: the students need more things to do than wandering around the campus "socializing." Besides, I need the exercise myself!

2. Olive's husband fled the Spanish legislature during the Spanish Civil War and taught at Rust until his death.

If I ever write you that I am having any trouble with discipline, mark me down as a poor teacher. So far absolutely none of that old problem. However, I have heard complaints from some faculty members about other years. I probably have an advantage in that I am not of their race and they are on good behavior for me. I also have the advantage of smaller classes than some. These students are working for me now. Learning? I hope.

On Tuesday the dean of women and a staff resident went with me to Memphis where we stood in the rain and heard [Vice President and Republican presidential candidate Richard M.] Nixon give a tremendous talk. He was in his best form. There were four Negroes on the platform with him. This is something in Memphis. Nixon started out with a strong statement regarding civil rights. He also came out strong on civil rights in Jackson, Miss., last Saturday.

After the speech we went to lunch—went in together then separated—they to the left, I to the right. This is one thing I don't like about this position. If I were alone I'd have experimented a bit; now I must think about the college with which I am associated. Maybe that is a good thing, but it does cramp my style.

The other highlight of the week you won't believe. Last Sunday I was singing as though I really enjoyed it—the way these young people do here at the college. A woman at the end of my pew rushed to me at the close of the service with hand extended. She introduced herself and said, "You must join our choir." Mrs. [H. L.] Smith, the minister's wife, came back from two pews up and said she stopped singing to enjoy hearing me sing. Together they took me up to the choir director and announced, "We have a voice for you!" I practiced with the choir Wednesday evening. The choir leader kept deferring to me about the anthem until I finally explained that I was a real novice, flattered to be asked to sing with the group, and thoroughly enjoying myself.

Had an official invitation to join the staff at Paine College, Ga., this week. It is a temptation to accept for next year. It has an international-interracial staff. Only Negro students but would welcome others.

Teaching in a small college town is really the life for me. I love every minute of it. However, I'm not making any decisions about next year now.

Oh yes! Mrs. Smith, the minister's wife, approached me before church Sunday to ask if I were happily located here at the college. She had a friend who would like me to room in her home with kitchen privileges. It was a very nice home, Mrs. Smith said. I was most grateful to her and to her friend for thinking of me, but I told her I had insisted on staying on campus as I wanted to get thoroughly acquainted with the college and felt I would be missing much of its life if I lived off campus.

Some of you seem confused as to the color of persons I mention. On campus all are colored. Off-campus acquaintances are all white. I know of no exception yet.

October 2, 1960

Dear Mr. [California Congressman H. Allen] Smith:

This name of Smith is becoming increasingly important in my life: the college president is a Smith, my pastor here is a Smith, and my Congressman is a Smith. And all three are upholding the honor of the name!

Some time ago in one of your "Report" issues, you mentioned a film on Washington, D.C. that you could rent or loan on request. How soon could it be sent to me here at Rust College?

In connection with the courses in American History which I am giving, I have arranged to show a film every Tuesday evening. Getting the films is proving a bit of a problem. Do you have access to, or knowledge of any more than this one? If so, how do I go about getting them?

It perhaps is presumptuous to even entertain this next subject, but I keep thinking what a shot in the arm it would be to my students here if you and Mrs. Smith could drop in and talk to us on issues of national importance. Politics are held in quite low esteem here. You could change all that with one appearance.

In this county, I am told there were and may still be about nine registered Negroes. The population of the county is about 75% Negro. If the college faculty is any indication, we are losing many Republican[3] votes because Negroes here are not able to cast their ballots. Even the president and his wife are not registered. One of the graduates of this college to whom I talked last Saturday lost her [teaching] position which she had held for ten years as a result of her husband's testimony in Washington, D.C. last January before the Voluntary Committee on Human Rights regarding Negro voting rights in Mississippi.

3. Before 1968, I was an ardent Republican.

I will be eager to hear from you as to how much you can help me.
I ordered an absentee ballot through the Republican Club before I left.

Saturday night, October 8, 1960

I am in the right place for me at this time. I find just enough need, enough challenge, enough opportunity to crusade in a subtle way (if I know how to be subtle) to be in my element. Also, we all enjoy having our egos fed, I suppose, and these folks have a gift for knowing how to do that.

Tuesday night one of my young men students came to see me about his history. Before he left I had learned considerable of his life's story. These young folks may not always be able to write a paragraph but they have "lived" through some pretty hard experiences. He said something that will keep me going in high gear for several weeks: "Mrs. Campbell, if I had ever had a teacher like you in high school, I'd sure know a lot more now. What a lot of money the state wastes on 'education.' " But I don't have to keep going on just that one remark. My in-service teachers are a delight to work with. "Even if I don't get a good grade from you, my mind is working; I can see my vocabulary growing, and I'm enjoying every day of this course." I might think they were just polishing the apple, but I get the same story secondhand from others. Right now these teachers are so excited over role-playing. One came to me today to ask if I thought she could use it on her 6th graders. She said, "I just love role-playing and I learn so much doing it!"

I always thought I could teach if anyone would *listen* to me! At home I always had to have half my mind on those "reluctant learners." Here I have such rapt attention it almost frightens me.

I use every help I've ever heard of: flannel board, Who Am I? stories, role-playing, time-line, bulletin board, and I just can't wait till I get some filmstrips and motion pictures going.

Everyone in my classes was assigned the Nixon-Kennedy debate yesterday. We had quite a discussion of it today. It was a better discussion for what little history we have studied. I watched the debate in the home of one of the faculty members. She has asked me a couple of times to come see her, so I decided last night would be a good time! She, Mrs. Griffin, asked me to bring Miss [Mary R.] Jackson with me. Miss Jackson lives here in the dorm. The three of us watched. Mr. Griffin went to a football game. We all have our own ideas of what is most important!

When Mother and I first saw these dorms [1957], they looked impossible to me. I admit to some weak moments before Mother left when I thought of living HERE. But, do you know, when you get in and clean the room, have a coat of paint, "new paper on the ceiling" (the preparation which they made for me, you remember), get your curtains up, your own things in, etc., it does take on a cozy homey atmosphere. I am lucky, of course, in that I do have the largest room and the only room with cross ventilation. I feel guilty about it but not guilty enough to give it up. I'm lucky, too, to have my room so close to the bath. The bath is freshly painted and the hall is in process of being done. I also signed up for the bell to be repaired and the front door painted. Oh, another thing for which I am grateful is that the bathroom has rather new fixtures. No shower, of course, but one can't have everything.

It seems that Homecoming is the time when the entire school goes out for raising money. They hope to get $10,000 this year. Every dollar we raise will be matched by the Nashville office. Every student is out to raise a certain quota by writing friends and soliciting anyone he can. Then each class puts on various activities to raise money. A basketball game was played Monday night between the sophomores of Rust and Mississippi Industrial (MI)[4] charging 25¢ admission. They made $77 but it was divided between the two schools. The faculty is divided in two groups and each group tries to outdo the other, of course. If anyone is trying to find someplace to put his money where it is really needed, I highly recommend Rust College to you.

The most important committee I am on is called the Faculty Committee. I thought it was to be a channel for grievances, but find we are also expected to work on salaries, tenure, and professional growth. We met with President Smith today, that is the chairman and I (the secretary), and presented him with four grievances. He said it was a good report.

October 14, 1960

My first motion pictures have arrived. I'm going to preview them tomorrow morning. If they are good I'll put up some posters advertising them to all the students and show them Monday and Tuesday evenings.

4. Mississippi Industrial College, across the street from Rust, was founded in 1910 by the Colored (now Christian) Methodist Episcopal (C.M.E.) Church, not to be confused with today's United Methodist Church which sponsors Rust College.

My concert[5] will have to be on November 13, Sunday afternoon, at 4. I wonder if I can get anyone to come out. Maybe I am beginning my ostracism that I had half way anticipated. I told Rev. and Mrs. Smith about it last night and asked them to save the date. November 6 has been declared Rust Day in this conference (white). They haven't had a Rust Day recently because of the fear of having anything. I tried to get my concert on Rust Day, but the choir is singing out of town then. I'll go to Sunday School Sunday with my gay colored tickets which I will attempt to sell for 50¢ each.

Tomorrow is the last day for my in-service class. Cotton picking will soon be over and they will be teaching again. I shall miss them. After they wrote an excerpt from the Declaration of Independence for me, one of them told me how hard she had studied for it. "I went around the house the whole week saying bits of it aloud. My sister thought I was crazy. I'd give her my copy of it and she'd hear me say it. When I went to bed last night I prayed, 'Dear Lord, don't let me forget the Declaration of Independence.' Then it was going over and over in my mind so I couldn't sleep. Finally I prayed again, 'Dear Lord, do let me forget the Declaration of Independence long enough to get to sleep.' " She also told me how much the course had meant to her. "I tell my neighbor—she's a white lady—all about you. I tell her things you say, what you wear, and how you look. She says she is coming down some day to *view* you herself." They live in Olive Branch about 15 miles south of Memphis.

Tuesday, October 25, 1960

Dear Patient Ones:

My simple and comfortable routine was completely ruined this weekend by our trip to Nashville. Dr. Dombrowski of the Southern Conference Educational Fund, with headquarters in New Orleans, wrote me soon after my arrival here asking if I would meet with the executive board in Nashville on October 22. I wrote back asking if I could take another member of the faculty so as not to make the trip alone. Thus Mrs. [Frances] Eaton and I went.

The trip itself was a revelation on the hazards of travel if you are of a dark skin. Mrs. Eaton kept warning me how we must leave early enough not to be

5. Miss Doxey's Rust College choir, which toured throughout the Midwest for many years to great acclaim, agreed to give a concert for which I could sell tickets to raise my quota for the financial campaign.

on the road after dark. I have no desire to travel after dark, myself, but this was more than a "dislike," I soon realized. Then she was terribly upset when we missed one highway (she was calling the turns and missed it), even though another highway was just as good. When I stopped to get a cup of coffee and a sandwich, not having eaten before I left whereas she had because she didn't have a class up to the last minute as did I, she locked all the car doors while she was waiting for me. Of course she traveled with her doors locked, too. Going around the courthouse in a town, she urged me to hurry and get out of this place before someone stopped us. Her concern was that we would be stopped on some pretense because we were of different races riding in the same car.

When I was getting my sandwich and cup of coffee, I asked if my colored friend with whom I was traveling could eat there too. I knew she didn't want to eat, but just wanted to get the answer anyway. I was told she could go around to the kitchen door and be served.

The meeting was at Fisk University. We stayed in one of the guest houses on that beautiful campus. We spent the entire day Saturday in the meeting except for my driving Rev. Fred Shuttlesworth (Negro) to the airport. You may have read about him. He is pastor of a large church in Birmingham. He has so many lawsuits filed against him that it is hard for him to remember them all. He says if he weren't involved in lawsuits, he'd feel he was slipping—ducking the issues or something. Every Monday night, about 400 people attend a mass meeting at his church. On my way back from the airport, I saw the Methodist Publishing House. Seeing its beautiful, modern building only made me mad. I would prefer a little less expense on it and a little more on a certain college.

I also met and talked with Dr. [Charles G.] Gomillion of Tuskegee. He is the one who has led the court fights and boycotts protesting the gerrymandering of the boundaries of Tuskegee. Those of you who read the *Southern Patriot*[6] are up on these people.

Mrs. Eaton's fears while we were driving to Nashville were not entirely unfounded, I learned. One of the members at the board meeting, Carl Braden [white], husband of the author of *The Wall Between*, was stopped en route to the meeting because he called on a couple of Negroes in Brownsville, Tennessee [the town where I had my snack].

Because Mrs. Eaton was giving a speech at 3:00 the next day, we had to leave at 6:00 Sunday morning. Returning home, the restroom became a prob-

6. The *Southern Patriot* was the newspaper of the Southern Conference Educational Fund (SCEF) from the late 1940s into the 1970s.

lem. The first place I stopped refused to let her use it. Later I reached the point—morning coffee, you know—where I had to stop. She said she didn't. I thought I was asking the attendant about her where she couldn't hear me, but she heard, and it hurt her that I had asked. She said she knew the policy and didn't like to put herself in a position to be insulted. Finally, *she* had to find a restroom, too. We tried to find a Greyhound bus station, but couldn't. At last I spied a sign in front of an independent station which said "White and Colored restrooms." Of course, the white was clean, the colored was not and was for both men and women.

By getting Mrs. Eaton back to Memphis she got an honorarium of $50 for her speech[7] which she is adding to the sophomore class's financial gift to the college at Homecoming. She is advisor for the sophomore class.

Last Monday I gave an alternate assignment to my classes—to attend a political meeting on the lawn of the courthouse at which there would be a speaker for the Republican Party, for the Democratic Party, and for the Unpledged Electors.[8] Mother, you know how many Negroes congregate around the courthouse. It never occurred to me that I was being indiscreet in my assignment. Then, in the last class of the day, I said on impulse, "I'll be driving down. If anyone wants to ride with me, meet me at my car. I can take up to five persons."

One of the young men went to Mrs. Eaton—he told me afterward that he went to her because if any of the students didn't return he wanted someone of long standing at the college to know where they were. Well, Mrs. Eaton met me at the car and said I'd only get these kids in trouble. All the white riff-raff will be at this meeting and you can't tell what will happen.

When I arrived at the courthouse I found two of my girls there so I asked them to return. After the meeting was in progress I spied three boys. It made me a bit uneasy especially since they were taking notes. Then as I turned to leave at the close I discovered a police car was parked right behind them. The boys and I ate dinner in the cafeteria that evening and had a good re-hash of the meeting. I was glad we all escaped unscathed. Actually, a crowd was needed. Only about 50 were there in all. Most of them were for the Unpledged Electors. However, only one other Negro was there and he was way off in the back-

7. In a large church pastored by one of her former students.

8. Mississippians led by Ross Barnett joined segregationists from other Southern states in sending some delegates to the 1960 Democratic National Convention unpledged to any presidential candidate.

ground so I guess they know when the courthouse is for their use and when it is not. Of course each of the speakers spoke for "our way of life" and against civil rights for Negroes, so none of them would have welcomed my students. I never realized before how much the Republican Party had done during the past 7½ years to advance civil rights until I heard the Democrat and Unpledged speakers relate these "offensive measures."

I'm afraid I'm up against a barrier that I can't surmount in this concert which I am promoting here on campus on November 13. Everyone is sure he is going to be busy on November 13 though as yet nothing is on the calendar when I pin them down to looking. One told me when I asked point blank—a lawyer of the Methodist church—that if I would indicate seats would be segregated, I might have better luck. One of the church women whom I have admired let go with some remarks about her fears that Negroes would demand use of the library here just because Memphis had capitulated. In the remarks I detected another side to her that I had never suspected—downright bitterness if not cruelty.

It sounds as though I had lost all sense of diplomacy when I look back over this letter. Where on earth can I mail it?

I think I'll draw in my horns for the rest of the year. I can't afford to do anything to get the college in trouble as I will only be here a year so wouldn't be suffering the result with the rest of them. This college is not one that is in the forefront of the movement for change. The policy here is that education is more important right now than anything else—and this may be right. At least education is surely *needed.*

Last night I gave a talk to the dormitory girls which seemed to go over big.

Even the town newspaper (a weekly) is segregated. One page is labeled as news of our Negro citizens. In this section I learn of the activities and interests of some of my students.

For example a baby contest was held in the church of one of my minister students. This seems to be a popular way of raising money—buying votes for a particular baby. In talking to the minister after class I learned that he has three churches quite scattered throughout the county; he has five children; attends school three days a week; and does carpentering when he has to meet urgent bills.

One of the real spark-plugs in that same class is another minister. He is from Phoenix. Said I probably would not be able to understand why he came to Mississippi but he found a girl while in the service who was from Mississippi. He received a call from an Illinois church and a Mississippi church at the same time. He and the girl, now his wife, decided to come here. He travels 50 miles each way to come to classes. Has been at his charge now four years. He was asked originally to take three charges but he refused, saying he preferred to build up *one*, giving his all to it.

One in my Saturday class drives over 100 miles each way.

November 4, 1960

I think I'll change my profession from teaching to writing—letter writing. Every day things occur that I want to tell someone, and so often they are such that I can't tell anyone here.

If I get to jail, or *in* jail, it will likely be because I write *too much*. You may have noticed the different postmarks on my envelopes.

I had such a good day at U. of M. I visited with one of my former profs, Dr. James Silver, for about an hour. He introduced me to other professors who happened in. Several are very much interested in Rust. Dr. Silver said he'd so like to get to know Rust College. I suggested he could start by speaking in assembly. He said he'd be happy to. "This is the first time I've ever been asked." (That solves the assembly program for which I'm responsible.)

Another faculty member came in just as I was leaving. Silver introduced us saying, "Mrs. Campbell isn't just *talking* as we do; she's doing something." The new entrant said, "You can't go yet. Sit down and tell me about Rust." Thus we talked till we were both late for lunch. He bought two tickets for my concert and says I can count on his being here. He wants me to show him the campus and introduce him to faculty members. He wants to come out some time to hold a discussion with a small group—such as my class or the Social Science Club.

My prof does not think I can last much longer on friendly terms in the community. He says it is *impossible*. I said if things should take a turn for the worse, I'd just chalk it up as part of the year's experience. Fortunately (maybe) I am in a position where I'm not dependent upon the local townspeople for friends. I always have my mail!

Mrs. Smith (the church Smiths not the college Smiths) told me about a meeting where the members of the Women's Club had a speaker on communism. We both warmed up on the subject. She said he was asked if the NAACP was communist, and he said absolutely not. I decided her speaker was authentic if he would say that in the South.

Suddenly she said, "Mrs. Campbell, may I ask you a personal question?" I asked, "You mean something like am I a communist?" She laughed and said she knew that would be futile for I wouldn't tell her if I were. But the question was, "Will colored and white sit together at your concert?" It seems she has been trying to encourage friends to come but they always ask this question. Mrs. Smith is a "Southern liberal" as regards race. Her husband sees the light but fears church dissension. She is more daring than he, but she is also a dutiful wife. Living in the South is very complicated for those who think.

I took an article to the local paper concerning my concert. I said, "Where do you plan to carry this piece?" The girl didn't know, and I asked to see Mr. [Grady S.] McAlexander. He said, "Our paper only has one section." I said, "Maybe, but I don't want this on the Negro page for this concert is primarily for the white citizens." He smiled and said, "OK." I'm eager to see where it is placed. We've had a jovial tit-for-tat ever since I met him and the owner. First I paid $3 for a subscription (1 year) then sold McAlexander two tickets. Then I inquired about an ad and agreed on a 3″ one at a cost of $1.95. Then I said, "Of course you'll carry an article in the news section, won't you?" I had already said I always seemed to come out wrong on the financial end in our trades—but at this he said, "You're doing all right!" When [I went] in, this time, I approached the owner for tickets. He'd be in New Orleans that day, he said. "Then for the support of a local institution, you could get the tickets and give them to someone." He capitulated and wrote a check for $1. I said, "Isn't there a Mississippi Senator around here named [George] Yarbrough?" "I'm it and also president pro tem," said he. "Imagine that!" I replied. "Talking to a celebrity and not knowing it!" (I was prudent enough not to mention the nature of his reputation.)

Last week I told you about a minister in my class whom I enjoyed so very much. He talked with me today after class. He feels his education at a theological school in Nashville and here isn't first-rate. Even though he is 33 and it would be something of a hardship on his family, he is considering going away for a graduate year where he has real competition. Finances would be a problem. His wife is willing to move out on faith. He can do hard work if necessary, he says. He has been here four years, turning down other openings because he believed in keeping a church long enough to make something of it. He speaks in different parts of the country and this is a welcome source of income. He is concerned for his children's schooling, too, realizing how little education they are getting in this little school they are attending. Coming from Phoenix he has had experience with good schools and so has a basis for comparison.

He feels the changes and opportunities for his people are coming now, and he would like to be better qualified to lead them.

November 12, 1960

Tomorrow is my Rust Choir Concert. I approached the owner of a drug store with tickets. "Sorry, I'm going to be out of town," he said. I answered, "Do you know, practically everyone will be away Sunday. This is going to be a mighty lonesome place." He took two tickets but of course I don't expect to see him.

A member of the church asked if there would be special seats. "Oh, no, you may have any seat in the house," I replied.

One of the local merchants and a member of the church succumbed to my request that he put a poster in his window. A few days later I had difficulty locating it, but persistence paid off. It was behind a large pillar.

To the pastor's credit, he put an announcement in the bulletin last Sunday (I didn't have the heart to ask for it again this Sunday). He announced it at prayer meeting last Wednesday at my request.

They'll all be happy when this concert is over. I've thought of selling guesses on the number of white guests we will have. I'll be disappointed if there aren't six here. More than that would send me into shock.

After traveling with my colleague to Nashville and having such difficulty finding her a restroom, I vowed never to buy gas again without putting the question, "Do you have colored restrooms?" I can't report my first attempt as an unmitigated success, though.

"Yes. New one. Tried to get Standard Oil to pay for it. Wouldn't do it. Paid for it myself."

After casing the place and finding only the usual rooms for whites, I returned to the owner now filling my tank and said, "You surely hid them well. I can't find them. Do you have separate rooms for men and women?" (Most do not for the colored.)

"No, ma'am. We just have one for men."

I'll learn to be specific.

Ministers of this conference (Central Jurisdiction[9]) had a three-day school of missions in the local Asbury Church. Wednesday evening they had a dinner here at the cafeteria honoring the new bishop. Faculty was invited. Many of the ministers plus the bishop had done their undergraduate work here at Rust.

I went to the church for the evening meeting where I heard my first *vital* sermon since being here. It was given by the bishop. Some excerpts: "The time has come when we may be called on to witness not just here between these church walls but between jail walls. There is a bit of God in each man. We have no right to subject that God quality in us to back door treatment for a meal we could do without. We can't talk about white folks keeping us out of their churches if we don't try to get them in ours. If you can *control* your religion, you don't have *religion.*"

I have been hearing *controlled* sermons. This was as refreshing as a summer breeze on a hot day. The bishop's name is [Charles F.] Golden[10] and he would be an excellent speaker for anyone looking for such.

One of my students was mentioned in a Memphis *Commercial Appeal* article headed "Miss. agog at church meeting—complains of church teaching." This student attended a conference at Lake Junaluska, N.C. He had told us previously how wonderful the experience was. According to the paper an "informant" was there who reported that some Mississippi youths went to camp segregationists and returned integrationists, that a white Mississippi youth, son of a minister, roomed with a Negro at the conference, and that Nat Green, a Negro student from Mississippi (in my class), rode the white bus as far as Birmingham.

November 20, 1960

Mrs. [Ardelia C.] Turner, one of the staff residents, and I have just returned from Water Valley, a fairly good-sized town as Mississippi towns go, about 50 miles from here. Mrs. Burley, wife of the minister about whom I wrote a couple of weeks ago, asked me to be the speaker for their Women's Day which was today.

9. The Methodist Church was at that time divided into Jurisdictions. The Central Jurisdiction was made up of African American churches and covered a large Southern area, overlapping white Jurisdictions.

10. Golden, who attended Rust College at one time, later became Bishop of the Southern California-Arizona Methodist Conference.

We arrived in time for church though the Women's Day program wasn't until 4. Rev. [Ralph Eugene] Burley is a powerful preacher. The church has a choir of about 20 children. They looked adorable in their short white robes and red ties. They sang with gusto. The congregation had no books for singing, but Rev. Burley did a good job of "lining." Those of you who have read *To Kill a Mockingbird* remember the description of lining.[11] There was never a dull moment in the service though it lasted almost twice as long as ours at home. At the end everyone sang "It Is No Secret What God Can Do" while we marched up and shook hands with Rev. Burley and all the deacons.

The Burleys have two children, a boy 11 and a girl 12. Mrs. Burley is a very capable person and had a good dinner for us. Mrs. Burley was bothered because I insisted on helping with the dishes. I told her after she had heard my talk she'd understand I had to do the dishes or be a hypocrite. (Camie's student who loved doing dishes, because she and her father had a chance to talk together then, was one of my illustrations.)

Rev. Burley and others appeared pleased with my talk. Maybe they were just nice. Knowing me I'm sure you understand it was very practical and down to earth. They gave me a beautiful corsage of three carnations and offered me an honorarium which I'm sure they were relieved I didn't accept.

When we first arrived I just had to find a restroom. Hating to rush into a strange church and ask right off for one, I said we'd find the church first and then hunt up a station. This we did. When I came out of the restroom there was Rev. Burley. I said, "You're not where you belong at this hour." He said, "I saw your car pass by the church and thought you were lost so left my handshaking to follow you." It would have been less embarrassing had I asked the usher.

The ping-pong table finally arrived and the students love it. They were so nice about offering to play with me. I think it an excellent addition to the school and I personally am going to get much enjoyment out of it. Thanks to you who helped to make it possible.

The concert last Sunday was tops. As for the town guests, I wasn't disappointed, and neither did I go into a state of shock. Just exactly six came—one of whom was a child of 12. Last Sunday at church I was buttonholing everyone I met saying, "I'm expecting you at the college this afternoon." One woman said, "You sure are a promoter." I said, laughing, "Well, no one can say I didn't try!" Another remarked, "You'll have to learn you're in Mississippi now,"

11. The leader calls the words of each line before the audience sings it.

which I thought gave the "lie" to all the excuses I had received even from her. The truth did out.

As for me I learned something about Mississippians—they aren't interested in concerts! Hereafter I'll use my energies in other ways. My only gain in this deal is a negative one; so far as I know I didn't make anybody mad at me. Thus the door is still open for further promotions.

Because my car must sit out in all kinds of weather, I had a good wax job from my regular service station. It meets my requirement of a colored restroom. However, I'm working on a strategy to enlighten the owner concerning the futility and undesirability of the sign over the drinking fountain, "White only—colored use cup."

[Thanksgiving Evening 1960]

Thanksgiving didn't seem like Thanksgiving. I came as near to homesickness as at any time since my arrival here. Highlight of the day for me was riding in the parade for Homecoming. The senior class decorated my car and furnished the driver. Two girls in the back seat and I in the front beamed and waved our way around the town square. I was particularly pleased to have my (white) church friends wave back. One man missed seeing me at first and ran a few feet to come up alongside our car and call, "Mrs. Campbell!" Here one gets satisfaction from such minor triumphs. Only last month one of the faculty told me I couldn't ride to town with these Negro boys. I never know what actions are avoided because of unwarranted fear and what are really taboo. Perhaps that is why I feel it necessary to try for myself rather than take someone's word for it.

November 28, 1960

Miss Jackson, one of the faculty members, and I had a delightful weekend in Alabama at Talladega College (Negro) with John and Verdelle's[12] friend, Mr. Harrison. We were entertained royally. Friday evening a dinner party in the hall where we stayed included the president and his wife, the dean and his wife, and others totaling about a dozen. The meal and company were equally good.

12. John and Verdelle Reynolds, African Americans from South Carolina, were my across-the-street neighbors in Pasadena.

Saturday morning we toured the beautiful rolling campus which to us seemed very large. The library gave evidence of being the "heart of the college" as we are so often reminded it should be. Miss Scott, the librarian, has many programs in progress including some for the community, with a storytelling hour on Saturday mornings and a mobile library that circulates throughout the county. Mr. Harrison's music department is well equipped with pianos and organs. Not only does the art building speak for itself, but the paintings in all the buildings evidence a strong emphasis on art appreciation. The library checks out paintings and prints to students for their rooms—even the president's home had paintings on loan from the library.

Miss Jackson [biology professor] was impressed by the science building. The Student Union is most attractive and functional—a part of the Physical Education building in which there is even a swimming pool. The chapel is of good size with grand piano and pipe organ. It also has facilities for the showing of weekly films. The school discourages students from exposing themselves to the segregated town facilities. The dining room is an experience in better living.

Everything is in good repair, well preserved with paint, and clean. Certainly what we try to teach is not found just in books; much must be caught, not taught. This campus appeared to be offering much that could be caught to advantage. Everything about the school gives students experiences in a way of life one would like to see the students become accustomed to.

The faculty has time for considerable individual work with its 300-plus students. Rust has 500-plus regular students and about 200 in-service teachers on Saturdays plus three five-week sessions for in-service teachers in the fall and summer.

Saturday afternoon we were invited to the dean's home at 4:00; in the evening to the president's home. We have never been better entertained. I couldn't help but be impressed by the apparent good relationship between the president and the faculty.

I say hats off to the Congregationalists. When they sponsor a school they make it one to be proud of. Tougaloo has a good reputation also, and Dillard in New Orleans, co-sponsored by the Congregationalists and Methodists, is well provided for.

As a Methodist, I am not happy with Rust. If we sponsor a college, it should be one to which we can point with pride. I'm sure few members of the Methodist Church realize the conditions that prevail in this college. We should see that our schools are of high enough standards to be accredited by something other than just the state of Mississippi. With the world in crisis over the problems of race, there is no place more in need of a good program than Mississippi. The good work that is being done here is due to the dedicated teachers who have stayed on year after year, underpaid and overworked, getting their reward in seeing their students go out better prepared to meet the world and improve it in their own small way.

On the way home we stopped at Rev. Shuttlesworth's church in Birmingham in the midst of typical, poor, Southern homes. This area made Richard Wright's *Black Boy* vivid in my memory. America, the land of plenty, has a long way to go yet. A gracious high school senior gave us a guided tour of the church and explained its program. This church was bombed a few years ago so has a new decorating job making it look fresh. Before the church bombing, the pastor's home was bombed. That is the price of freedom of speech in Alabama. I had met Rev. Shuttlesworth when I was at the meeting of the executive board of SCEF in Nashville. The *Southern Patriot* frequently mentions him and the many court suits in which he is involved.

Fortunately Rev. Shuttlesworth was out of town or we'd have stayed for the church service, in which case we'd have had a flat tire in the dark on a lonely stretch of road. We had it in front of a small church and were glad for some daylight, fading as it was. We were indebted to two Negro men who stopped and changed the tire for us.

At Birmingham, en route to Talladega, I wanted to check on my ticket to New York for Christmas. We stopped at the Greyhound station, beautiful and spacious. The swinging glass doors of one waiting room carried the inscription "COLORED INTRASTATE WAITING ROOM." The door of another larger room read "WHITE INTRASTATE WAITING ROOM." We circled the building looking for an "interstate" waiting room. Finding none, we decided to go in anyway and ask for the information I needed. Miss Jackson is not very dark and it seemed altogether possible to me that she might go unnoticed.

Without further hesitation, we walked through the doors marked "white" and went directly to the ticket counter. I made my inquiry. The clerk turned his back to me and went to the other side of his little office. When he returned to me a policeman said, from behind me, "Did you know you *tend* to disturb the peace? You can't bring *her* here."

I explained that we had looked for the "interstate" room but couldn't find it, that I only wanted information regarding a trip to New York by Greyhound.

"There isn't any interstate room and you *tend* to misconduct by being here with *her*."

I assured him I wouldn't want to *tend* to anything like that. "I won't be long getting this information; then we'll leave. All right?" Miss Jackson afterward laughed over my "All right?" She says I repeated it three times and he never did answer, just stared at me.

I took his silence for consent and turned back to the clerk. He curtly answered my questions, and I requested him to give me the figures in writing. He wrote them on a scratch pad, tore off a corner and thrust it at me. There was no evidence here of the Greyhound courtesy I had always been accustomed to receiving.

I turned to face the policeman who was still at my back. He still had the same stern expression. I said we had planned to eat at this terminal, thinking that due to the interstate nature of travel, we would be allowed to eat together.

"She'll have to go to the colored room."

"May I go there, too?"

"We put a United States Senator in jail for that once," he said.

"You did? What was his name?" I ventured to ask.

"Taylor."[13]

Dear Miss Jackson. Such quiet dignity as you never saw.

Miss Jackson and I went to a grocery store and bought food.

Coming home we stopped at an attractive roadside place to eat. The man who greeted us said to me, "This colored lady will have to go to the side door." I asked if I could go with her. He agreed and directed us to the door with the canopy. When we found the door led to the kitchen, I recalled the bishop's speech and said, "No, thanks." Leaving, Miss Jackson said we should give the man credit. He was courteous and he called her a "lady."

Next we tried a drive-in, but there proved to be no open window from which to order. We walked in to get a hamburger to take out. The man at the counter turned red with rage and shouted, "Get her out of here! Get out, I say!"

I said we merely wanted a hamburger to take out. He repeated, louder, if that were possible, "Get her out of this place!"

Somehow I had always clung to the idea expressed by the Dallas Grey-

13. Sen. Glen Hearst Taylor (D-Idaho) served 1945–1951. While campaigning for vice president on a third-party ticket with Henry Wallace in 1948, he attempted to make a speech to the integrated Southern Youth Congress in Birmingham. He was arrested for disorderly conduct, treated roughly, and released on $100 bond after he declined to enter the Alliance Gospel Tabernacle by the "white" entrance and tried to go in the "colored" entrance. *Newsweek* of May 10, 1948, carried one of many national articles about the incident.

hound clerk: "We can't enforce these segregation signs, but we don't have to; the people by tradition observe them." It is hard to believe that people, actually confronted with two quiet, dignified ladies, can be so abusive and hard. We ate again from our bag of groceries.

Miss Jackson is a wonderful companion; she is quiet and objectively interested. No one can insult her. She has a rich sense of humor. We decided it was time someone wrote a book similar to Carl Rowan's *South of Freedom.* You never can tell; we might be the ones to do it. I really need some justification for taking such chances that obviously don't do much good except to satisfy my curiosity. As far as doing any good is concerned, the greatest good I can do is to help my students learn. If I get sidetracked and end up in some adverse situation, don't bother to "know" me.

We had better luck this trip with restrooms. My technique has improved. I drive up and say breezily, "Two questions: first, will you accept a Mobil credit card?" When the operator answers in the affirmative, I continue, "Good! Second question: Have you a restroom for us?" At the first place, on second look, the operator said, "She'll have to use the colored room." I replied that was o.k. I'd use it, too. He called to us as we were on our way, "The ladies' room is just around the corner." We never did find the colored room and decided he had had a change of heart and was sending us to the white room. The other two places were without incident.

December 6, 1960

In pulling to the side of the road after my puncture on Thanksgiving weekend, I ruined my tire. I first inquired about a new one at my regular Standard station. For some time I have been annoyed by the refrigerated drinking fountain at this station. Above it hangs a plastic cup with a crudely written sign, WHITE ONLY—COLORED USE CUP.

After the attendant gave me the price, I asked if he gave green stamps.

"No, ma'am, we don't give stamps," he said almost apologetically.

"Shucks!" I said. "I always like something a little extra when I buy. I'll tell you what—I'll accept in lieu of stamps one large one—that sign over your drinking fountain."

Stunned, he replied that the owner would have to be consulted. Returning the next day, I was informed the owner said the sign was not for sale. I said I had no intention of buying it—I just wanted him to *give* it to me. I thanked him and drove to another Standard station.

While the proprietor was figuring the price of a tire, I noticed the same situation regarding the drinking fountain there. I said in what I hope was a jovial manner, "When did you people last study hygiene?"

"Why?" asked an attendant.

"Don't you know that cup might spread disease?"

"Oh, that's only for the niggers," he explained.

"Disease knows no color line," I continued. "Let a disease start with the colored and it will hit the white people, too."

"How could it? We don't have anything to do with the niggers."

"Maybe you have a cook or a maid in your home. The fruit and vegetables you buy in the store are often picked and handled by colored."

The owner interrupted with the price, and I expressed appreciation for the discount he was allowing. "Throw in the sign and we'll call it a deal," I said.

"Why should I do that? I'd only have to make another."

"That's up to you," I answered.

Then slowly rising to his full height, he declared, "NO! I'd rather not make the sale!" And he didn't, though I don't know who won these little bouts as I bought my tire in Memphis and paid *full* price.

December 13, 1960

I don't know why I didn't pick up some extra programs to show you what an advanced concert the Methodist choir (white) gave with my "help." I was on the front row and when the notes went too high for me, I just opened my mouth wide, taking care to let no sound out to mar the beauty of other voices. When I had to carry a second soprano part on occasion, I often had to resort to the same technique because I couldn't find the pitch. However, when it was over, the director put her arm around me and thanked me for helping them.

Two things bothered me throughout. One, why anyone bothered to come hear us. Remember these were the ones who "didn't like music, made it a habit to go out of town on Sunday afternoons, usually had guests visit them on Sundays," ad infinitum. Two, I looked up at the balcony originally built for the slaves and now not generally used; I saw the lone Negro caretaker listening intently to our rendition of the Christmas story—Peace on earth, good will to all mankind. At least he was allowed to listen. Given another 2000 years, he might be able to sit on the main floor.

I had such a good letter from a Pasadena friend who used to teach at Washington [Junior High] with me. She said in part: "Years ago, Margaret Mead came to Washington and spoke [on race] at a faculty meeting. Afterwards I said to her, 'What is the good [of talking to prejudiced people]? Nothing you can say will change them.' She said it was of value just to make them uncomfortable—to force them to realize that other people did not agree with them—that they held unpopular ideas."

This is about all I can do here. It was a comfort to know that someone might see value in doing that much.

Oberlin, Ohio
December 26, 1960

Dear Keith and Camie,

Perhaps it's time to explain my comments on Rust.

When the ping-pong table arrived, the students took to it just as I had hoped. After three days of playing, the paddles and balls disappeared. Tracing them down by asking who last used, last saw, etc., they were found to be in the possession of Mr. [Theodore R.] Collins, the business manager. I approached him regarding them and he, folding his arms across his chest, said, "Yes, I'll have to see Mr. [Earnest T.] Battle and work out some rules."

I asked if the students had abused the privilege. "No, but they might. Anyway, the president told me to do something about it." I replied that was queer because I had cleared the whole matter with the president before I ordered the table. "How long will it take you and Mr. Battle to figure out the rules?" I asked. "I don't know," he said.

A few days later when at the Smiths' home, I casually said, "By the way, what is the story on the ping-pong set?"

The president knew nothing about it. Said no mention had been made of it since he told Mr. Collins it was coming. I asked him if he would please straighten it out and he said he would. We continued to talk of all the possibilities—even a tournament, etc.

Nothing happened. After another week, I was in his office on other business and brought up the ping-pong again. He had forgotten to say anything. As I left, he walked into Collins's office to tell him right then.

Next day, Smith went to Mayo Brothers [clinic] in Minnesota for surgery. Nothing happened for 10 days. Then a notice went up on the bulletin board saying ping-pong hours were from 9–11 a.m. and 2–4 p.m. (all good class or study hours). At the bottom was, "These rules apply to young ladies only."

In the cafeteria, I said to Collins, "I see you and Mr. Battle are making progress on the rules. Are the boys allowed to play any time?"

"No, they have a table in the men's dorm."

The paddles and balls were still locked up and had to be requested from the cafeteria dietitian. Of course my whole purpose was defeated anyway. I expected this to be a social game. From after dinner until 7, for instance, there is so much "boy-girl" relationship with nothing to do but look at each other, get a little closer, and wish for more. The ping-pong gave at least a few of them a chance to enjoy each other but with minds focused on something else. Always some were watching so quite a few benefitted.

Just before vacation, my first chance after Smith returned, I told him that you had asked what you could do by way of a Christmas gift to Rust and the best suggestion I had was a dustcloth to be used on the ping-pong table.

He said, "What *is* the problem about this table?"

I told him I didn't know, but as far as I was concerned until we used what we had, there was no use asking folks to send us more. I also said it was most embarrassing for me to have students ask me why they couldn't play. That I was really disturbed when the YM president called at the hall one evening asking permission to use the table and saying they would promise to take good care of it (as though *I* had a table that *I* was keeping the students from using like a dog in the manger). I said either all students used that table at any hour other than meal hours or I'd send it to someone who *could* use it. I said the greatest problem in this school is not lack of facilities but failure to use the facilities we have, and this ping-pong table is just *one* example.

The president agreed and said he'd give me his word that the matter would be settled when I returned from vacation.

If I can believe President Smith, he and I think alike on this whole matter—and many related. He is an excellent speaker, a good public relations man, very intelligent, but administration is not his forte.

On the faculty committee, I have the job as secretary of writing up all our suggestions. I'm finding it really a task, as everything we touch is a problem.

January 2, 1961

It was wonderful in New York, Chappaqua and Oberlin, but I can't say as much for the homecoming. I arrived Sunday afternoon. My dormitory was locked. Mr. Collins was out and no one else had keys. I visited with the president and his wife until the superintendent of buildings and grounds returned home. He had no keys either but managed to get in the dorm. By this time a student, Miss Jones, had arrived. The president told her to stay in my dorm for the night. Inside there was no electricity on first floor; second floor was o.k. My room was locked—for first time since I have been here. Someone probably thought he was doing me a favor. Superintendent returned to president for instructions. Was told to break in my room. Did—another repair job to do now. Turned on gas heaters. We went out to eat. Returned to upstairs where there was light. Miss Jones and I huddled about the heater and read. Kept worrying about the sound running through pipes. Didn't know if it was gas or water. No water was turned on so if it was water making the noise it must be running someplace it shouldn't. I traced the sound to the water heater. Couldn't figure whether heater was on or not. At 9 Miss Jones and I began a tour with my flashlight. Found broken water pipes, wet walls, some first-floor ceilings sagging from weight of water-soaked plaster boards. Whole boxes of toilet paper soaked. I went down to president again. Told him I was going to a motel and he could figure out what to do with Miss Jones. I said I was afraid of fire. President came up to get Miss Jones. He said to leave a heater on because it would take a long time to dry this damp cold place. I ended up staying at the president's home. Miss Jones stayed with one of the secretaries who lives near campus.

Today Mr. Collins arrived with the keys. The plumber came. Said he knew he should get in here during the vacation period but he didn't have any keys. "I only take orders." This isn't the only dorm that has frozen pipes. I hope not so much damage is in the others. Fortunately my room is spared. The room next to me has the whole ceiling off the middle. The bed covers are soaked. The clothes in the closet are wet. The books are practically ruined. The ceiling is falling down in our bath. We still have no water though it is now 3 p.m. The men's dorm has no water either.

Students are arriving all the while. The blessed students. They are what make this life worthwhile.

One encouraging thing is that several things the Faculty Committee urged in its reports have produced results. Latest—a math teacher is being brought in for night classes. Our poor science teacher was beside himself because there is no adequate math course for his students. This was blamed on the [attempted] merger—MI was supposedly responsible for the math program [but didn't supply the math teacher as agreed].

January 7, 1961

Of course, the president and all hands have been busy trying to get us dug out of the mire caused by the frozen pipes. I didn't like to hound him about the ping-pong table when he was so discouraged about more important things. (We just tonight have a toilet that flushes. Just today got water on second floor.)

Yesterday the ping-pong table appeared again—in a corner where no one could possibly play. This morning I asked a young man to help me move the cafeteria tables and get the ping-pong table out where it could be used. I asked the cafeteria manager for the equipment and said I wanted it left out. I went to my room and made a sign: "Note Change—Both men and women may use the ping-pong table in the cafeteria. Playing may be done any time the cafeteria is open except for meal hours and scheduled events." Returning to the cafeteria at noon, the ping-pong equipment was again in the kitchen. I asked the cafeteria manager if Mr. Collins had spoken to her about the ping-pong table. She said no. Just then he came in and I approached him. (The president left last night for 10 days.) I asked if the president had mentioned the new plan for the use of the ping-pong table. No. So I said, "The president gave me his word of honor that after the holidays that table would be out; the equipment would be left out; both men and women could play at any hour the cafeteria is open except for meals. You can tell him anything you want, that I was obstreperous, blame me as you like, but I want that table used. I've made a sign to that effect and will give it to Mr. Battle to put on the bulletin board." I think I out-kingfished him. He just said "All right" at each appropriate pause. Now I intend to be in the cafeteria from 6:30–7 every evening—just to be sure the cafeteria stays open until then. About a half hour of playing every night would be fine. That wouldn't interfere with studying which is supposed to begin at 7.

Rust College, Holly Springs, Miss., January 8, 1961

Before I left for Oberlin, Dr. [F. W.] Schaefer, a white visitor at Rust for the past several weeks, made arrangements for me to leave my car at the home of some friends (colored) of his in Memphis. When I talked with Mr. Harris on the phone, he insisted on my staying overnight with them, promising even to take me to the bus station at 5:30 in the morning. Always one to appreciate new friends, I accepted the Harris hospitality. Mrs. Harris teaches school; Mr. Harris is a postman and works evenings in a gas station he and his father own. They have three fine children, the oldest of whom is in a Wisconsin college. I was given her room. The Harrises live in a nice home in a rather new subdivision.

On the way to the bus the morning after I arrived at the Harris home, I asked Mr. Harris to give me a tire while I was gone. When I returned, he said, "Did you know you don't have a spare wheel?" Now I have to go back to that dealer here and tell him that just because we couldn't make a deal on the tire was no reason for him to keep my wheel. Mr. Harris asked if this would be embarrassing for me to go back with a tire I bought someplace else. I said no, it would just give me another opportunity to attempt to drive home a point. I hope I can keep it all in a light vein. At first I thought I would not buy any more gas from this dealer, but he has been very nice to me. It was only the tire that was involved in the sign issue. And, I can't possibly have any influence if I just cut all relations with him. He certainly isn't going to feel the absence of my business.

The Harris family was wonderful to me. I never felt so well received by someone who had no reason to be so good to me at all. I haven't received the bill [for the tire] yet. He said he'd have to get to the station to look up the wholesale price. I told him I didn't want a wholesale price. It is enough to have the storage and all the hospitality.

The trip to Oberlin in itself was interesting. In Memphis, buying my ticket at the Greyhound station, I mentioned my surprise at the large "Colored" sign over a door. I said I had heard that Memphis had desegregated. The clerk said, "We have. You should see this place when we are really busy. Colored and white all mixed up in these two waiting rooms." I asked if this were also true of the restaurants. He said it was not; there seemed to be more trouble there. I asked who objected, management or patrons. "Both, I guess."

Before leaving Memphis, I went into the colored eating room. The waitress said to me in an aside, "You don't have to eat here. You can go to the other room." I expressed satisfaction with service there. During breakfast I conversed with a friendly lady next to me. There were glances in our direction, but nothing of more moment than that.

At noon we stopped at an attractive place to eat. As we entered I asked the hostess who met us so graciously if colored were served there. "Yes, we have a dining room for them. We also have a colored cook. Why do you ask?" I explained that while we had colored traveling on our bus, I didn't see any in the room and so, naturally, wondered where they were. She seated me at a table. The waitress came for my order. After giving it, I said, "And will you please serve me in the colored dining room?" She looked a bit startled, I thought, but recovered quickly and agreed. "Where is it?" I asked. She led me through the kitchen to a lean-to at the back in which there was crude furniture. There were only two tables. Of course none of the men would sit down with a white lady so I ate alone while several servicemen stood—the price they had to pay for my little research. I received very good service from the waitress of the white dining room who kept coming back to see how I was getting on. The kitchen help served the others—all men—with loud calls of "What do you want?" etc.

In Chattanooga I had a sandwich in a small dingy colored waiting-lunch room. Though the white section had an attractive food service, this only had a small counter with high stools, no menus, just a few sandwiches listed on the board.

As I was waiting for a taxi and enjoying a cup of coffee, courtesy of the St. James Hotel in Knoxville at 5:30 Sunday morning, December 18, I inquired of the hotel clerk regarding the schools. The clerk failed to answer. A local resident, who for some reason was visiting with the clerk at that odd hour, said they had begun to integrate in the lower grades with no special problems resulting. I remarked that they must have an enlightened citizenry in Knoxville. This brought the gray-haired clerk out of his shell. "I'm a segregationist myself. I just can't believe it's right to brainwash little children. If they're going to integrate, it should start at the top where they are old enough to know what they are doing. This way they'll marry each other and not know any better." I suggested it might comfort him to know that in California, my home state, we had always had school integration and intermarriage is very rare. He said, "Don't tell me about California. You sent all your Japanese to concentration camps."

Breakfast was in the Colored Luncheonette off the integrated waiting room of the modern Knoxville Greyhound station. Service was from the same kitchen, but it was hard to know what was offered without a menu. We had to stand at the counter to get served, then take our food to tables. All the empty tables had food spilled on them. I asked if my table might be wiped off. "Come in here and you'll find a clean table," was the answer from the white room. "Can't these be clean, too?" I pressed. "The man hasn't been able to get around there yet."

But as soon as we crossed the Virginia line things were different. There were still signs, but the restrooms for colored had "Out of Order" signs plastered over them. I always engaged the clerk at each stop in conversation. "I'm pleased to see that you serve all people at your cafeteria. How long has this been going on?" The answers were all quite similar—to the effect that Greyhound had lost a million dollar lawsuit which had originated in Richmond. "We try not to make an issue of it; we just put up 'Out of Order' signs on the colored restrooms and direct them to use the others. If they expect service in the cafeteria we serve them, but we don't suggest it to them." I usually ended the discussion with something like, "Isn't it interesting that everyone just accepts the situation as natural? No one seems a bit concerned." One clerk said he liked it better this way. None seemed to mind it much. I asked one of the colored girls on my bus how she knew when she could expect service and when not. She said it was so confusing that she just asked at every place we stopped.

Coming home there was not much segregation because I came through Ohio, Kentucky and Nashville. Nashville is more progressive than most of Tennessee. One colored lady came up to me in the station there and asked where the colored room was. I said I didn't think Nashville had such. She said she just wanted a drink. I looked around and found a fountain. She stood back and looked the situation over carefully. I said, "No, there's no sign." So much for my Christmas trip by Greyhound.

We had a tremendous talk by the college president last Thursday. Speaking is his forte. He must have been a great preacher.[14] He has clever ways of presenting his ideas. For instance: "One of the most philosophic nursery rhymes is:

> Pussy Cat, Pussy Cat, where have you been?
> I've been to London to visit the Queen.
> Pussy Cat, Pussy Cat, what did you there?
> I frightened a mouse under a chair.

He went to London with high purposes. He was going to visit the Queen. When he got there, what did he do? He fooled around playing with a mouse. Pussy Cat, where have you been? I've been to college—to study—to learn—to

14. After leaving Rust, Dr. Smith was a popular speaker at General Conferences throughout the nation.

prepare. What did you there? I fooled around; I played; I forgot my high purposes."

And from this, of course, he launched into the opportunities here to accomplish real study and the lack of interest the college has in keeping any who just want to play.

Ping-pong table was in lively use yesterday afternoon the way I envisaged it in the beginning. Even I played. I hope nothing happens to give an excuse for rescinding the privilege of using it. I hope I have made my peace with Mr. Collins. Maybe my human relations haven't been too good.

During 1960 I tried to write only what would reflect to the honor and glory of Rust. This was partly because I kept holding out faith that all really is honor and glory here. I have worked by speaking my concerns directly to the administration and through the Faculty Committee. Everyone agrees with all I say, but nothing much happens. Now I have decided that someone has to be the goat and it might better be I than anyone else. I have a good position to return to—and I realize more every day just how good.

I think the trouble may be that everyone here has been so concerned with presenting a good facade that no one has dared probe too much. Much of the distress here is caused. First, headquarters in Nashville, in my opinion, should give more supervision—at least should know what goes on. Second, right down the line of administration something is lacking.

I had such a wonderful letter from Mobil[15]—the Secretary, no less. Of course, as I expected, these Standard stations are not under Mobil supervision. Mobil cards are accepted as a courtesy in Kentucky, Mississippi, Alabama, etc.:

> "We would, however, like to take this opportunity to make Mobil Oil Company's position clear. If the kind of practice you describe were to exist at any given Mobil station, we would not hesitate to discuss it with the dealer concerned, even though nearly all of our 30,000 retail outlets in the United States are operated by independent businessmen.
>
> "Mobil Oil Company's official position is that we do not discriminate because of race, creed, color, or national or ethnic origin. This is true in every aspect of our business, including our recruitment, employment, and personnel development policies, and in our relations with our customers.
>
> "Although we regret the displeasure that caused you to write, we are grateful to you for having taken the time and trouble to direct our attention to this matter.

15. My husband Harold worked 31 years for Mobil Oil Company (under one or another of its corporate names).

We are forwarding your letter to the Standard Oil Company of Kentucky in the belief that they will wish to be aware of your comments."

Next time Miss Jackson and I are in Tennessee, we will check on Mobil stations. If they are that good, every Negro should know it and patronize them.

early January, 1961

Last night one of the teachers came in. She was restless. No wonder. She does nothing but work. I was restless. No wonder. I had played for two wonderful weeks and couldn't get back into the routine of work with no play. Upshot of it all was I said, "Let's go calling. I've never seen one of these halls when occupied." We went.

Just now I heard over the radio: Every man must either oppose the evil of his time or accept it. Here is one evil I don't intend to accept.

That hall is one that Mother and I went through in 1957 when it was unoccupied. Mother will tell you it was no incentive to get a college education then. Even Mother would be shocked at the difference now. At the time I don't think either of us knew it could be worse. It is in one word a slum. Of course last weekend's flood didn't help it, but everything can't be blamed on it. Plaster off in small and large breaks. Inadequate baths. Rickety floors. One is a very small room that has only two girls in it. Most have 3, 4, 5, and 6. Room after room had girls studying in light only sufficient for a dance or a cocktail bar. I assume this is one way Mr. Collins has balanced the budget and I don't blame him for trying to balance the budget.

The men's dorms have long been notorious for what they are not. So much so that our Faculty Committee carried a protest to the president, and in assembly last Thursday he told the men not to return to classes until they had cleaned their dorms.

This is a little different way than I intended to serve this year. But certainly someone must call attention to all this. The frustrating part is to know how to do it without wrecking the institution. I can't think of a more needy place for education—in the whole world—the influence of America being what it is. Now that the merger is started with MI is a good time, I should think, to have some people come in and look the place over in detail. That is all I ask. That someone in authority come and stay long enough to see for himself. Just talking to the president and staying in his beautiful home isn't enough.

Dr. James Silver, my professor from Ole Miss, spoke in assembly today. He brought the head of the History Department, Dr. [William T.] Doherty, [Jr.] with him. In his speech Dr. Silver said he was ashamed to admit it, but although he had lived in Mississippi 25 years, this was only the second time he had ever spoken to a Negro audience. The previous time was 13 years ago. He also said he did not know any Negroes. "This means that practically half of the people in the state of Mississippi are unknown to me." His point was that communication between the groups is lacking.

As he rambled on, I began to wonder if his opening statement might be true—that he hadn't quite made up his mind what to talk about. Finally, he got around to a scholarly history of race relations in America beginning with the Declaration of Independence. It was a most appropriate subject for a history professor to give a Negro group.

After prophesying that within the short future—perhaps five to fifteen years—they would have first-class citizenship even here in Mississippi, he said he would now indulge in about five minutes of preaching. Then he pulled no punches in relating some responsibilities that accompany rights. In Tennessee one out of every three Negro babies born is illegitimate. Such records as this might explain why his wife, Alabama born and bred, was so concerned about the possibility of their daughter's having to go to an integrated school with perhaps a large number of Negroes. "I am not excusing my wife, nor do I excuse the record." He urged them to attempt to register if they were of age and to join some organization that is working to speed the day of full rights for all. And, finally, he urged the students to make every use of their opportunities to learn. Equipment and buildings are not too important. It wouldn't even matter an awful lot if you didn't have good teachers. Learning is an individual matter and anyone who has a book and is willing to study can learn. "Maybe you *are* taking advantage of all your opportunities," he said. "If so, you are doing better than the students at the University of Mississippi."

One of my colleagues almost had me in a dither before he began. She is the one who tends to distrust most white people—with good reason, I'm sure. She said to me, "I hope he doesn't say 'Nigra' because these students just won't stand for that." But, then I remembered he had pronounced the word correctly when teaching my summer class in '56, so I stopped worrying on that score. Apparently from the comments I keep hearing, he was well received.

Prof. [William Spencer] Hamer, the one who plans to come [from Ole

Miss] for a discussion group, told me last Tuesday that Dr. Silver was telling them he was speaking here at 11:00 and expected to get a good meal out of it. We had our worst menu today—fish with so many bones that you can hardly get a nourishing meal out of it. I kidded him about the meal he was expecting—when we were alone, that is. He had just asked me, "How much pay do you get for this job?" I said, "A little more than you. I get board AND ROOM." He said, "I knew you were rich."

January 15, 1961

I'm so glad to be on campus. A person living off campus would never get behind the window dressing. It is disturbing to know the situation as it is, but I want the true picture—not just the dress parade such as I gave the visitors yesterday. I didn't even show them where I live, though I would have, had we not still been so torn up from the New Year's frozen pipe debacle. I felt it unnecessary to show them a worse picture than is representative.

I'm finding it a good idea to give the students a choice of writing a book report or coming in to discuss it with me. This gives an opportunity for us to get acquainted and discuss other subjects. Tonight I was asked how I felt about dancing. One young man told me he was writing a sermon on an idea I gave him in class. The idea was not original with me, however; it was from one of Harold Case's sermons: When self-discipline breaks down, law takes over.

The ping-pong table is being used constantly now. It's breaking me up in business buying balls for it. Do they actually burn up from hard usage or do you suppose we have some pack rats? I think I'll supply the book store with some and then they can buy their own.

I play once each day, right after dinner. The playing is supposed to cease during the line-up for the cafeteria as it isn't very pleasant to have players bumping into you or stepping on your toes when you are queued up. But last night and tonight I went in to find them utterly disregarding this rule. So I took the ball each time. I wish the students had more self-discipline, but it does have one advantage for me. I can be the first to start the game after dinner—thus I don't have to wait my turn! Tonight and night before last I was able to play four games before I was beaten. Last night I was skunked right off.

This week I at last met the owner of the gas station where I have my car serviced. He breeds bird dogs and is seldom at the station. When he started waiting on me, I said I had asked about everyone else, now I would ask him,

"Are you Mr. Cottrell?" He admitted the identity. I said, "I tried so hard to see you before I bought my tire." He said, "That's what I heard." I pressed a little further, telling him how I hated to drive all the way to Memphis for that tire and did so hope up to the last that we could get together on a deal. With that we dropped the subject and went into other talk. The manager still has business in the other corner of the station when he sees me drive in. But in time he may thaw. In the meantime, I'm sure just seeing me reminds both of them of the sign. Whether that augurs good or evil, I'm not sure, but I trust Margaret Mead's idea is right.

January 22, 1961

There are more hazards to this work than I anticipated. First I thought I'd do well if the townspeople put up with me; then it looked like the administration might be my Waterloo; now it appears it may be the students that will get me out. This is exam time. Shall we say there were some irregularities on a wholesale scale? I am still trying to ferret it all out. But there will definitely be some failures as a result.

Religion here is a fancy variety. We need more basic integrity. Of course, I keep reminding myself that they don't have much opportunity to learn basic integrity [if they haven't learned it at home]. They don't even see it displayed often—certainly not in the law. I keep thinking of the remark Keith made once: Do we really ever get down to teaching these moral concepts that we expect them to know?

Last Sunday afternoon Mrs. Smith, Dr. Schaefer (white) and I went to the art museum. I had remarked [to the president of the museum] that Mrs. Smith was interested in art and I would ask her to go with me to the museum. She said, "She's colored, isn't she?" I said yes, though I could have said no, for she looks white. Then it was that she told me I could probably get permission to go some time during the week when the museum was not usually open.

Mrs. Smith said the Rust art classes were being allowed to go this year, but she refused to go with any special groups. She didn't feel it was right not to allow all to go at regular hours. I said, "Who's going to challenge them? If you just sit back and accept their little rulings, they get away with them." She hesitated and debated, but agreed. On duty was Mrs. Wyatt from the church. I introduced Mrs. Smith. Imagine having to introduce the Methodist college president's wife to a leader in the local [white] Methodist church in this small community! Mrs. Wyatt was very cordial. Dr. Wyatt, her husband, came before we left. I told him I was looking forward to his presentation of the lesson on alcohol that evening. So a good time was had by all.

Last night I was caught without money since I had forgotten to cash a check at the business office. At first I thought I didn't dare go to my gas station asking for that favor. Then I thought, why not? It worked. I got my first nice words out of him. And I learned the place had changed hands. Now this manager is half owner. Now that he doesn't have to defer to "the boss" maybe I can ask him again about his sign [over the water fountain]. Did I tell you that Anne Braden, editor of the *Southern Patriot*, wants a picture to illustrate my letter about it? We thought we might accommodate her, but one of the faculty "cased the place" and decided the photographic problems involved were too great for a quickie take. I figure we have other more important things to do than to get in jail for a picture, so I've given it up. The dean of a Negro college in Tennessee was caught doing just that and arrested.

Dr. Schaefer and I visited the Rosenwald[16] (colored) school. It runs from 1st through 12th grades and has 1900 students bused in from all Holly Springs districts and a few from the county. The elementary building is new. The high school not quite so new—restroom was awful—library had a few World Books and other old encyclopedias. Mainly the shelves were just plain empty. No librarian or adult was in the room, and it was a general visiting area. The junior high was a partially completed building—never really finished inside—rough boards with cracks for walls, etc. No playground. We had a very good lunch there thanks to the surplus foods program of the government. They must have a good cook and cafeteria manager. They have a good inside gym room but it is at the center of the high school with all classrooms opening onto it so there is no physical education program. The elementary as yet has no playground. With so much rain the yard is clay. Their exercise is in the halls and classrooms.

That same evening Dr. Schaefer and I were invited to dinner at the rectory by the four fathers and a brother. The brother is the cook, dishwasher, housekeeper, chauffeur, etc. They have charge of St. Mary's school where the local colored send their children if they want them to have better education, more discipline, smaller classes. The priests and the brother are white; the sisters who teach at St. Mary's are also white. I haven't met any of them yet. One is teaching a math class for us here at Rust next semester. I'm so glad we are getting that math class.

16. About 1920, Julius Rosenwald of Sears, Roebuck and Company gave generously to Southern states for African American elementary schools.

If I had met these priests earlier, I could have doubled the white audience at my concert! They are all good company. We had a good evening of conversation. This invitation came through Dr. Schaefer, who has known them and worked with the [Catholic] school over a period of years.

Dr. Schaefer will soon be taking off. He has made things more interesting here.

[January 1961]

Dear Hildred [Armitage]:[17]

All your comments and suggestions about the college are appreciated. I'll try to comment on a few of them in return. As for reaching the townspeople—I'm doing better than anyone, including me, anticipated as possible. In fact this is a plus on my score card, I think. I like Margaret Fleming's expression of "gentle law breaking." Everyone has to work in his own way. Mine is to continually break some of the unwritten or un-spoken laws gently and then turn around with a big smile. Actually, I don't see how you can believe some of the things I write, for I wonder if they sound at all like me. I am a different personality here than at home. I am aggressive, really. I hope in an acceptable sort of way. Anyway, I am not ostracized at all. I don't say I have made any deep abiding friends. There is one to whom I can talk more freely, but her husband is a traditional Southerner so she can't do much. Anyway she is rather timid, she says herself. I am quite satisfied, however, with my relationship as far as the town is concerned.

Upgrading the college is, as you say, a vicious circle. Until the elementary schools and high schools do better, the material we receive is not ready for college work. So we turn out students who have inferior educations—they go back to teach and produce more poor students for us. On the hopeful side, our students do know more when they graduate than their teachers in elementary and high did, so it is a gradual up-swing.

Bringing white students in is ideal and can be done where you have colleges up to standard. Talladega, Fisk, and other good schools are doing this.

Retired people, I think, is an excellent idea. If I were sold on other things,

17. Reading this today, it sounds arrogant indeed. But at the time of writing, it expressed my frustration and hope. This letter went only to my very close friend, a professional educator.

I myself would urge others to come at the prevailing rate. They would be excellent teachers.

Money is a problem—but only one. I came thinking the greatest problem was money. No more. We simply do not use what we have—this includes money, buildings, personnel.

As for a mixed faculty and administration—it is, in my opinion, a must. This college, contrary to what I thought when I left home, has a history of a mixed faculty. Within the past few years, this has changed. The entire personnel should be made up of the best persons available regardless of race. This is true in any institution, but so much more so here where these people have been cut off from the best practices and procedures in conducting a school.

I just had a call from the Student Council president. Our Student Council folded last semester. We heard from it but once and that was in assembly at the beginning of the year. The officers resigned. I don't know the details. Now a new group is in. The first act or nearly the first was to come see me. Would I object if the ping-pong tables were put away before each meal because they made it crowded for the meal line and as a result there was some cutting in on the lines? I immediately recognized the indirect hand of the one who originally made all the rules about only girls using the table—only between 9 and 11, 2 and 4, get balls from cafeteria manager, etc. I told this young man—who is a fine chap doing the errand of him who sent him—that I did mind. "Have you noticed how damaged that table is already? That happened when the table was put away on Saturday for cleaning floors. I bought the best table because I knew it would have hard usage, but no ping-pong table can stand being put up and down three times a day, especially with the careless treatment it gets here. Now if you don't want the table, I'll give it to a church or another school that does." Protestation here, of course.

"I spoke to Mr. Battle about forming the line inside the cafeteria room, which would leave only one column for the lobby. You could pick up the balls and paddles at the beginning of each meal line and not return them until the end of the meal. You could even work to teach self-discipline. This is more important to learn than history, even. The less self-discipline we have, the more laws we will get. True here, in the community, the nation. This is our business to teach self-discipline. I am convinced, the reason this college has so little is that it does not use what it has. You have a $50.00 ping-pong table. Rather than figure a way to use it, we would put it away (you know how often it would fail to get out. I even had to retrieve it from the lavatory Sunday morning after the Saturday cleaning). I got this table because I believe students need recreation. It is as important as study, and I think you already know I believe in real study. We have very little for students in the way of recreation. They use this table constantly. I think we can figure out a way to leave it up." He interspersed a few remarks, of course, but I gave it to him straight and I'd like to see the faces of those who sent him when they get the report.

Much of this I said to the business manager yesterday morning in regard to his locking the lobby doors Sunday afternoon. He gave as the excuse that it was too easy for people to get into the cafeteria from the lobby. Any file would open those locks. I gave him my song and dance about the need for recreation and suggested he get a couple of bolts.

It's been both a heart-breaking week and a fascinating one. One fellow, the only good student involved [in giving out test answers after someone lifted them from my room], I think, said, "Didn't any of my work during the year count?" He can't understand why taking answers to class and helping others to do the same should give him an F in the course. I asked if he were old enough to remember when West Point students were dismissed for no more. These that I can't pin anything on, I am insisting that they get in a book report and a notebook if they didn't already. "Your grade is incomplete until you do these two things and take the test over." They've done more reading and working these few days than all semester.

One young man said, "You've taken everything out of me. I'm going home." I said, "You can get the measure of a man by what it takes to get him down. If one F or one mistake gets you down, you never were much of a man. You'll make more mistakes and greater ones than this in the future. The important thing is to get up after each fall and try harder. Let each mistake be a stepping stone to something better. Learn from your mistakes," etc. He has been back three times to see me, always with some way out that he has figured. "Make up work? It's not worth the paper it's written on. I never give make-up work. If you can't keep up, how can you make up along with your regular work? If you could learn so much in a few weeks, we'd close schools the rest of the year and save some money."

One fellow returned last night to tell me he had decided to face reality. He was staying on. He was going to show me yet that he had something worthwhile in him. Let us hope he can remember this bold decision day after day. Last night he wanted me to help him with a speech on race relations to be given in a church in February.

Three young ministerial students were involved in this ring. I told one, I wondered if they didn't realize the seriousness of it. Perhaps they just thought of it as a lark, snitching a test paper, having fun putting one over on the instructor, not realizing that a final examination taken illegally is rather serious.

Some others not involved, hearing that I was requiring these students to come to me and report orally on their book, have been in to report on theirs that they failed to turn in. "We hear if we didn't get our book report in, we might get an incomplete or an F. Is that true?" I just say, "If you didn't, you'd better." Two have reported thus. One came and said, "Mrs. Campbell, I turned in my book report, but you wrote on it 'see me' and I never did. Should I see you now?" I, with a straight-face answer, "Yes, you'd better. Do you have the report with you?" "No, but I'll get it and be back."

I won't have many signing up for class this semester. But those I have will surely know I mean business, I guess. I do hate to have them learn it this hard way, though. It leaves such a bad taste in everyone's mouth, after a good term, too.

Time to eat. I never miss a meal.

January 27, 1961

This afternoon I stopped at the courthouse to inquire concerning procedure of registration. The clerk asked where I lived before, and I admitted to California. She said I'd have to pay a $2 poll tax now and then again next year. After my second poll tax and residence here of two years, I could register.[18] She offered me a form to look over, but when I asked for a copy of the Mississippi Constitution, I was told the office only had one. Demonstrating the thickness with her fingers, I concluded that, allowing for exaggeration, it was fully three inches thick. From this volume the registrar chooses a section to be copied on the top half of the page. On the lower half, the applicant interprets what he has copied. Here the personal touch is possible—the registrar can fit the section to the applicant. I said, "What happens if I fail?" She said I could take it again in six months. I asked if there were a review board to whom I might appeal if I should fail, and she said she knew of none. This is contrary to what Father Monley told me last week. However, it is not surprising that she did not know of it as Father Monley understood from his friend on the board that no one had ever appealed to the board. Probably no one knows of its existence—if, indeed, it does exist.

18. I paid only one year's poll tax before Congress outlawed it in the 24th Amendment.

You are required to take an oath to "faithfully support the Constitution of the U.S. and of the State of Mississippi" and to "bear true faith and allegiance to the same. So Help Me God." (Capitals theirs—not mine.) Apparently it is realized that mortal man unaided could not possibly do both.

Stopping at the office of the *South Reporter*, our local weekly from which we learn who visited whom, I was greeted with a cheery, "What are you selling now?" (shades of concert ticket days). I said, "Nothing, but I'd like some service. The American Legion in your *Reporter* offered to show a film on communism. This I'd like for my students at Rust, and I'd like two members of the top echelon to show it—you and Sen. Yarbrough." He said that would not be possible as they were both speakers and each speaker was teamed with a projectionist. So I agreed to settle for one of the top echelon.

He proceeded to tell me how hair-raising this film (filmstrip, it turned out to be) is. "It shows four phases to the communist program. Three phases have been completed. It's really frightening to see how near we are to being taken over by them. And the cure is so simple." "Really?" I said. "What is the cure?" "JUST SIMPLE PATRIOTISM."

"That sounds well and good, but it's so general. What do you mean by patriotism?" "Just this. When there's a parade and you see the flag go by, it makes your spine tingle." I said, "You think a tingling spine will combat communism?" He said, "I know it sounds corny." I, perhaps foolishly, prattled on, "Personally, I think communism can only feed on injustice. If we make our country strong by weeding out corruption and poverty, if we treat all people with equal justice, I don't suppose communism would have a leg to stand on in America." I wish I had added something about obeying the laws, but that thought didn't come to me in time. He just stared at me. Finally I closed the incident by saying I'd call tomorrow to see when Senator Yarbrough, who does the booking, could schedule the film for us. Mr. McAlexander, to whom I was talking, I always find interesting. He's always good for a little banter on the light side and we always hit a serious note obliquely.

Last night our Faculty Committee toured the big Rust Hall. I had begun to wonder if I hadn't exaggerated the conditions when Miss [Martha E.] Couche and I went through the first time, but now I know I hadn't even seen all the details. Just yesterday morning the third floor bath overflowed again—toilet troubles. The bedroom under it was flooded. The bedroom ceiling is rotted from so many similar experiences—plaster off, some boards out. The whole hall beggars description. Tuesday night it was bitter cold and the girls couldn't keep warm. Many of them took their blankets and marched over to the student center saying they were staying there all night. Administration told them some very harsh things, I understand, and sent them back. When I heard about it, I shocked some of the faculty and staff by saying "Bully for them!" This is the first display of life I've heard of. Tonight again, it is bitter cold. I have the best room I have seen on this campus this side of the president's home and the dean's room. Even so, my feet are freezing tonight though otherwise the room is comfortable. Those girls in Rust must really be cold. Even the upstairs of *this* hall is indescribable. We went through it, too. Also there are several real fire hazards. I no longer marvel that so many buildings in Mississippi burn. I now marvel that any of these old structures are still standing. I'm going to try to get some individuals to come out.

January 30, 1961

This afternoon the Faculty Committee [chaired by Prof. Berry O. Wilcox] toured the men's dormitories. The fellows gave the high sign all the way down the line that we were there. Having any ladies in their dorms is quite unusual.

The first was the best. The halls were clean. Some rooms were well kept. Others not so good. Rooms were very small and crowded with two to four beds. The lights again were inadequate. Everything needed painting. The bath facilities and toilets were dreadful—you'd have to scrape the filth off with a knife. Two out of the three toilets were out of order and covered with boards. The hot water was running in one dirty basin because it needed a washer. The floors were dirty. Mr. Wilcox said he didn't need to wait for administration to do something on that. He asked whose responsibility it was to clean the bathroom. Asked that he be sent in. He came. Mr. Wilcox asked if he couldn't get cleaners for this room. The student said he had Ajax. Mr. Wilcox said that wasn't strong enough to touch this. Told him to request certain chemicals. If he had trouble getting them, let us know. Get that place cleaned up! Another small bath at the other end of the building put on an act for us just as we arrived. It shot forth water from the toilet plumbing, flooding the bath and two adjoining rooms.

The next dorm was much worse. Dirty halls. Walls bashed in evidently from scuffling. I suppose it doesn't take much to knock in those plasterboard walls. As we stepped in we had to be careful to avoid the hole in the floor. The rooms were smaller yet, with two beds each. Again the baths were horrors. In fact as we entered this dorm the stench was noticeable. I couldn't help but wonder how these fellows could possibly come out of those rooms appearing as neat and clean as they do. I couldn't help but think of the young man who took advantage of my motherly qualities to explain his problem of constipation. I thought how could anyone be otherwise, for surely one would put off the call of nature as long as possible rather than use one of those contraptions.

You can believe there is real resentment at our going through these buildings. I would resent it, too, if they were my responsibility and they were in the condition in which we are finding them.[19]

I think I shall never be willing to give to any cause again unless I KNOW how the money is used. Not only the money I give but other monies.

I can't understand why the Methodist Church does not supervise its institutions adequately. This is a $300,000-a-year operation, and while it's not large enough for a college, it's too much money to be unsupervised. On Race Relations Sunday you will all be asked to contribute to our Negro colleges, and heaven knows they need money. But—? (I really don't think the others are like this, but how can one know without going to stay at each a year?)

Now another subject by way of contrast.

Today I visited the Catholic school. I have never been so impressed. (Wonder if I'd find a different situation were I to stay a year.) The place is spic-and-span clean everywhere. The bulletin boards were thrilling to see. A movie was shown at noon—part of a series on occupations and vocations.

The lunch was excellent. The teaching that I saw in progress was good. The children answered questions for the sister who was showing us around. They were eager and wide awake. The charge is but a token charge of a dollar a month, if they can pay. Lunch is 15¢—they get government surplus food to help there. The children do have to pay for bus transportation which the sister said ran quite a bit. There is no compulsory law for education in Mississippi[20] so the public schools have irregular attendance, but here there is regular attendance. One of the teachers said the discipline problems were negligible, but he admitted the fact that the teachers were white made quite a difference in this

19. One of the most rewarding gifts I ever made was a small Sanitation Scholarship to a student chosen and supervised by Mr. Wilcox. In one of his frequent letters, the student reported, "I am proud to say that I am having splendid cooperation with my project. Freshmen and upperclassmen seem to be very appreciative in my remarkable upkeep of the shower room."

20. In 1956 the legislature repealed the compulsory education law so white children would not have to attend school with African American children.

state. No Negro in his right mind here crosses a white person unless he's ready to pay the penalty. This is just a law of life in Mississippi. And I mean "life."

There is a very fine library and it was being used as a library should be used. This was a contrast to the public school for Negroes here.

If one were to believe the scripture, "By their fruits ye shall know them," it would go hard on Methodists by comparison to these Catholics. I am fast losing my Methodist loyalties. When I get home I may be Catholic!

February 3, 1961

I wasn't planning to start the volunteer grammar class this semester, but several asked for it so I put a notice out (with proper permission, you can bet): HAVING VERB TROUBLES? COME TO THE VERB CLINIC, THURS. AT 4. I tell those who come that they need only continue until they conquer their verbs, then they should quit until we have another clinic that hits one of their needs—such as one on capitals or possessives. It was so exciting this week to watch one of the students discover the third person singular of the present tense. All these students—almost without exception—have trouble with that. This fellow had about 10 errors on his paper and when he discovered the relationship between the conjugation and his errors he was so thrilled; he wanted to conjugate every verb he had missed.

I must tell you donors that the ping-pong table is never, never idle—I wonder if everyone goes to class when he should. Never idle, I say, unless the balls are gone. I've asked the business manager to order balls, but he isn't "just sure where he can get them." I wanted them stocked in the bookstore so students could buy their own. I've bought out the town.

I made bold to ask the minister of the Methodist Church if he wouldn't like to have our men's quartet sing on Race Relations Sunday. He said he'd have to take it up with his official board. "Some people feel pretty deeply on these matters, you know," says he. I suggested that people might not resist so much if we just didn't expect them to, and it would be so nice to give them a musical treat. Our poor church choir hasn't had much to offer lately. The last three Sundays we've had to pull a hymn out of the hat at the last minute because of absentees including the director and soloist.

All the good homes around here are built of brick. It's easy to see why when it rains. I pulled off the campus driveway a bit too far when I met a car and got stuck—but good. My wheel was lost from sight. The fellows had to stop their painting and pull me out with the tractor. That's how little I cooperate with the painters.

February 8, 1961

Secretary, Rotary Club
Lorain, Ohio

Dear Sir:

We continually are reading such captions in our newspapers as NEGROES FARE WELL, MISSISSIPPIANS TELL; FILM AIMS TO SHOW NEGROES LIKE MISSISSIPPI JUST AS IT IS.

The Sovereignty Commission, an official agency of the state, is telling its story far and wide. Being intelligent people, I'm sure the members of your organization have not been completely convinced by these talks. Even so, I wish to state that as the lone white member on the faculty of Rust College, I have been in a position since last September to learn what Negroes like. I can assure you they do not like conditions as they are in Mississippi.

Every sign over a drinking fountain FOR WHITE ONLY—COLORED USE CUP (a tin cup) stabs them in their innermost being. They resent having to enter a doctor's office through a door marked COLORED. They intensely dislike going to the balcony of the theater. They marvel that it is possible that as Christians they cannot worship with any and all Christians. They do not appreciate the fact that their education, improving as it is, still is not on a par with that given white students. One could go on ad infinitum.

I do not have a state behind me to pay my expenses, but if you care for a speaker who is having one of the most valuable experiences of her life by living on this campus for a year, I would be glad to pay my own expenses to speak to you during Easter vacation or this summer after school is out. If you'd like to pay the cost of a student's travel, I could bring one with me to tell his views firsthand.

Whether I ever see you in person or not, please do not be taken in by these fabulous stories about Negroes enjoying the denial of those rights Mr. Jefferson described as "unalienable."

February 9, 1961

Now is the time for all good people to come to the aid of—RUST.

If you read the article in the February 3rd issue of *Time*, you may want to write a letter to Dr. J. O. Gross at Methodist Headquarters in Nashville, Tenn. or to *Time.*

You have my permission to use anything I have written that you think will add strength to your letter. Some of you have not received information about the conditions at the dormitories. Two are meeting the need fairly well. Four I am afraid to describe, as you wouldn't believe what I would tell you about them. I'll just say this: Anyone who feels any sense of responsibility in sponsoring this college would be very ashamed were he to see these four dormitories. Physical facilities are only the beginning of our needs; I mention them because they are more easily measured than other less tangible matters.

Students, with the help of their families, are making great sacrifices to attend. It is not easy for them under the prevailing economic conditions here to raise even the modest sum of $600 plus a year. They deserve to graduate with an education somewhat on a par with that obtained by others who put in four years of study. They, at the very least, should graduate with a firsthand experience of living conditions that are acceptable in American society.

The following is what I have just mailed:

Rust College-38
Holly Springs, Miss.
Feb. 8, 1961

Editor, TIME
Time and Life Building,
Rockefeller Center
New York 20, N. Y.

As a visiting instructor at Rust College, I was particularly interested in your article, "College-Building Church." To me, a life-long Methodist, it is difficult to understand why my church has not concentrated whatever effort is required in money and energy to make Rust College newsworthy for its superior qualities rather than for its deficiencies.

Rust is located in the heart of the South where educational opportunities have been all too meager. Mississippi will soon be faced with the necessity of extending civil rights to include all its citizens. This transition will be less turbulent if the Negro is educated. Because so many Rust graduates become teachers, educating a Rust student is the equivalent of educating many times his number.

World problems will be more easily solved if we first correct our own inadequacies. We, too, are a part of the world. What we do here speaks louder than what we say in the United Nations.

I trust your article will spur my fellow Methodists to demand such immediate improvement in this—their oldest Methodist college for Negroes—that Rust will again make *Time*—this time as an example of the best in colleges.

Sincerely, Clarice T. Campbell
Home address: 1758 Casitas Ave., Pasadena, Calif.

Copy to Dr. J.O. Gross

I urge no one to write (Not much!). Write only if you sincerely feel compelled to do so.

Monday while driving to the University of Mississippi to register for some seminar courses, I heard over the radio that police were gathered at Ole Miss to prevent a couple of colored graduate students from registering. When I signed in at the Alumni House for my night's lodging, the clerk expressed surprise that anyone from Rust could be white. It suddenly struck me that I might have been the cause of the panic—a graduate student from Rust planning to register at Ole Miss! I had a good smile over the possibility; no person of color appeared.

February 12, 1961

Dr. Wyatt, Chairman
Christian Social Concerns Commission
First Methodist Church
Holly Springs, Mississippi

Dear Dr. Wyatt:

You may have read in the February 3rd issue of *Time* an article, "College-Building Church," which states that of 136 Methodist schools only Rust College is unaccredited.

As a Methodist, I feel this condition should be corrected as soon as possible. If I were also a citizen of Holly Springs, I think I would feel the urgency of the situation even more. Certainly no community can take pride in having an institution within its borders that is substandard.

Is this perhaps something the Christian Social Concerns Commission could consider? As a first step I would like to suggest a visit by your entire commission to see firsthand *all* the facilities here.

Speaking for myself as an individual, I have written *Time* and am enclosing a copy herewith.

[In class discussions, students frequently voiced concern that nothing had been done about the lynching in south Mississippi of Mack Charles Parker. On April 25, 1959, Parker, 23, was dragged from jail in Poplarville, Pearl River County, Mississippi, by eight masked white men—three days before he was to be tried on a rape charge of which he was likely innocent. He was beaten, shot in the heart and thrown into the Pearl River, where his body was found 10 days later. The lynch mob, which included a Baptist preacher and the jailer, went free. Governor James P. Coleman hoped Mississippi would not be "punished by civil rights legislation."

[Seeking information for myself and students, I wrote to my California Congressman. He replied, "The FBI {Federal Bureau of Investigation} found out who did it, turned the evidence over to Governor Coleman on May 25, 1959, and it was presented to the local authorities who refused to take action.

["There isn't any Federal jurisdiction as far as can be determined at the present time. However, the matter was presented to a Federal grand jury, but they refused to take action, I suppose on the basis that they were somewhat the same local citizens who declined action by the local grand jury. The case is still pending, but I doubt very much that there is any Federal law which would extend jurisdiction in this matter.

["This is one of the types of things that causes so much trouble in that it is no wonder we have arguments on Civil Rights when the local authorities just will not act in accordance with good American custom.

["I don't know how much I want to be quoted on this, but at least I thought I would let you have the facts."]

February 12, 1961—and a Happy Birthday
to Mr. Lincoln

Dear Mr. [Cong. H. Allen] Smith:

Thank you for your prompt and forthright answer to my query concerning the Parker lynching. My students were very impressed, as they were also with your monthly letter. They have never had any experience with responsible representation at any level of government.

Since living here, I am more convinced than ever that the Un-American Activities Committee is off the beam—however much it may have intended to be a force for good in the beginning. It harasses every individual and every organization in these parts that is attempting to promote a way of life consistent with the Declaration of Independence, the Constitution, and the Supreme Court decision on school segregation. When the Un-American Activities Committee will investigate the White Citizens Councils which constitute the power behind the governments in these parts, I may again have faith in it—and the perpetrators of crimes such as the Parker lynching may be brought to justice.

I do hope that my Congressman (I'm sure you know I admire and respect him very much) doesn't, nor ever will, cooperate with these Southern Congressmen to the extent of helping them maintain the status quo denying civil rights to Negroes in the South in order to get the Southern Congressmen's votes on measures my Congressman may favor. I can see there might be a temptation to do so, for in many ways your and my ideas of local responsibility in government coincide with the Southern ideas of states' rights. But basic rights guaranteed in the Constitution should not be confused with lesser matters which can better be handled by states and communities.

March 2, 1961

To all those who responded by sending a letter to Nashville or *Time*, thank you. I loved the note I received from a second cousin: I thought that you might like to know that I did write a letter. It may be only a feeble voice crying in the wilderness but "she hath done what she could."

Probably I told you about the District Superintendent of the (white) Methodist church who spoke so very effectively on alcohol about six weeks ago at church. He made a remark that gave me the cue to his more liberal attitude toward race: "You have been getting so excited about communism, but America is in much more danger from two other problems—race and alcohol." Thus, I immediately asked him to speak here on alcohol and to show his interest in the college by spending the day with us.

He came today. I asked the chaplain if he'd like me to put up a couple of posters announcing his talk as, usually, we have just a handful at chapel. The chaplain said he'd take care of it. He did—with a typed note on the bulletin board. Thus I took matters in my own hands and put up two bold posters. We did have a good crowd with some standing. And [Dr. G. H.] Holloman was as good or better than I had represented him. After eating lunch with us—a thing no well-brought-up [white] Southerner would think of doing—he toured two dormitories. (I asked permission from the president first.) Then Holloman visited with Dr. Smith and came into my Recent American History class and discussed with us many things pertaining to present-day race problems, but in doing so he gave us several dips into world history. He is a well-versed man.

When we of the Faculty Committee started visiting the dormitories, there were some objections. Dr. Smith and I have since talked about it. My point is that if we are doing the best we can, we have nothing to hide. Only by letting our Methodists see us as we really are can they know our needs. He agreed.

Prof. Hamer [of Ole Miss, in an evening discussion with a small group of Rust students] gave us an interesting experience. He led off with some general statements about the Constitution and how it has been variously interpreted throughout the years. This, of course, led into civil rights. The students were very interested. One of the fellows, a hard-working student but quite limited, remarked at how glad he was to know enough of the Constitution to understand the references made to it. It was his way of telling me all the studying and memorizing of it which I had required were worthwhile.

Another, a member of the Student Council, said he was sorry that this man could not have spoken to the entire student body—that Dr. Silver had caused some resentment, not only toward Silver but also toward me for having brought him here. (Then he was embarrassed for telling me this and hoped I wouldn't feel too bad.) It seems they resented the part about one out of every three Negro babies born in Tennessee being illegitimate. They thought the bare fact presented a distorted picture, as colored families do not have the money to send their girls away or have abortions as do the white families. I concurred with the argument to a degree, but told him the problem was still great enough, I was sure, to warrant concern, and Dr. Silver was addressing himself to the students as leaders who could help bring higher standards and understanding to others of their group. I also told him I thought it was too bad if the students couldn't approve my bringing a well-known historian, and a man far more liberal in his thinking than most Southerners, just because they took exception to one statement. After all, the way to learn is to hear what others are thinking. Of course, the very fact that this young man would tell me this indicates we have a fair rapport. Others whom I thought I knew better had said nothing but nice things to me about Dr. Silver and my inviting him to come here to speak.

At the university a week ago, Dr. Silver excused our seminar early so we could hear a Mr. Lowman speak on communism. It was the grandest indictment of everyone who had ever raised a finger for the extension of civil rights to all our citizens. Whenever he mentioned Bishop Oxnam he emphasized the G-Geeh! Bromley Oxnam, in a slurring manner. He referred to Kennedy as "our boy president." Hodding Carter was the recipient of the *P-ee-ew*litzer prize. W. Russell Bodie (whose book Bobbie and I used in Bible School one summer) was denounced for his membership in commie front organizations. This Lowman is a member of the Circuit Riders, a Methodist group to counteract the "radicalism" of the [Methodist] Christian Social Concerns Commission. The Mississippi Sovereignty Commission is reported to be paying Lowman a fabulous salary for making these speeches, but he insisted he was speaking without remuneration of any kind. Of course that statement could be based on a technicality. Lowman had booklets listing 2,109 Methodist clergymen who were affiliated with communist front organizations; 1,411 Episcopalians, 614 Presbyterians. The "purest" of all were the Baptists.

Dr. James Dombrowski [of SCEF] is "a greater threat to our American way of life than [Communist Party USA leader] Earl Browder." I felt insulted because I wasn't listed in his book as having entertained Jim Dombrowski in my [Pasadena] home. The only reason for the omission, obviously, was that I'm not considered important enough.

Dr. Silver stood immediately when questions were permitted and said he had no way of checking on all names mentioned, but of one he had firsthand knowledge and a life-long friendship. He knew Hodding Carter, Jr., had even been cleared by the F.B.I. for several important government missions, one quite recently. He knew he was no front for communists, and when his name was so listed it made Silver discredit other names given. Before the evening was over there was a running verbal battle between Silver and Lowman. It was almost hilarious. Each was emotional and each deadly serious. However, the encouraging thing was that all the questions were not of sympathy with the speaker. One student in my seminar who is so typically Southern that he can't even refer to the Negro by his scientific name, stood and objected to Lowman's indictment of [Robert C.] Weaver, [black, New York City] housing authority administrator, on the ground that at the time Weaver was a member of the executive board of the organization cited, we were allies of Russia. Though this young student was opposed to Weaver on other grounds, he stated it was unjust to condemn him for something considered patriotic at the time.

Shortly after my neighbor, Yas Ikeda, wrote that Dr. Jones is the uncle of one of our [Pasadena] neighbors, Mrs. Turner, a staff resident here, and I called on Dr. and Mrs. Jones. We had such a delightful visit we hardly had the manners to leave before our welcome was worn out. I knew it was a mistake, though, to associate with a doctor. Just the thought of one makes me conjure up symptoms of illness. So I was soon knocking on the door of his office. Nothing seriously wrong with me—just the inevitable result of too many wieners and bologna. Before Christmas our food was very good, as you recall from my letters. Since Christmas (we must be trying to make up for all the cost of frozen pipe damage, we are concluding around here), we have been getting less quantity and more wieners and bologna. Dr. Jones thinks I should eat off campus. He wants to find me a place to board for dinners. I told him I was sure I could augment my diet morning and noon with fruit and such as the collards I am now nibbling like a rabbit. Actually, I am more concerned for the students than myself. They complain of being hungry and I'm sure they must be. Of course the students supplement with soft drinks, donuts, popcorn, and other things offered at the Student Center—but that doesn't give them a balanced diet.

We have been having more plumbing trouble. The new linoleum in the bath has been flooded so many times, it no longer looks new. Also the plumbing in the bath above went bad again, so the second paint job in our bath this year is now water streaked. Such is life with old buildings.

The first of the week we awoke to snow. The next day it was like spring. Today I discovered some violets courageously blooming.

These dittoed letters go to friends who have shown the slightest interest in Rust or my being here. Though I love to hear from all of you—my day is really made when your letters arrive—yet I do not feel a dittoed letter primarily beamed at my family obligates you in any way to answer. So please never feel you must apologize for not writing more often.

Someone asked about the ping-pong balls. Students are buying their own now at the Student Center. I am still trying to supply them with paddles but find it impossible to keep them in good ones. They break the handles. They get so upset at missing a point that they bang something with the paddle. They seem to be able to play just as well with a handleless paddle but I can't so this hampers my playing. I hope Western Auto gets some in soon. I had to send to Sears for the last ones.

You also asked about the quartet I suggested to the minister of the Holly Springs Methodist Church for Race Relations Sunday. He said he took a poll of official members and he had no "ayes." I remarked that they surely believed in cutting off their noses to spite their faces—that they were the losers, for the quartet is really good.

March 8, 1961

Returning home last night from Oxford, I found the students had been on a strike for four meals—the entire four of my absence—protesting quantity and quality of the food. These students can be so deceiving. To look at them and talk with them, you wouldn't guess anything was bothering them. But underneath something is going on. Maybe this just proves that I have not penetrated the mask which they put up to one of my kind. They all came back to breakfast this morning. The kitchen wasn't prepared for them and ran out of eggs. It switched the menu back to the old reliable wienie-type sausage—looks like a wienie but tastes a little different.

The president called them all together and talked to them at 8 this morning. He said it was like a child having a tantrum and refusing to tell his mother why, for them to make a protest when they had not first talked to him. He reprimanded them quite severely but ended by asking them to stop by his office if they had grievances. I hope they do.

When Dr. Smith happened in the conference room this afternoon, I told him I had wanted to see him before I left Monday to tell him that I wasn't getting enough food and was getting too much bologna and wieners—but on returning I found the students had told my story for me. I said I was really proud of them. I had begun to wonder if they had no spirit at all. He admitted it was a good sign, but was sorry that the situation made it necessary. Anyway, I told him that I *had* seen Mr. Collins before I left and enlightened him as to my grievance.

Today's mail brought four boxes of ping-pong balls from the Bryans. Very nice and thank you! These ought to see us through the year. I finally sent to Sears for 10 boxes which are now being sold at the Student Center. I noticed they were down to three boxes though and was just thinking about sending for more. Glad I didn't. If the powers that be continue to take down the table at every possible excuse, the balls may last longer! It always takes a while to get the table back up. They act as though they are ashamed of the ping-pong table which is in the lobby—and to me of no bother even if a few guests are expected in the cafeteria. I finally got the new paddles last Saturday—handles again so I can play—but had to wait until Monday to play and then had to plead to get the table up. Guess I don't understand. There must be a reason.

March 15, 1961

Today Mr. George Sisler from the Memphis (newspaper) *Commercial Appeal* came to show the filmstrip "Communism On The Map." The state senator from this county, who I understand is a leader in the White Citizens Council, was instrumental in getting Mr. Sisler out, saying that probably no one around here would be competent to answer all the questions students would ask. True. It didn't take long for the questions to be pointed toward civil rights. There was considerable heat generated on both sides.

I will say Mr. Sisler is a good sport to come out at all, for he had about the same problems with two other Negro colleges—Owen and LeMoyne in Memphis. The film is o.k. It shows the steady advance of communism. My only quarrel with it is that no notice is taken of what we can do to improve our democracy. The film affords such a perfect opportunity for promoting local action to correct inequities which, to my thinking, would strengthen us as a nation and build a bulwark against communism. At least Mr. Sisler said afterward to a group that his 13-year-old girl knows that if her school is integrated she will continue to attend; she has been taught to accept all people with respect. This was an admirable and unexpected statement. Not many people in his position would put themselves on record before they had to.

When Mr. Sisler came, three American Legion men came also—one in the uniform of the Mississippi Highway Patrol, which gave him a formidable appearance. One was the manager of the local theater. The students have not been patronizing the theater for a couple of months. This has been a quiet protest against segregated seating. It is part of the movement I did not feel free to write about before, but I suppose it is no secret now. The students didn't want it talked about, in fact they still don't talk about it.

Friday evening we had an unexpected visit from Dr. Charles Satchell Morris II, recently of Benedict College [black] in South Carolina. Sunday I drove him to Memphis, where he preached in a Baptist church. Afterward we had dinner with the president of Owen College.

Driving home by way of Somerville, we visited Tent City, made up of [black sharecroppers who had been evicted for registering to vote] last fall. It was hard to believe this was America. It had been raining, which left the clay-like soil soft and full of puddles. Children were swarming about. We had a long talk with Mr. and Mrs. Frazier, who were just evicted last Friday. They had sharecropped for 12 years for the woman who owned the place. She wrote him a letter which he received on election day, saying his services were nearing an end and he should concentrate on getting the crop in. Last week the sheriff and two deputies, plus two Negro prisoners to do the actual work, came and moved everything out of their house to the street. They had no car. There were seven in the family—an odd collection of children, grandchildren, and brother's children. Their cow, two mules, meat in the smokehouse, share of this year's corn and hay crops are still on the place. They do not know if they should go back for them or not. They are afraid of arrest for trespassing and yet they were told they could have "what was outside." I should think the NAACP could give them legal advice. He is a member—probably another reason for his being evicted.

They owe a bill at the store that supplied them with farm commodities, food, etc. The store has not pressed them thus far though it refused to sell them anything after November. The Fraziers' tractor was sold to give the landowner the amount owed her on it. Because Mr. Frazier wouldn't sign a release, he was sentenced to jail. He said he had been advised to sign nothing unless he understood what he was doing. The justice of the peace got him off the jail hook. Through it all, neither Mr. nor Mrs. Frazier showed bitterness—only bewilderment.

We stopped to meet Mr. [John] McFerren [black], who owns a small country store a mile or so from Tent City. It was McFerren who sent a truck up for the Fraziers' household effects and moved them to the only vacant tent.

I was very impressed with Mr. McFerren and his wife. He planned to call Robert Kennedy Monday morning. According to our understanding, there is a temporary injunction against evicting these people. The McFerrens seem to be assuming leadership for these dislocated people, and they appeared very capable, but that alone does not assure success here where the law works against your every move. (This is in Tennessee.) I wonder if we can imagine what it would be to have the law against us.

McFerren has not had gas in his pumps since October 13. No oil company will supply him. I asked if he had tried Mobil. He said he had tried every one of the companies.

The Freedom Packages which some of you, no doubt, have sent are distributed through McFerren's store. This, however, is not the only center for these people. There is another tent village near Moscow and one in Haywood County.

Mrs. Frazier had that tent as neat as a pin. The furniture was good. Of course sanitary facilities are deplorable.

In the McFerren store there is an appealing poster showing a boy and a girl about 12 or 13 years old. The caption above reads, "We're too young to vote." Below, "What's your excuse?"

When Mr. Frazier registered, there was a long line out in front of the courthouse. It was a day of hard rain. Only a few were allowed in the courthouse at once. He said the merchants did a good business that day in raincoats. After lunch, someone called the Attorney General in Washington, D.C. and then they were allowed inside the courthouse.

Yesterday I brought back a couple hundred books for the library here—a donation from Dr. Doherty at the university. (For those of you who don't understand my contact with the university—I enrolled in a seminar on Monday night and another on Tuesday afternoon. I stay overnight, having no classes on Tuesday here.) He is moving to the University of Kansas next year so is getting reckless with his books, thinking he will use the library more.

Another university professor has agreed to come out to talk with our science students. He is a chemist and it will be a strictly professional talk. Also Professor Hamer is planning a return engagement. Some students expect to come with him for a discussion group. These little acts probably don't seem much to you, but I assure you they have significance.

My real-real Southern classmate says he'd like to come out for a discussion group. He wanted to know if I thought he'd be lynched if he came. I told him I was sure he'd have to alter his semantics in some respects. He asked if the term "Negro" was acceptable or must it be "colored." I told him both were in good standing, though maybe I shouldn't have. Rev. Burley objects to "Negro" strenuously, but I tried to argue him out of it explaining that surely it was a more scientific term than "colored" and to me, at least, it sounds more respectful. I suppose it's not too important how it sounds to me; more important is how it sounds to them.

Spring is beautiful here. Students are beginning to sing again. I was concerned because we haven't heard them in spontaneous song as we did when school first opened.

Lois Scott[21] speaks of people saying to her, "You just don't know the situation. You've never lived in the South." This was the remark which after the umpteenth hearing finally drove me South to see what was so peculiar about the "situation." I can say of a certainty that when people tell you the Negroes are satisfied with the Southern way of life, it is *they* who do not understand. The Negro is expected to smile and beam when he meets a white person. One of the faculty is so disgusted with this ritual that she bends over backward to impress the white citizenry with her dignity. "I've done business with that bank for thirty years and no one there has ever seen my teeth yet," says she.

Lois asks how one can reconcile the strong Christian belief of Southerners and others with the prejudice so evident. I, for one, just can't reconcile it, except to say that Christianity has become an empty shell for many.

Lois asks if the students treat me as one of their kind. I never thought much about it, but I suppose the answer is some do and some don't. Same with faculty. On the whole I think the acceptance is as good as in any other situation. I suppose those who object to me are the ones who don't get the grades they hoped for. For them there must be a tendency to feel that I don't understand and am not one of them. One minister in my in-service class on Saturdays evidently thought I was expecting too much and asked if he should drop the class. He didn't want an F against his record. Then he expressed concern lest I didn't understand the meager background that most of his generation had. I told him I tried to accept everyone as I found him, that no one would fail in my class who tried. However, he should learn to appreciate a C as being a good grade. I talked it up as being what most college students get after working quite hard. B means superior and A really outstanding. I still can't make myself give a B to one who can't write a sentence without help—no matter how hard he tries. We have been getting along fine since.

One of the faculty members resents, and openly so, that I can flit in and out of the University of Mississippi campus and back to this campus. "Those white people can walk all through our campus, but we can't set foot on theirs." She has a point, I think.

One of my pre-minister students brought me a big slice from a home-

21. My roommate when a freshman at the University of Southern California, 1925–26.

made cake given him by a member of his church. I said, "Your parishioners must like you." He answered simply, "I *hope* so." He is such a fine chap. We have often talked of his future. He plans to go to Gammon Theological School—a colored school. I said, "You evidently are planning to stay in the South." He said, "If I were a skilled laborer, I probably would go where I could make more money, but a minister should go where he is most needed and I think I am most needed in the South."

No, I haven't read about the John Birch Societies, but they were mentioned at the university this week. My going there keeps me more in touch with the world. Monday Mr. [Claude] Sitton, a reporter for the *N.Y. Times*, came to see Dr. Silver just before time for our seminar. Silver brought him to class to interview us the last hour of the session. Mr. Sitton is after a story on Mississippi. Specifics that interest him are: the payment by the state of $5,000 a month to the White Citizens Council; Mr. [Bill] Higgs's lawsuit against the state for using tax money from all citizens to pay for the Sovereignty Commission's campaign to keep almost half the population from obtaining their civil rights; the state's bringing Mr. Lowman in for a couple weeks' speech-making at a cost of over $3,000; Silver's remarks about Lowman at a meeting of the Historical Society. After class Silver asked as many as wanted to go to his home to continue the talk. Because one of the students (whose grandfather was an organizer of the KKK [Ku Klux Klan] in his county—the one I have mentioned as being so ultra-Southern) asked me to go with him, I indulged in later hours than is my wont.

This Mr. Higgs, a young attorney fresh out of Harvard, may come out to speak to us on April 12. A number of the professors at Ole Miss are trying "to keep him alive" (giving money to him). Silver says Higgs is an idealist "like Mrs. Campbell—expects the Lord to feed him."

My ultra-Southern friend is fascinated with my being here at Rust. He thinks my life must be interesting—not "boring" like his.

April 4, 1961

I completely forgot about choir practice last Wednesday so went to Asbury[22] for Easter service in company with others here. It was a lovely service followed by a coffee hour.

22. Asbury Methodist Church, where Rust College was organized in 1866. Its outgoing minister, Rev. Merrill Lindsey, became active in the civil rights movement and lost a primary election for Congress in 1962.

We had intended going to another tent city on Sunday, but I suddenly discovered I had no insurance on my car. Harold [who died in 1959] had always taken it out with the company. Of course, under the circumstances, I was not notified of its expiration and never gave it a thought. I'm grateful to my guardian angel that I didn't have the oversight called to my attention in a disastrous manner during the past three months. Once I realized the lack, I refused to drive the car even to church—thus Mrs. Griffin, one of the faculty who lives across the street, took the three of us. Sunday was a beautiful sunny (cool) day. We were sorry not to make use of it with a little outing. Especially since the dogwood is out now.

A week ago Sunday we attended a student's church. It was really in the country though near a small town. The building was a rough one with plank pews that encouraged one to sit up straight. Behind the church is a cemetery. The week before, the members from the two churches this student pastors had spent a Saturday clearing the cemetery of growth. Things grow so luxuriantly around here that a cemetery could soon be lost to sight if it were not cleaned periodically.

I hope no one else feels, as did one of you, that the criticism of my being able to go to Ole Miss was too personal. As long as people feel free to tell me these things, I take it there is a good open relationship. Maybe I haven't the good sense to take it otherwise. Anyway, I'm sure this lady is my friend. I hope she feels toward me as the little Jewish girl asked her friend to, when she said, "Honest, I didn't have anything to do with killing Jesus."

A couple of my students have enlightened me as to some town talk. One was questioned about me by a white citizen where he works. Allegedly (note how careful I am), he said I was creating a stinko in the church—that I had tried to get some colored persons in the choir. This, I suppose, is the way my suggestion for inviting the Rust quartet to sing on Race Relations Day developed with a few tellings. Also, it seems I am being credited by some of the white citizens for the absence of Rust students from the theater. I think it good, and I'd like to take credit for it, but can't honestly do so.

When I get to feeling a little smug because I don't labor under some of the prejudices others around me do, I think of Harry Tyler's[23] remark in a recent letter: "I would be unhappy if I had to live with people whose prejudices were so totally different from mine." I know he's right in implying we all have

23. Executive Secretary of the Pasadena Education Association.

our prejudices—of one kind or another—and I probably should be seeking to correct my own brand rather than always thinking on the other fellow's.

The Centennial of Fort Sumter—April 12, 1961

We really hit the jackpot in speakers today—a quiet-mannered slow-speaking young lawyer—Mr. [Bill] Higgs, who currently has a suit filed against the Mississippi State Sovereignty Commission. You can well guess he is not too popular in Mississippi, though he said, upon questioning, that he still has some friends who either agree with him or tolerate him.

Mr. Higgs said the new federal administration is very different from the old and that everyone senses it—even the Mississippi government and police force. Negroes are going to have to make sacrifices before things get better, but probably not as many sacrifices as most of them think. Every time a Negro is knocked down, or bitten by a police dog, the picture is flashed around the world. Mississippi knows that and doesn't want more of such publicity. Mississippi knows now that the Justice Department means business. While the read-in at the Jackson, Mississippi library[24] was blown up for the world to see, more recently students bought tickets in the white waiting room of the bus station in Jackson and rode to Vicksburg without interference. With so many FBI men standing around, the police knew it would be futile to take action.

Mr. Higgs urged students to vote. In Mississippi you must have paid a poll tax two successive years before you are eligible to register except when you are just 21. He said we probably had a number of students who were 21 and had been at college one year. Thus they could claim this as their legal residence. He stressed that they should go down and ask to register; if refused, they should call the FBI or Mr. Burke Marshall, [white] Assistant Attorney General in charge of civil rights in Washington. Keep going down in an attempt to register; always go in company with others so you have witnesses. If you are arrested, submit to it without violence. NEVER commit violence. If you get knocked down—maybe your teeth knocked out—it won't be any worse than many a fist fight you've had and thought nothing of it. If you think you might be killed in the process, call the FBI before you go—but the likelihood of being killed is very slight now that the government is showing its intention of enforcing the law.

24. When nine black Tougaloo College students entered the municipal library and tried to read, on March 27, 1961, they were jailed on charges of disturbing the peace.

Until Negroes let people know that they don't like things the way they are, matters will be no better. Write letters constantly to those who do something of which you approve and to those with whom you disagree.

I felt vindicated on this point as I have harped all year on the necessity of being articulate. Just this morning I had said to a class, "President Kennedy receives 3,000 letters a day. Has he heard from you? You had better believe he has heard from people of the Citizens Councils, the KKK and the John Birch Society." Then I assigned a letter of commendation or disapproval to someone in the news—naming several possibilities and including Mr. Higgs, who would speak to us today for no honorarium whatever. "He deserves a letter of appreciation or at least of your reaction, whatever it is." I have made this kind of assignment before. I never insist on their sending the letters, saying that is up to them. I am interested now in their learning how to express themselves and hope they will. If they send a letter merely because I ask them, it loses its sincerity (to say nothing of the trouble I'd have with administration—and I feel rightly so).

I could have said a bit more about Mr. Higgs himself. He is a graduate of Ole Miss and Harvard. Though he was on the University of Mississippi campus yesterday, he was not permitted to speak; he merely visited with sympathetic professors. Mr. Hamer was instrumental in bringing him to us; in fact, Mr. Hamer drove him out here.

Last Thursday Mr. Hamer brought four university students out for a discussion with about 50 of our students. We got off to a worrisome start. The guests were due at 3:30. Our students were gathered and waiting on *time* for once. At 3:40 I suggested we sing while we were waiting. For my part they could have gone right on singing—it was that beautiful—everybody taking part in the spirituals with deep rolling basses coming in at the most exciting moments. However, I was fast growing an ulcer thinking Mr. Hamer and I must have gotten our wires crossed or something. Finally, in the midst of a quartet number, the university group arrived—just 35 minutes late. Was I ever glad to see them!

With a sympathetic audience of five, our students seemed to just let all their dammed up grievances tumble out. It occurred to me that we were doing all the talking, so I leaned forward and whispered to the student seated in front of me, "Direct a question to one of the visitors because we're monopolizing the discussion." This student, himself most guilty of monopoly, proceeded to tell a story of some officers who were traveling with handcuffed prisoners on the bus. When the passengers stopped for lunch, the prisoners went in the front door and the colored passengers on the bus went in the back door. Then, obedient to my suggestion, he asked, "How do you feel about that, Mr. Washburn?" You never saw such a red face as poor Mr. Washburn's, and I concluded students might do better without my help.

As we were breaking up for dinner, someone asked if we could meet again after we ate. Mr. Hamer suggested we limit the post-session to 30 minutes, as he had some work to do. We did, but after we adjourned everyone stood around talking for another half hour—pretty good evidence that the occasion had been successful.

I had spoken to Mr. Collins ahead of time, suggesting he might want to put our best foot forward with one of our better menus—which he did! We had fried chicken, string beans, rice with gravy and a fruit cup. I was very pleased and told him so.

Last Sunday the lesson on Wisdom was well presented as always in Sunday School at the Methodist Church in town. One of the facets of wisdom, according to somebody's definition, is RESTRAINT or control. After class, the teacher asked me if it were true that Mrs. Sainz had inspired me to come here. I told her Dr. McCoy (former president of Rust) was the one who sparked my interest in Rust in the summer of '56. She was quick to acclaim his greatness. "He understood that it was better to accept the conditions as they were, and his attitude was responsible more than anything else for the harmony which has always existed here between the races." I made no reply and didn't realize I allowed any expression to betray my feelings, but she said, "I can see you don't agree." I answered, "Then give me credit for practicing RESTRAINT." We both laughed and went our separate ways—mine to the choir.

Friday—fish day—President Smith ate in the cafeteria. I stopped by his table and said to him and incidentally to all at the table, "I think it's a WONDERFUL idea for the president to eat in the cafeteria. In fact, making it mandatory might be a solution to all our problems." He laughed and said it probably wouldn't help because he doesn't eat much—"food isn't very important to me." I said, "That's what I used to say, but I've found food, like money, is not very important so long as you have it." He's a good kidder and I hope got the point without any undue hard feelings.

I asked Mr. [James Luther] Moody, president of MYF [Methodist Youth Fellowship], if his group would be interested in using the money some of you have sent me to furnish one dish each Sunday night, so long as the money lasts, to supplement the sandwich and apple ration. He was pleased with the idea, as I knew he would be. I know they'll all be grateful to you who made it possible, though they know you only as my good friends. I anticipate that attendance at Methodist Youth Fellowship will increase!

Tuesday we had a beautiful dedicatory service for our new cafeteria which, though we have been using it all year, is now bricked and finished. Many alumni were here and officials of the church. Dr. [James F.] Thomas [black] came from Nashville Methodist Headquarters. I talked with him a bit. He said the office had received many letters of concern for the college as a result of the *Time* article. I stressed the need for his office, in my opinion, to make our church aware of the great opportunity here for a strong college, saying no other place in the entire world was more in need of our efforts at this moment in history than this, and once our people realize this, they will respond generously, I'm sure.

To return to the dedication: The cafeteria was named for the Shaw family—seven children, all graduates of Rust except one who died while a student here. Their parents both started life as slaves. Bishop [Bernard F.] Shaw, now of Los Angeles, is known to many of you. All in the family distinguished themselves—some in medicine, education, music, the ministry. Bishop Golden and Bishop Shaw both gave excellent speeches.

The luncheon served was such that I was prompted to remark that a dedicated cafeteria seemed to produce better food. However, today when Mr. Higgs and Mr. Hamer were here, we were on our usual diet. Because I told Mr. Collins they were coming and suggested that, if the meal were as frugal as sometimes, he might want to add a fruit dessert or something, the two guests were served ice cream. It was a bit embarrassing because no one else—not even at their table—received it.

April 19, 1961

I am pleased that the Pasadena City Schools has approved another year's leave for me. This is the last I shall be able to get for the time being, as two years is the maximum.

You may be surprised to hear me say it, but I think I'd prefer staying here. Mississippi has captured my heart for some inexplicable reason. It takes a while to get the confidence of people, especially with the barrier that has existed throughout the years to overcome. This semester has been so much richer than last just because of the improved confidence in each other. Also, I am beginning to make contacts that should be more rewarding as time goes on. And again, Mississippi is just beginning to stir. Even our students are moving out.

April 27, 1961

I imagine several of you are disappointed at my attachment to Rust. Actually, I am trying to be sensible; I've not made any commitments here and hope not to for a while at least, though it is hard when I am flattered by students asking if I will have a class this summer, next year, etc.—students whom I have not had. (The most flattering experience for a teacher, I find, is having students audit your classes. I only have two such, but two more have tried to and been unable to schedule it.)

Hildred's boxes of lovely clothes arrived this week. Mrs. Turner, one of the finest of housemothers, is matching girls to the clothes—choosing them for size and need. She has remarked about the quality of the clothing—which, I'm sure, surprises none of us, knowing Hildred. They were, indeed, very nice and well cared for in packing and all. Our girls all are well dressed. They amaze me in that they always look so pretty. After seeing the crowded conditions in their rooms, I wonder how they do it. But some of them have to rely on help for their clothing as they have so little cash. This is surprising, too, to learn how little actual cash some of these students ever see. Then, of course, others do have more. Anyway, Hildred, you can be sure your contribution will be much appreciated.

Dr. [Barton] Milligan, the chemist, came yesterday and spoke in assembly on fallout. Afterward he spoke in the science classes where he could answer questions. It was one more opportunity for our students resulting from my acquaintances at Ole Miss. I hardly have the time for those courses, but in many ways they are rewarding.

Rev. Holloman, the [Methodist] District Superintendent I asked out six weeks ago, returned with another man to show him the college. The report is that he has money. One can hope.

Day of triumph—Alan Shepard did it!—May 5, 1961

The Sunday night snack provided by some of your checks was a real success if judged by attendance—about three times normal, or around 200. The students were delighted with the jello made with salad fruits and bananas. Several said they had never had such before! We also had Ritz crackers and Kool Aid enriched with pineapple juice. The girls are eager and ready to do it again this Sunday.

Tonight's menu was one medium-sized hamburger patty which was low on meat content (we couldn't figure out the substitution, though) and a serving of canned peas and carrots mixed, plus bread. This was their dinner. The lunch was that same bony hard fried fish we always get on Friday. This is merely to explain the enthusiasm for Sunday night snacks. (Usual fare Saturday and Sunday night is one sandwich and an apple or orange.)

I drove with Mrs. Smith, wife of the president, to her childhood home near Yazoo City, about 200 miles from here. It is a nice comfortable home back in the woods on the kind of road I always wish I had time to follow. Beautiful country abounding in trees, wildflowers, birds (including brilliant cardinals), hills, canyons, and ponds. Mrs. Smith's brother lives there with their mother and farms the land. We were there overnight and enjoyed three meals of Mrs. Gooden's superb cooking. Greens from the garden and steaks from the range! Why do people ever leave the farm?

Last Sunday Mr. [S. T.] Nero and Mr. [Henry] Reaves and I drove to the Regional Conference on Negro Leadership in Greenville, about 150 miles away. I was introduced as one who "is comfortable with our people." I met three extraordinary men, all excellent speakers: Dr. [Aaron] Henry, a pharmacist from Clarksdale[25]; Dr. [Edwin P.] Burton, a physician of Mound Bayou, an all-Negro town; and Wiley Branton, an attorney from Arkansas who argued the case for integration of Little Rock schools. Mr. Branton was one of the first Negroes to attend the University of Arkansas Law School.

There were several interesting sidelights to the day. First, it was a problem seating me in the car. Mr. Nero's wife is almost as white as I. (She couldn't go.) We decided as long as people were used to seeing him with a light woman, I wouldn't be particularly conspicuous on the front seat. Out of Holly Springs, Mr. Reaves became worried about my being on the front seat. We stopped and I changed to the back. Then there was the fear of driving into a gas station with me. I said if it would help, I could get out and let them get gas without my presence—adding, "Please don't forget to come back for me!"

But when they were ready for gas at Water Valley, I suggested the station

25. Long-time president of the Mississippi NAACP, Dr. Henry was a member of the state House of Representatives 1980–96.

at which I had traded before. I gave my credit card from the back seat to the owner. I thought he was quite natural, but the men felt he "eyed me right smart." I requested Mr. Nero to ask for a restroom as I wanted to know what facilities this Standard (Mobil) station offered. The colored helper said there was no colored room, but the owner spoke up telling him to go through the office and he'd find a restroom. No signs out in front of facilities for anyone, which probably has its advantages from the standpoint of the owner. Mr. Nero is sure the man relented on account of my presence.

One of the ladies at the conference, Mrs. [Vera M.] Pigee [of the Coahoma County NAACP], and I went to a corner store to get some peanuts to stay our hunger until the delicious home-cooked dinner was served by the church women. As we were walking out the door of the store, a frowzy white woman approached me and pointing to Mrs. Pigee said in a rasping voice, "Is she your maid?" I said, "No, she's my friend." She harangued, "Well, isn't that kind of unusual?" "Not for me. I have several friends and find it enjoyable." She continued, "Where are you from?" I should have ignored her, but I said, "California," thinking the magic word might save a riot. "I suppose you are going to CHURCH now!" All the time we were moving away. Mrs. Pigee turned around to say sweetly, "And I'm not a maid; I'm a beautician." The retort was, "You LOOK it!" Mrs. Pigee said, "Thank you."

It felt strange to hear them talk all through the conference about the "white man." There was a good spirit throughout—nothing of revenge. Open repudiation of any help from communists. A clear determination to see this thing through even though it landed some in jail or worse first. Dr. Burton, the new president, said he never could reconcile the Negro's religious bent with his timidity. "My religion makes me bold because I know we are not fighting alone."

A dynamic young high school senior who at some time in the past—I gathered it was several years ago—had been beaten by police because he would not move to the back of a bus, asked me to talk to the few young people there because it was "unusual for them to talk with a white person on these subjects." Several persons said it was "encouraging to have a white friend in our midst." And again, "We feel we are making progress when a white lady will come to our meeting." At 8 p.m. we were eating a supper in the lovely home of one of the members.

The Pilgrimage is over and I didn't see any of the antebellum homes. People have, with understandable pride, been interested in my seeing the Holly Springs counterpart to our Tournament of Roses. When my insurance man, such a delightful old gentleman, showed me the picture of the interior of his home and hospitably expressed the hope I would take in the Pilgrimage tour, I said, "Well, Mr. Francisco,[26] this poses a bit of a problem for me. It hardly seems fair that I, a stranger in Holly Springs, should be asked to participate in your Pilgrimage when my friends at the college can't. You can see that it is a bit embarrassing and I haven't quite decided how to resolve the problem." He said, "Yes, I can see how you feel, but these are private homes, of course." I said, "But when you advertise your tour all over the nation and sell tickets, it does take on a public aspect." In defense he added, "Even President Smith segregates. There are many people in this town he wouldn't have in his home." I answered, "Oh, for that matter, I'm an arch-segregationist myself. But I segregate on the basis of character and interest—not on a God-given characteristic."

Last week I noticed the big sign in front of the theater announcing the sale of the Pilgrimage tickets. I went in and asked if I might bring a couple of my college associates on the tour. "Why of course, but you'll have to pay for them." I assured her I was willing to pay, but thinking this was a bit too easy, I pressed further. "You understood, I'll bring two instructors from the college?" Then light dawned and she said, "What color are they?"

She sent me to a man at another table where also sat one of the church women. I asked the man. "Sure, we're here to sell tickets. $3 each." I said, "Good, I'll take three—two for my college friends and one for me." "What color are they?" he asked with a puzzled expression. "At present I'm the only white person out there."

He gave me about five different and highly involved reasons why he couldn't sell me the tickets. Finally, I said, "I just thought I'd ask because sometimes we think we can't do something, when we really can. Though I'd love to see the homes, I wouldn't want to go without my friends. Thank you, anyway."

This seems to be my week for conversations. One more interested me. I arrived too late at the university Monday night to check in at Alumni House before class. At 10 there was another person at the desk, a young law student. When I signed giving Rust as my address, he said, "Do you have any trouble out there? How's the discipline?" I said there was no problem that way at all, that I'd never had any discipline problems, though I might wish they would study a little more. "Do they resent you?" I told him I wouldn't know, but they don't show it if they do. "How do people in Holly Springs react to you?"

26. Senior partner of the young agent with whom I had dealt.

I said I couldn't say how many real friends I had, but four had been willing to come to the college to visit me and that might mean something—that I had many acquaintances who were always very pleasant and nice to me. "You know, I like you, I really do, but I don't think I'd have the courage to come see you at the college." I laughed and said I had not counted him as a friend so I was no worse off for his admission. "What do you think will happen if a colored student applies here for admission?" he asked. "I think he'll be admitted and you'll like it. I don't mean that sarcastically, I mean you'll really like it." He didn't think so. "Barnett (the Governor) will close the school first, and I'm all for him. I can understand the Negro wanting to vote and go to school, but why does he ask for social integration?" I answered that as far as I could learn they weren't much interested in social privileges with whites. "Then why do they stage these sit-ins at lunch counters?" I suggested that sitting at a lunch counter was hardly a social ritual—that when I think of social life I think of inviting friends to my home, going to the theater with them, to church, etc. While *I* do these things with my friends of all races, I wouldn't expect him to do it unless he wanted to. A person is privileged to choose his own friends.

I told him about the conference Sunday, the capable leaders and said, "After seeing those men and women, I'm sure they mean to get their full rights or go to jail or worse in the attempt. And, I think if Mississippians are smart they'll start planning for a smooth transition." He said, "Just wait till their credit is cut off, wait till they begin losing their jobs, then you'll see all their leaders run for cover." I said, "Do you realize what you are telling me about Mississippians? You're not painting a very pretty picture of the people of your state." "Well," he said, "It's a matter of survival with us."

I told him he was interesting to talk to because I could see he had convictions—just as I did. "Now the person I have difficulty respecting is the one who sits quietly through a conversation on these lines and then seeks me out afterward to say he doesn't believe as does that other fellow who was doing the talking." I told him I wasn't going to give him up and in parting said, "You are too young to think as you do. At your age you ought to be out on the fighting front working for a better world." He just about spoiled my compliment of his being a man of conviction, at least, when he asked me not to tell about our conversation. I asked why, for it seemed to me that if anyone should want it kept quiet, it should be I. He said what I thought very revealing, "It isn't considered good taste to talk about these things."[27]

27. This illustrates the theme of James Silver's book, *Mississippi: The Closed Society,*

A student in one of my classes has asked me to help him choose a school for graduate work. This young man will have to work his way. He is a hard-working student now, but his background was very poor and it will be a hard pull for him wherever he goes. I think he will make good though. He insists on an integrated school, for which I am pleased. Rev. Burley has settled for Atlanta University, I think. It is a Negro school so in that way, I'm disappointed. Segregated schools, to my way of thinking, are never as good—if only for the reason that there is not a sufficient cross-current of ideas. Being shut off from the mainstream of ideas is devastating.

School is out May 31. I'll work on my university papers the first week of June—and perhaps go to Highlander School[28] in Tennessee the second week plus a few other places I want to take in.

May 17, 1961

Guess what? I'm the proud owner of a Kodak Signet 30 camera! These dear people presented it to me last night at a "Campbell Appreciation" party.

It was a beautiful party. The M.C. said enough in the way of appreciation. But then she called on Rev. Burley, the young minister. He gave an appreciation speech. I'm going to ask him for a copy so you can see it. The dean spoke. Miss Jackson said some more nice things and made the presentation of the camera. Mr. [Lynell] Stubbs, a student in my American History 202, gave me a scarf from the class, doing it with a clever short talk. Mr. and Mrs. Holmes sang two numbers. The entire faculty knows how much I enjoy their voices. They have been on concert tours in years past. The male quintet sang several numbers. We had sliced ham and several other goodies to eat including strawberry shortcake.

And all the time I ached my way through this, thinking they were putting

which made the 1964 best-seller list: Mississippi's problem is not so much race as that most people are afraid to speak their own thoughts.

28. A folk school in the mountains of Tennessee founded and directed for many years by Myles Horton, son of white Tennessee sharecroppers. Highlander, one of the few places in the South where blacks and whites could meet together, hosted seminars and opportunities for individual studies to promote better understanding and cooperation between the races. Most major civil rights leaders met there and exchanged ideas. A picture of Dr. Martin Luther King, Jr., at Highlander was widely circulated, including on billboards, as "proof that King was a communist!"

on a good act—thinking I had wrecked my whole year with a few words at the faculty meeting that probably had alienated them from me. I knew they would go through with this because, after all, it had been planned before the 15 minutes of catastrophe took place in faculty meeting.

It came about because I [as secretary] tried to read the reports of the Grievance Committee in the faculty meeting [the night before the appreciation party]. The president and I got involved in some verbal gymnastics. The only thing I can say to my credit now is that I kept smiling all the while and even tried to kid him a bit about what I thought was the absurd position he was taking. He finally pulled rank on me and reminded me that in the hierarchy his word was the last word. Mr. Wilcox, chairman of the Grievance Committee, stood and boldly asked a question. I finally said a faculty committee could do nothing without rapport between committee and administration—that there would be no point in reading these reports without such rapport, and sat down.

I went to see President Smith before I left for the university, as he would be off to conference before I returned and I didn't feel I could leave with matters as tense as they were. We talked more sanely though just as diametrically opposed. I had no idea that the faculty could do anything but loathe me for disturbing their quiescent status quo. It wasn't until the party was over last night (I returned from Ole Miss just in time for the party) that I learned I was a "hero" of sorts! "She said what we should have been saying and were too chicken to say. I'd rather contribute to a 'staying here' gift than a 'going away' gift."

There was even talk of forming a committee to ask for my return. This I discouraged. They tell me they are going to have more spirit in speaking out themselves. Had I known this during the party, my heart would not have bled so, and I might have responded with more verve.

EXPRESSION OF THANKFULNESS
to
MRS. CLARICE CAMPBELL
May 16, 1961
RUST COLLEGE, HOLLY SPRINGS, MISSISSIPPI

When I was approached a few days ago to represent the student body of Rust College at a surprise farewell affair in your honor, Mrs. Campbell, the first thing that came to mind was a poem by John Donne.

This poem is the prelude to Ernest Hemingway's book, *For Whom the Bell Tolls.*

> No man is an island, intire of itself; every man is a piece of the Continent, a part of the Maine; if a clod bee washed away by the sea, Europe is the lesse, as well as if a Promontorie were, as well as if a Mannor of thou friend or of thine owne were; any man's death diminishes me, because I am envolved in mankinde; and therefore never send to know for whom the bell tolls; It tolls for thee.

Your devotion to Christian service, and your untiring work on our campus are the words of the poem put to action.

You are well prepared, both educationally and economically, but you realize that you are not an island intire of yourself, that you are a part of the main. Therefore without reservation yours is a life dedicated to service regardless of race or creed, that others may benefit.

It may have seemed at times that we did not care, that we were lazy, unconcerned, or unthankful concerning your given assignments in class. But we want you to remember us in the light of a story about a forester who desired a great forest of timber.

He planted. Many times his courage waned, his faith grew dim, as he wondered, will there be fruition, or is my work in vain? But mother patience was with him. When he had finished the seeding of his vast land, he waited. The sun rose, the rain fell and days became weeks, and weeks became months, and months became years. Alas! one morning as he awakened, as the sun shone brightly over the horizon he saw his great forest with timber as far as the eye could behold. Tender and tall, large and small. Here was his answer, as he sighed in relief, "my work has not been in vain."

As you head for the sunny shores of your native state, where the stars of both the celestial and terrestrial parade, and men of all the world sometime or another desire to promenade, let mother patience be with you, and soon you will see your labor, the seeds you have planted here blossom forth. Not only in us, your immediate students, but even our posterity. The nation and the world shall also be benefactors, because from here, many shall go forth, far and wide to serve.

To you we extend our gratitude, our love. Not surface love, but love that has no limits to its height, width and depth.

The Greeks had two main words that described love, eros and agape. Eros has been termed the "orange squeezer" love. No one really loves the orange; it is only the juice he seeks. But unlike eros, we extend agape, that divine love which is eternal.

Mrs. Campbell, on behalf of the Rust student body, I would like to paraphrase from a portion of a poem and dedicate it to you:

> And when that one Great Scorer comes to
> place beside your name, oh what joy shall
> fill your heart to see the score you've
> gained (by having come to Rust).

Your elder student,
R. Eugene Burley

We have about a dozen members of NAACP, I understand. Before, few would allow their names to be used. If they joined it was in the name of "A Friend" or they just gave two dollars and refused membership. I said to one of my students interested in getting members, "And you have done all this?" He said, "No, you did it." My part, on inquiry, was in an answer I gave when I was asked as I entered the classroom one day, "What do you think of the NAACP?" In no uncertain words I told them in about six sentences. Those bold words were all a few of them needed—especially this one leader.

Glad the Southern Route [to California] suits you, Don [my son]. If you can bring back a couple of sleeping bags, I'll be game for some nights out. Any and all the places you mentioned are fine with me—as far South as you want to go.

May 23, 1961

President Smith sent word he'd like to see me at 1:30 today. When I went in he said he had bad news. He had talked to Bishop Golden while at conference. Golden was agreeable to my staying another year. Yesterday afternoon he just happened to be talking to Dr. Thomas at Nashville. Told him about my desire to stay. Thomas said Dr. Gross [also an official at Methodist headquarters] had a letter from someone in Holly Springs indicating a resentment on the part of the townspeople over my being at Rust. Smith asked Thomas what he would recommend. Thomas said since the Board of Trustees had already met, it would place sole responsibility on Smith for hiring me. That evidently was a big responsibility.

President called in Dean [W. A.] Waters. Explained the situation. Yes, the dean had heard such comments from someone named Smith (the florist Smith,

I'm sure). She cornered him one day and told him of the town's grievances over me. President asked the dean what he would do if he had the privilege of hiring me. Dean said, "Well, I don't know. It would be quite a responsibility without the board to back you."

"You see my position," the president begged me to understand.

"I see that you are allowing white segregationists to dictate to you whom you may hire. You say they have nothing definite against me. You know they are against me because I represent a way of life they don't want.

"Yesterday my car insurance was canceled. I was notified by certified mail. I stopped in last night to ask why. Was told it might be because I am leaving so soon for California. I said that didn't sound logical. Surely insurance companies did not require that people stay in one state always with their cars. Finally I was told that it was my privilege to crusade if I wanted to, but when I went against the mores of the community it made me a poor insurance risk. He said the company in Chicago probably felt just as I did about integration, but it knows that anyone living as I am at Rust in the heart of Mississippi is bound to create hostility. Therefore, someone is more likely to throw a match in my car. The agent continued to say that he imagined I was 100% for integration. Well, he was not even 1% for it. If those Freedom Riders were to come to Holly Springs he'd be the first to pick up a rock and heave it at them—or a club, whatever was handiest.

"Now," I continued to the president, "you would play right into their hands. They would feel they had gotten rid of me by canceling my insurance and writing a letter to Dr. Gross at Nashville. And Rust would be retarding the cause of civil rights at a time when others are riding for freedom and conducting sit-ins."

He was, of course, surprised to learn of the insurance deal.

"Now," I said, "I can understand it if you find me difficult to get along with and want me not to return for that reason. I know I am inclined to be independent and I imagine it is annoying to you."

"No, no, no—it isn't that at all. I'm glad for you to speak out. I wish others would, too."

"And, regardless of whether or not I return, I shall still have to speak out when I feel there is need. I feel so strongly that all the while we are working for an extension of rights we must work even harder to upgrade our school. In short, our standards are not high enough."

"Don't you think I know it? After four years I'm only beginning to be able to sleep nights for it."

Then I brought up the financial statement, asking for clarification of the $36,000 profit on cafeteria, the $15,000 loss on athletics. [He explained that] they were just work-aid scholarships dumped in those categories. No wonder I didn't understand them because the auditor whom we paid $200 didn't understand it either. But the board at Nashville understands. "You don't think they would let me make and lose such fabulous sums, do you?" I suggested that if we received value for the work the students did, it shouldn't make much difference whether we paid them in the form of tuition or someone else in the form of wages. But we are not getting value. Our dormitory right now is dirty. Miss C. has to clean her own classrooms. (All buildings including restrooms are just as segregationists would expect of the stereotyped Negro.)

There's the matter of classes and study. These work-aid students are taken out of class to work. They cannot get their assignments. They need class help because they are not good enough at figuring out the books for themselves.

He said that was why he wanted syllabi. Then it wouldn't matter if they were out of class. I disagreed flatly with him on that. He knew. He had taught. "Of course, you may be teaching a high school method where you just want them to learn what you say, but they must be learning to think and do and choose for themselves."

I suggested that this was always puzzling to me that he expected students to be more mature than faculty members. (Denial here.) You tell us our classes should be so interesting that students will want to come, but you tell the faculty if they don't attend a meeting, a day will be deducted from their pay. ("No, only a day of their allowable leave.") Then I said, "You want us to conduct our classrooms democratically and not expect the students to accept at face value everything we say, but you won't let *us* discuss anything of importance in faculty meeting."

He thought we understood after he wrote us the letter that we shouldn't report in faculty meeting.

"We understood that you did not agree with our [written] reports in every case, but we thought we were a faculty committee and the group ought to hear the reports so they could approve or disapprove—and incidentally we might by pooling our efforts find a way to overcome some of our problems."

Finally he said he would see the bishop again tomorrow and Thursday. He would call and let me know what the bishop thought about my staying.

Dr. Silver had told me he would bet anything I wouldn't be able to keep on friendly terms with the town for the whole year. Everyone is still friendly, but evidently they do their complaining where it does the most good. According to the insurance man, my greatest sin was in asking for tickets to the Pilgrimage. I said, "I just asked—didn't argue."

[May 23, 1961]

Another thing the town probably has against me is the drinking fountain letter to Mobil—and my badgering of the local station—always in good nature but the sting isn't missed, I'm sure. Guess I will have to concentrate on education and leave the town alone—except for the choir [at the white Methodist church].

We have been having police circulating through our campus recently. We've all wondered why.

Yesterday after I found that "some people might love to throw a match" in my car, I decided not to come home after [my university] class last night. If anyone molests me I want it to be in daylight so I can see his face. Thus I stayed overnight again even though I had to be back by 8 this morning.

Received one check for $20, another for $10, and another for $2 this week. Supposedly for the suppers, but we are through with them for the year. I have a [good] student I want to help get in graduate school. He's been on his own financially since he was 13 so doesn't have much. Perhaps this will help him a little.

Another thing the [younger] insurance man brought up in our full hour's talk was the film on communism we had. Said he heard the students weren't interested in communism—only in the right to vote. I tried to explain that there did seem to be a relationship—but he couldn't see it.

Of course with the students still boycotting the theater, with others joining the NAACP, the letters being written to newspapers by the student body, you could know there would be a reaction.

May 31, 1961

At the moment I'm so happy! I've just returned from town and not everyone is "agin" me; after talking with President Smith, I began to wonder. But in the post office I was cordially greeted. Beth Ayers, friend of Olive Sainz, came in and asked so everyone could hear her why I hadn't been to see her recently. She insisted on my coming over for an evening's visit. I stopped at the Rev. Smith's ostensibly to use the phone. Right off Mrs. Smith wanted to get me a coke (this is the symbol of Southern hospitality 1961—coke). I declined and asked her just to sit still and not bother getting anything. Soon she had to go to the kitchen to take an apple pie out of the oven. She insisted on my having a piece of that and made me a cup of coffee. When she found I was walking she wouldn't allow me to hike back but drove me in her car. On the way back I explained why I was walking and she was horrified. She said the man who told me all this, the insurance agent, though a member of the church, was a rather odd person so I shouldn't let what he says bother me. I wasn't letting it bother me, of course, except insofar as walking bothers. Mrs. Smith offered to drive me anytime I needed her until my policy arrives.

Yesterday I had a most interesting talk with Dr. Thomas (colored),[29] who is the director of all the Methodist Negro colleges. He seemed to picture me as being persecuted by the townspeople. He said he often wondered how I managed to look so cheerful whenever he saw me about campus. He is the one who was shown the letter [sent to Nashville] objecting to my presence here. I explained to him that I could imagine there were some White Citizens Council members or type of people who would object to me, but even they had been courteous and nice. I have felt no pressure against me. I even appreciated this insurance man's willingness to discuss the matter of our beliefs for a full hour—and that we could do it with spirit and yet without loss of control—we could even smile and laugh a bit at intervals. I asked him if he would recommend me for another Methodist school. He said he certainly would and gladly. [He said he would like me to go to Claflin, his alma mater.] I told him that while I had been happy to serve this year without salary other than room and board, I could not do it again—that I would not haggle over salary but would have to ask the going rate because my bank account was too low. Now—this next bothers me in view of the fact that the president had written me a letter, a beautiful letter of appreciation for my year's work and said the Board of Trustees directed him to write it. Dr. Thomas *did not know I was working without salary.* Dr. Thomas is on the Board of Trustees. I had supposed that was why—working without salary—the board directed the writing of the letter. No one else received a letter of appreciation and why should I if the board thought I was getting a salary?

When Mrs. Turner learned last evening that I would not be back she started to cry. She tells me today that she slept very poorly last evening for thinking about it.

I hate to give in to these segregationists—and regardless of the real reason

29. Currently, Dr. Thomas is a bishop.

for my leaving, the segregationists will think it is because they wrote to Nashville and canceled my insurance. On the other hand, if I can see another Methodist college, it will give me a better picture of Methodist schools. As I told Dr. Thomas, this was one of my purposes in coming, and I imagine I do not have a fair picture—it probably wouldn't be right to judge all our Negro colleges by this one. He said for that reason, if no other, he would like to see me go to another school next year.

Commencement was interesting. We had three good speakers. Dr. Thomas was the best commencement speaker I have ever heard.

President Smith just met me on campus and told me enthusiastically about the progress toward merger of Mississippi Industrial [College, across the street] and Rust. He talks with me as though I had understanding and intelligence about these things. Too bad we can't work together.

One of my students tried to explain to me what segregation meant to her. She said after you are told in so many ways that you are inferior, you begin to wonder if it is true. You cannot drink from the same drinking fountain, you cannot sit at the same counter, you cannot attend the same church, you cannot go to school with the whites. The implication is you are not good enough, you are inferior. This girl is one of the sharpest students I ever had. If even she felt this doubt, think how it must weigh on those of less ability. Actually these people have suffered a systematic brainwashing over a period of 300 years.

June 7, 1961

It is true that I am hopeless and unsuited for this school. I can't even control my tongue when I am under fire. This morning I had my tooth filled. This dentist—a nice young fellow—is easy to talk with. After he shot me with Novocaine, I said, "This is a beautiful office you have now (just remodeled). I'm surprised you didn't go modern though." He: "What do you mean?" "I thought you might have just *one* waiting room." He: "You can't do that here. People have been living this way for hundreds of years. You can't change their habits overnight. That has to be done gradually." "I agree that the longest journey must begin with a first step. What would you consider a good first step—to accomplish a gradual change, you know?" He: "Well, in the first place, the colored are treated better here than in any section of the nation but it's dangerous even to be talking about these things." He worked on me and I was at a handicap because I couldn't say anything with my mouth pried open and a drill boring away at my tooth. When I came up for air I said, "Either I'm awfully brave or a fool to discuss the subject with you when you have me at such a disadvantage." He patted my shoulder and said, "Oh, we'll get along." I said, "Don't bother to lie awake nights thinking of a way to put me in my place because I'll be leaving very shortly anyway." From there we talked about where I was going and my family, etc. He was very nice but that is a Southern custom—which may not always mean much.

Friday morning I leave for Nashville. Everything is up in the air because I haven't yet received my insurance. I called the [Southern California] Auto Club. The man I talked with believed I was covered from time of order. I told him I'd rather he *knew* I was covered. Yesterday I wrote Harry[30] asking him to check for me. Why that Auto Club takes so long just to acknowledge my order, I'll never know. I won't go to Nashville without hearing definitely. [Later Harry called.] Auto Club said it was highly unusual to order from so long a distance. They seem to think I'm trying to put something over on them.

Don't let Mr. [President Harry S.] Truman or anyone else lead you astray on the Freedom Riders. They are good. Say all you want about not forcing people—they just don't move until they are forced. If they would come up with any gradual plan or show any willingness to move, I'd be for gradualism; even the way the demonstrations are going, it will still be gradual. I think the Kennedys are tops in the matter of civil rights. Had any president come out so forthrightly years ago, we wouldn't be in this situation today.

My Nashville trip, you may have guessed, is to see the Methodist Board of Education—at least one member of that great august body. Don't know that I can do anything, but he is gracious enough to give me a Friday appointment at 3 so that if we don't get through with our talk we may continue over the weekend.

Two students come to me every day for help in grammar. I am impatiently waiting to get started on the journey that will lead to your doors.

June 14 [1961]—still at Rust

Jeanette has asked my opinion of the Freedom Riders, saying there are such conflicting reports of them in the papers. Being so close to the scene I should have given you my views on them earlier—for whatever they are worth.

30. My lawyer and long-time friend in Pasadena.

If I were not so selfish, I would join the Freedom Riders. Monday night I heard James Lawson [black] speak at a mass meeting in Nashville. He is a young man of Christian depth. He is now working to meet a deadline for his book on nonviolence and you will want to read it when it comes out. You recall, I'm sure, that he was expelled from Vanderbilt for participation in the sit-ins a year or more ago. He finished at Boston University. He recently served 10 days in the Jackson city jail, finally bailing out because of his ill mother, his pregnant wife, and his church needs. Anyway, I don't know that there is much point in staying in jail too long. He asked us to picture what the result would have been had the rides ended with the beating of the original group in Birmingham—six of the group returned home to be hospitalized and all were discouraged and beaten in spirit. What might have been defeat was turned toward victory by the entrance of the seasoned Nashville veterans of the nonviolent technique. These inspired others to come in from various points of the nation. It was impossible for these people to let the movement die, for then the segregationists would have become even more firmly entrenched in their methods of getting their own way despite law and constitution.

Privately to me, he said he felt they were thrown into this before they were ready. They should have had about 500 ready to go when called—all thoroughly trained in the nonviolent technique. This has been a spontaneous development. People have gotten into the act without adequate preparation. Even so, the violence has come from the whites—not from the Negroes.

The papers have recently taken to deprecating the rides in various ways. I was heartened by [New York Governor Nelson] Rockefeller's statement which I found in an obscure section of the *Nashville Banner*: "These young people are showing great restraint asking in a quiet way for their rights. [It is] time we accelerated in making a living reality of the basic precepts on which this country was founded. Martin Luther King [is] a good American. We can be very grateful that some of the minority groups in this country have been as patient as they have and as considerate in their approach to these questions. One would visualize that this country could have a very much rougher time." Rockefeller announced he would attend a rally in a Negro church where King is speaking.

The refrain among the white people here is that these things must come gradually. I have a stock question reserved for those who say this to me. "What would you consider a good first step—a second step?" I have yet to find anyone who has any idea of how to proceed.

On the whole I think the prevalent feeling among the articulate white people is similar to the Washington County Superintendent of Schools whom

I talked with in the summer of '56. She was proudly showing me pictures of the 18 new schools for Negroes that were replacing the 81 old shack buildings. I exclaimed over this very real accomplishment and said I imagined the court would accept this as a first step, as obviously they couldn't integrate in shacks—there had to be good buildings. "Have you thought of submitting this as a first step?" Her answer: "Never! A first step implies a second."

True, these Freedom Ride demonstrators are setting up an artificial situation—they are not on normal business. I WAS on normal business last November when the police put Miss Jackson, one of the faculty members, and me out of the Birmingham station. We had a dinner date for that evening and weren't interested in going to jail. We left, leaving the white segregationists just that much stronger. Every time they get away with these extra-legal and illegal acts they are more firmly entrenched and harder to dislodge. It almost has to be done by someone who makes a project of it. As one of the students at the mass meeting [in Nashville] Monday night said, "Have you decided how you will spend your vacation? I can highly recommend the Hinds County jail [in Jackson, Mississippi]." Another point is that court cases require money. Had Miss Jackson and I gone to jail, we would have been without backing financially. In a project, there is this backing. It isn't going to do any good to go to jail if no one knows you are there or if you don't have the money to see your way through the maze of court procedures.

The NAACP has for years gone through the courts to get Negro rights. What could be more legal—more constitutional? Yet, the Negroes are still denied the very things the court decisions said they should have. We can count ourselves lucky they are dramatizing their situation nonviolently rather than in a bloodbath. How they ever learned these Christian ethics from the religion we taught them, I'll never understand—as so few of us have such ethics.

Yesterday I visited the Highlander Folk School [in the eastern Tennessee mountains]—an amazing place. The school sets up citizenship schools to teach illiterates to read and prepare them to register. Their reading books are mimeographed and deal with adult interests: state laws necessary to understand in order to register, how to fill out mail order blanks, money orders, job applications, etc. A very good lunch just seemed to appear without any obvious effort on anyone's part—tomato soup served from a pitcher, a large macaroni salad and another tuna salad, with a dessert of pineapple. Dr. Lewis Jones, a writer who is finishing a book on the Southern oligarchy, returned thanks. I remarked that I was surprised to hear grace said at a "communist" institution! When anything or one is labeled communist in the South, it is safe to suspect that it or he is working for Negro rights.

On the way back to Holly Springs, I stopped at [a black] church in Shelbyville where Rev. Lawson preaches. It is a small rural church 53 miles out of Nashville. Afterward a Mrs. Wilhoite invited me to have dinner in her home. Rev. and Mrs. Lawson were expected but I was a last-minute addition.

I imagine I'll be home around July 4th. I expect Don to arrive from Berkeley on June 19th. We shall take about two weeks to drive out.

I thank you all for making me happy while here with your interest and love. My mail has been a real support to me. I even rushed home from my little trip these past five days to get my mail. I have a new definition for home: Home is where you get your mail.

Claflin College, SC, 1961–62

[Mother and I drove all the way from Pasadena, California, without any difficulty with directions until we reached Orangeburg, S.C., where we could not locate Claflin College. We asked several people; not even those at the black-owned service station just around the corner from the school's football field would give us any help. Evidently two white women asking for a black school were suspect by both black and white citizens of Orangeburg. We finally stumbled on the school, quite by accident.

[Mother had come for the trip and the visit it afforded us. Soon after our arrival, I put her on the bus for Washington, D.C.]

Orangeburg, S.C.
September 8, 1961

Dear Mother,

Our Faculty Institute was very good. All the complaints I ever had—almost—were dealt with in an attempt to ward off the need for such complaints here. I found myself in agreement with general policy. If the implementation is as good as the statement, this will be a great year.

The radio is announcing a meeting of the KKK tomorrow night three miles out from Claflin on Highway 301 for all white people. The truth about integration will be told there. I feel "obligated" to attend to learn of this "truth."

Notice of a boycott by the NAACP was on the cafeteria tables—enough copies for all yesterday. I did buy a fan after I received the notice, and feel guilty about it every time I turn it on. I'm sure it will give me a cold or something as punishment. I shall try to comply hereafter.

Claflin is making a real fight for extension of civil rights and for equal treatment. *You* did not get equal treatment—you realize—but preferred treatment. You and your soldier boy were put on that bus, which was the better bus. Most of the others had to go to the second bus, which had no restroom and was obviously a second-rate bus. Perhaps you'd better write the lady a note—or maybe I'll figure out how to thank her. Anyway, I was glad you were on that bus!

It was wonderful having you with me on the way back. I'm glad we have these opportunities once in a while for an extended time together. Gather together enough fun, rest, inspiration, etc. for the coming year of service which you will give—as is your habit.

Claflin College
September 13 [1961]

Dear Esther [Thompson],[1]

I think the article is excellent! You have improved upon my efforts markedly.

Because there has been so much said about communists entering the movement, I think it might be well to include a paragraph some place on it. My thoughts: Perhaps a few communists have entered the protests—it would be unusual if they did not. After all, they enter every worthwhile thing trying to bring about confusion and disruption. Even in churches. But we must not let them take over a cause which is essentially Christian. More loyal Americans—I'm sure most Freedom Riders are substantial and loyal citizens; a number are ministers—more Christian Americans should join the movement—join any movement which seeks to make our country stronger, better, more democratic. Communism thrives on injustice. If we are interested in combatting communism, we should strive to make America just, see to it that the gap between what we profess and what we are is narrowed—and hope it will eventually be entirely closed.

Elmer Wells's article [in the Pasadena paper] may have been "good" but I hope it never reaches Holly Springs. It sounds as though I thought I had really done something—daring to break tradition—raising standards, etc.; and it sounds as though I had made no white friends. It has caused me to examine my own heart to see what my motives really were—and perhaps they were not always the highest. But I'm sure I told him some of the other side, too, mentioning the dedication of the teachers at Rust, some white people who were big enough to openly befriend me, even visit me on campus, that I sang in the [white] church choir by invitation, etc. I've been rather low since reading the article, not only because of my fear that Rust or Holly Springs will get it, but also because I realize how hard it is to get a complete picture across to my listener—a balanced picture.

1. A cousin who was trying to write some of my experiences for publication.

September 16, 1961

Now comfortably settled here in this relatively new women's dormitory, my thoughts this Saturday night turn to you—my family and friends scattered so far.

Mrs. [Leone M.] Young and I have adjoining rooms sharing the same bath. She is a charming woman, somewhat younger than I, here also for her first year. Her husband is a doctor in Anderson, S.C. She is home now and plans to make the trip every other weekend.

The faculty of about 52 persons is an interesting group. According to my unofficial count, eleven of the men have doctorates and three of the women. There are four Chinese—all with doctor's degrees; Dr. and Mrs. [John W.] Tait, Dr. [Percival] Robertson, Dr. and Mrs. [C. Ross] Milley, and Dr. [Arthur W.] Calhoun are Caucasians. Dr. Calhoun is of the illustrious senator's family, but I'm sure [1800s pro-slavery politician] John Calhoun wouldn't own him. Though known as a Negro college, Claflin has made a good start toward integration of the faculty.

Mrs. [Harry Lee] Kelly, the full-time nurse, and the doctor have given VD tests to all freshmen and I understand it is routine each year for everyone. The clinic has a men's ward of three beds, a women's ward of the same number, and three isolation rooms. Mrs. Kelly has her apartment there, too. At the moment, though, there are six girls temporarily stowed away in the clinic because the enrollment is swelling to greater proportions than had been expected.

During this week the freshmen also are instructed in the use of the library, are given individual conferences with the chaplain-guidance director, Dr. [Jonathan] Jackson, are taught the alma mater, and generally indoctrinated with the ideals of Claflin. Several social activities, including the dance in the gym right now, probably please them most.

Last week President and Mrs. [Hubert V.] Manning had the faculty and staff plus their families at their home for a barbecue. The place abounded with babies, little children, and a few teenagers. Just watching the children and holding the babies was fun.

Classes are scheduled MWF and TThS. As long as the students are on campus, it does seem a good idea to have them in school on Saturday. I'm glad, however, that the TThS classes are not scheduled for afternoons. This means we can have a bit of a weekend—from Saturday noon until Monday morning.

The library is open Sunday afternoon. I always did feel library reading was a good Sunday activity.

Food is well seasoned and servings are large. The menus are varied and well balanced.

I've seen a number of schools worrying and working with the problem of students' cutting in cafeteria lines, but this student body has a simple, foolproof system. A student representative hands each student a cardboard tag with a number on it as he enters the cafeteria. Another student representative collects the tags as the student approaches the food counter. Each number must be in proper sequence, of course. I am also impressed with the dispatch with which all are served. The line moves right along.

I took Mrs. [Nancy B.] Davis and Mrs. [E. Blanche] McNeil, dean and assistant dean of women, to hear Senator J. Strom Thurmond speak at the ball park Labor Day evening. He spoke on the danger of communism in our country. The radio had said it was everyone's "obligation" to attend. So, we had no choice, you can see! Before the two ladies would go with me they called Rev. M. D. McCollom, pastor of the colored Methodist church here, and president of the NAACP. He suggested I call the white minister, Dr. Frampton, to see if this "obligation" extended to colored people. I did. Dr. Frampton said, "You have asked a big question. I will call the Youth Council in charge and let you know." His answer later, "There will be arrangements for colored though not just as you and I might prefer." We went and, though we saw no other colored there, we were accepted without difficulty—oh there were a few glances our way and no one sat next to my friends until driven to it by the rain. (We were under cover.)

About half way through Thurmond's speech extolling God and country, the storm became so severe that we were dismissed to reassemble at the white high school auditorium. My friends didn't feel quite up to that so we came home. After we left he made his remarks about the muzzling of the Pentagon and army officers. Our papers have been full of little else since.

Don't misunderstand me. I'm all for God and country (and against communism). It's just that I can't square such things as our not feeling welcome in the white high school with his remarks on religion and patriotism.

The next day Rev. McCollom of the Trinity (colored) Methodist church showed me a large ad he had tried to place in the local paper. It commended Thurmond and the Youth Alert (sponsors of the meeting) on their concern for America and the threat of communism, but reminded them that any right denied any citizen might become a right denied all citizens in time. The ad, need I tell you, was refused.

One has to admire Rev. McCollom on many counts. His sermons both intellectual and inspirational are based on sound theology (my interpretation, of course). He is a good pastor, always calling on his members and constituents. He is a leader in the community and after 12 years is still here. His NAACP pin is openly displayed. He is president of the local chapter.

I missed the Ku Klux Klan meeting that the radio repeatedly invited all WHITE people to attend to learn the truth about integration. It was held last Saturday night three miles south of Orangeburg on Highway 301. Perhaps it was my guardian angel appearing in the form of Mrs. [Daisy D.] Johnson to lead me away from temptation. She asked me if I'd like to drive her home for the weekend. Her husband is a Baptist minister in Georgetown about 120 miles from here on the coast. Mrs. Johnson is secretary to the dean of instruction and is also new here this year. I thought she was a very young person and then found she was in college 25 years ago. A friend of hers invited us to dinner Saturday night. Sunday we returned by way of Charleston and I had my introduction to that historic city. Then we stopped at the country home of another of her friends. It was a beautiful drive all the way—and often a wet one. I think the expression, "It never rains but it pours," was coined for this area.

One of the men working on the new men's dorm fell off the scaffolding. An ambulance was called. "Is he white or colored?" On hearing the reply, "Then you'll have to call __________."

I hope you don't expect a letter to be well organized. Back to the NAACP which I presume was responsible for the mimeographed papers on the cafeteria tables the first week.

"WELCOME STUDENTS

"With the sound of School Bells, there will be no sound of Freedom Bells in Orangeburg. However, the time is not as distant as before. And even this can be made shorter with your cooperation.

"Several cities in the South have desegregated Lunch Counters and have hired Negroes in department and chain stores. This was done only because the Negroes applied the pressure by not spending their money.

"This is the only way we will get results. So we urge you to get with the movement that will mean your Freedom.

"Stay away from downtown—Buy your clothes at home—let no one talk you into giving up your principles.

"The theaters are segregated too. So adopt the policy that you will BUY NO MORE SEGREGATION THAN YOU CAN HELP."

"FREE BY '63"

Saturday evening—9–16–61

A letter from President Smith of Rust says, "The University Senate is sending an investigation committee on November 2–4—this will make or break us—I am confident that we are worth more support from the church than we have ever received before."

You've no idea how much I miss Rust and all those there. It is an odd thing. I can't quite understand it myself. I keep thinking of different ones. Of course as I know *these* people better, that will occur less.

CONFIDENTIAL

September 18, 1961

Dear Dean Waters [of Rust]:

You recall the episode involving some eight or more of my students at the time of final exams last January. Mr. X was in some way involved. I was never able to get at the bottom of it, but the whole affair did seem so contrary to his character as I understood it.

Actually I have no proof of his involvement though there were about 4 points that he wouldn't clear with me because to do so would, he said, involve others.

This past week, the matter has been plaguing me anew. I keep thinking of the hard work he put into that class and of the possibility—remote as it seems in the face of the circumstances—that he could have been innocent.

Is it too late, and do you think it advisable, to remove Mr. X's F in American History 201? If we change it at all, we may as well make it what he would have received—a B—had he not been involved, giving him the complete benefit of the doubt.

All others involved, except for Mr. Y, did not earn a passing grade anyway, though they would have received D's but for this occurrence. As for Mr. Y, I think he was relieved to take the F and have no more said about it.

The part that saddened me then and now is that these students see so little integrity in others. All the discriminations they are subjected to—economically, politically, and socially—indicate a basic lack of integrity on the part of our society. Sometimes I think I expected too much of them and was too harsh.

I know it is unkind of me to pass this problem to you, but will you please give it some thought? I would appreciate knowing your decision.

September 22, 1961

I'm so busy trying to keep ahead of my five classes, Monday through Saturday, that I haven't time to get out and see much nor write about it if I did. Aside from classes in American History and English 101, I have three subjects I've never taught before: World History, Negro History, and South Carolina History. If anyone has any helps, send them along. For me it is a growing experience—I can only hope the students find it so.

Incidentally, those VD tests came back—everyone negative. This could refute many arguments I have heard against integration.

[September 30, 1961]

We had our first vesper service this afternoon. It was very good. President Manning gave a serious talk on which he had put much thought. He is not the fluent speaker of some presidents but he is a good speaker from the standpoint of having something worth saying. Then he is a good administrator. Besides that he is courageous enough to be a community leader in a community where to lead in the matter of civil rights means sure condemnation.

It was so warm today that the organist was literally dripping. I hope his suit was shrink-proof.

All the men wore suits. The South is as intransigent in dress as in other traditions. (No air-conditioning on campus either.) Trinity Church is air-conditioned, so wearing suits there is not difficult.

One professor on campus, Dr. Calhoun, is a nonconformist throughout. He is an ultra-liberal (white), way past retirement age, educated on all fronts (he's one who knows more about all my subjects than I do); he is stooped, bony, and always wears a shirt with short sleeves, collar open, wash trousers that are too large for him so are pulled up with suspenders, white socks, and sandals. He rooms in the home of one of the Negro families adjoining the campus. He walks uptown—which is quite a hike—once a day for a meal. The rest of the time he prepares something in his room. Well, today with all the girls dressed in their best with hats and gloves, with the men suffering in their suits, Dr. Calhoun comes in as usual. How I envied him—his being so secure within himself that he could do the sensible thing.

October 1, 1961

Yesterday I took time off my books to attend a Human Relations Conference in Columbia—41 miles from here. With me went Dr. Calhoun, Dr. and Mrs. Tait (both white) and two students (colored). It was encouraging to see such fine people trying to find a way to break through the segregation barriers. I never found nor heard of such a mixed group in Mississippi though there may have been such.

The cafeteria packed lunches for us so we wouldn't have to waste time eating before we left. It was an all-day meeting and we couldn't leave until 12:30 at the end of our last class. Coming back Mrs. [Bula M.] Tait offered to treat us all to dinner in a restaurant. I said (by this time one student had left us for her home in Columbia and the other was in a book store for the moment) I didn't suppose we could all eat together in a restaurant. She said Mr. Manning (the student, no relation to president) would have to be served in the car but that could easily be arranged. I expressed shock and surprise and refused. She thought we should ask Mr. Manning—maybe he'd be glad to have the food even in the car. But I wouldn't even go for asking him. Instead, Mrs. Tait and I went in and ordered hamburgers and coffee for all and took them out.

This morning I thought we should have gone to a bus station. I believe they are desegregated now in Columbia. At least I'd like to see. The new ruling of the ICC [Interstate Commerce Commission] of course isn't effective until November.

I must get a S.C. license tomorrow. The Taits told me it is required after one week. I also have to take a driver's license test. At such times as this I wish I didn't have to give my address as "Claflin."

All over the campus there are posters saying JOIN NAACP NOW. Rust was never like this! I attended an NAACP meeting at Trinity church. The group was small but was busy planning a selective buying program to put the financial pinch on local merchants who discriminate.

My hairdresser who has a shop in her home eight miles out (I don't buy in town) said, "If I'm not being too personal, why did you come to Claflin—I mean you must know how we feel." I said, "Just how do you feel?" She tried to tell me of their love for the colored people but integration of schools couldn't be accepted because it would lead to intermarriage. I pulled out my best arguments ending with the thought that she probably should be more concerned about the possibility of her daughters' marrying an unworthy white man than about their marrying a Negro—whom they probably wouldn't think of marrying anyway. That very day this hairdresser had a toothache and had been to the dentist asking that the tooth be pulled. The dentist said he was on his way to the doctor himself. He was too sick to pull a tooth. And guess who the dentist was? A Negro! I asked why she went to a Negro dentist. At first she told me because he was so good and gentle—then she added, of course, he doesn't charge so much. "People like us just can't afford the prices of these white dentists." Yesterday I read in a book on South Carolina that many white people patronize Negro doctors and dentists because of the price differential; Negro doctors cooperate by giving them separate waiting rooms. I should have asked her where she waited.

A letter from Dean Waters of Rust says Rust has over 550 students enrolled this year. That is more than last year (regular college students). President said he was going to be more selective this year but I guess not. They must be terribly overcrowded and the classes must be larger than before, which is not good.

October 8, 1961

This morning the children's choir sang—36 of them—led by Mrs. [Geneva B.] Williams, a music instructor here at Claflin. (Incidentally, she is auditing my Negro History class. I have two faculty members auditing and it costs them $15 each.) Trinity has three choirs—adult, youth, and children's.

This morning's sermon was taken from the theme "whosoever shall offend one of these little ones, it were better for him that a millstone were hanged about his neck." Three ways we tend to cause little ones to stumble: our actions, our attitudes, our acquiescence with a social order that limits them. The first two were well developed but you would expect me to elaborate on the last and I won't disappoint you. These little ones could drift into sin because we have not prepared a good community for them to live in. Many of our youth grow up to be anti-Christ, anti-American, anti-democracy saying Christ is the white man's God—democracy has nothing to offer us. We must invest more of our money in our people. You may say, "Oh, he's talking NAACP again." Yes, he is, but only because the church has failed to be concerned for its people. When the church lives up to its responsibilities there will no longer be a need for an NAACP. You may say, "I can't work with the NAACP; I'd lose my job if I did." No place in the Bible does it say you are obligated to protect your job. We will have sin in our town as long as we want it—no longer. By cooperating with a system that is destructive of human values, we sin against Christ's little ones.

I always feel I do an injustice to a speaker when I try to report what he has said so well, but maybe this gives you an idea.

Today I joined Trinity [Methodist Church]. Rev. McCollom may renew my faith in the church before the year is out. He may even help me to rebuild some of my own spiritual fences that have fallen into disrepair.

One Sunday he brought out the question, "Can you remember that God loves the man who would deny you your freedom as much as he loves you?" I like that man.

When I attended the NAACP meeting he was relating how, when he was talking to a group on speaking out, one man in the audience whispered to another, "Hmmph! If he'd kept his mouth shut his wife would still be teaching." Rev. McCollom said, "As though my wife's teaching were more important than our freedom and our responsibility to speak out. Friends, I'll have you to know, she hasn't missed a single meal by not teaching."

Don't repeat these next items to Elmer. I'm sure I couldn't stand it to see them under "Mrs. Campbell says, . . ." but I would like to pass on to you two encouraging remarks of the week.

1. Yesterday as I was driving off campus I passed a group of half a dozen girls. I waved and they returned the greeting and I heard one say, "She's so sweet!"

2. For the third time I suggested that a certain young man be transferred from my English D section (lowest entrance test scores) to a higher-achievement group. An English faculty member said, "Would you be willing to keep him, Mrs. Campbell—give him extra work, but keep him? Your class is doing so well in the reading clinic—we can't help but see the difference. You have inspired them to want to improve themselves. I said to the dean, 'Why did you put Mrs. Campbell in social studies when we need her so in the English department?' " I informed her that I had asked for social sciences—she acted as though she couldn't understand why anyone who might teach English would be satisfied with social science. Isn't it wonderful to believe our own subjects are most important! I also told her I hadn't had these students long enough to get any credit for their attitudes. They're just a good group, that is all. This is

the truth. Quite different from teaching a low-ability class—these are just low achievers—but all seem smart enough.

Any secure teacher wouldn't bother to mention these incidents. I've always thought that one reason for my feeling inadequate was that I came in the back door through summer classes—afternoon sessions for in-service teachers—evening classes, etc. They were as watered down for me as my class in American History last year was for the three-hour Saturday sessions with in-service teachers. I do know one thing for sure—if I know my subject I am a better teacher. Down with the philosophy I was educated under (my post-education) that if you know how to teach you can teach anything! Maybe *you* can, but *I* can't.

A letter from Mrs. Turner of Rust indicates that several improvements have been made. The meals are better with a new dietitian; a young lady is in charge of chapel and the programs are much improved; the E. L. Rust Hall is beautiful, she says, with new baths, new floors, new walls, soft two-toned paint job, and beautiful draperies.[2]

Negro Students Turned Away From Church

ORANGEBURG (AP)—Two Negro students from Claflin, a Methodist college, were turned away from the St. Paul's Methodist Church at Orangeburg Sunday.

The two were told to "go worship with your people" by a man at the church entrance. Then Orangeburg Mayor Clyde S. Fair came out of the church and confirmed the refusal.

The two students left.

Claflin is located at Orangeburg.

The students identified themselves as Dorothy Vann and Emmanuel Hixson.

They said the mayor told them "this is a segregated church."

The Rev. T. E. Jones, pastor, said he did not know of the incident until told of it after the services were over, and he had no comment.

October 9, 1961

At the same hour that I was joining Trinity (colored) and being warmly accepted by pastor and members.

2. This is the girls' dormitory which was in such bad condition: plumbing, lighting, water, walls, etc.

I joined—not *because* it was a colored church but because I could feel a Christian atmosphere there in the 5 Sundays I have attended that I missed all last year in the white Methodist church.

On way to class now.

October 15, 1961

Last Sunday at the very hour that I was welcomed so warmly into the fellowship of Trinity, two of our students attempted to worship at St. Paul's Methodist Church (white). (Mother will recall the large and beautiful building.) You may have read that the ushers denied them admittance. One went inside and brought the mayor out to turn them away. Orangeburg criticizes the students for bringing their photographer along, but I consider it smart of them. Thus the mayor was photographed in the act of telling them they could not worship there. Orangeburg radio says the story and pictures were in the hands of the news services and magazines almost immediately (a tribute to the efficiency of these students, I'd say). Radio said yesterday that the mayor had received newspaper clippings of the story from all over the nation—California was mentioned as sending its share. Yesterday Dorothy Vann, the girl involved, showed me a very fine letter she had just received from a Methodist minister in the Midwest apologizing for the action of St. Paul and assuring her that most Methodists did not feel that way—that she would be welcome in their church always.

Dorothy came to see me and for an hour or more she regaled me with stories of their protests last year. When they were sitting-in at Kress, so many were arrested that all the jails were filled. The overflow was put in a stockade—a pen with pigs and other animals. Fire hoses were turned on them, tear gas was used, and some of the time the temperature was 23 degrees. Through it all the president of Claflin was working in their behalf, the [Claflin] nurse kept in constant touch with them administering what relief she could to those who had colds, etc. It was an incredible story.

This year Dorothy is president of the student chapter of NAACP. She spoke at assembly Friday—a very down-to-earth serious message she had. The student body sang "Battle Hymn of the Republic" at the beginning and the official NAACP song, "Lift Ev'ry Voice and Sing," at the end. I always thought that a beautiful song, and with the aroused student body singing it, it became a stirring song—a call to battle.

Now the bandstand has a booth on it labeled in foot-high letters "NAACP." Memberships are being sold with some significant success if I can judge by the number of buttons I see being worn by students.

When I applied for my S.C. car license, I was told my Southern California Automobile Club insurance was not acceptable in S.C. I said, disturbed at the thought of more insurance trouble, "What shall I do?" She said in an aside, "Well, you can always go back to California." I picked up my papers and returned to think about it. She had said I would need a driver's license too and therefore gave me a thick booklet to study. In reading it I found I could pay $20 in lieu of insurance and that I didn't need a driver's license as long as I was a legal resident of California. I returned to pay my $20 and get the license. She started figuring my bill and said, "Is this the address you want to give?" I answered that it was my address; I had no other in Orangeburg. "You *live* at Claflin?" I confirmed it. "You understand you'll have to pay $40—20 for '61 and '62?" "Oh, no," I said. This time facing me directly she said, "As I told you before you can always go back to California." I said, "I thought that was what you said the other day, but I couldn't believe my ears. It sounded so inhospitable." "That's right; we have enough white niggers now." The entire bill was $51. I said, "I'll have to think about this a little more," and picked up my papers. Her parting words were, "Remember you are past the 10 day limit already." I half expected to be pinched on the way back to the college.

I dropped in at the office of an attorney. He looked up the law and it required insurance with a reputable company. Armed with this information I went to Columbia. The clerks were very nice but the charge would be the same $51. I sought the insurance commissioner. No luck in getting my insurance accepted. I then looked up the head man of the Department of Motor Vehicles. He was very sympathetic toward my problem. I was as nice as I knew how to be. I said I realized that it was necessary to have a list for the clerks so they would have some guide as to what was a reputable company. I also knew that if the law said one of these specific companies was essential, I was stuck with it; I was to be here less than a year and hoped that he could o.k. my insurance. Even though it could not be sold in S.C. (no license) it would pay off just as surely as any other company and therefore the citizens of S.C. were protected. He asked what I was doing. I said I was teaching in a private school. He didn't ask what school and I did not volunteer that information. He said if I would come back another day with all my papers he would personally fix me up. I said I had my papers with me then. But he said his office secretary was off for the day. I asked when I should come back. Any day, he said. I explained that it was a 41-mile trip for me so I would appreciate knowing when his secretary would be in. "In that case, we'll take care of you right now." He got on the phone and called in a man telling him that he personally was going to o.k. my application. The man took me to his office—told others waiting that he couldn't help them for at least 20 minutes as he would be busy on a special job for the chief. I walked out with my plates in hand for which I had paid a total of $7.50, which included a 50¢ fine for exceeding my 10 days. No one was more surprised than I.

Sunday, October 29, 3:30 p.m.

Returned from Chapel Hill—University of North Carolina, 250 miles from here, at 2:00. Took three girls including Dorothy Vann to a SCEF conference on the First Amendment. Many leading lights were there. It was well planned; very good. Attended the board meeting yesterday as a guest. Conference was Friday. Met Bob Zellner again. First met him last June at Highlander School. He is now [the first white] working with the Student Nonviolent Coordinating Committee [SNCC].[3] He is just out of Huntingdon College in Montgomery, Alabama; is son of a Methodist minister; was beaten up in Mississippi in the McComb troubles where high school students picketed in protest of the dismissal of a couple of students who were involved in getting people to register. Have your papers told of another murder in Mississippi? Our papers don't stress some of these happenings, I find. Man killed for trying to register.

We stayed at the home of a white lady. Tried to stop at two drive-in-type restaurants this morning for breakfast but were refused both places. Finally, at 9:30 we inquired for a colored restaurant. Suddenly decided to stop at the next white church we found for service. One of those pretty brick churches in the country town of Patrick. As we greeted folks standing around outside we evoked a few reluctant greetings. Only one man on guard at entrance. We got by him. Sat down in next to last pew. Everyone in that pew got up and moved forward.

3. SNCC (pronounced "snick") was formed in Atlanta in 1960 by students from several campuses to organize passive resistance against segregation across the South. Through the mid-sixties, dozens of subsistence-paid SNCC staff were very active in southern community organizing efforts.

Everyone in pew behind likewise. A man came up behind me and tapped my shoulder. Asked where we were from. "Trinity Methodist in Orangeburg." He said, "We don't want any trouble here. We have reserved these two pews for you—just don't give us any trouble." I assured him we wouldn't and thanked him. The minister welcomed all visitors worshipping with them. Afterward two men engaged us in conversation until most of the congregation had "escaped." One asked for my name and address and I gladly obliged. We talked pleasantly and left. The church really rose to the occasion and I think is quite proud of itself—rightly so.

I have forfeited my California driver's license but don't feel too bad about it now that I have learned I can write to get it back when I return to California. When I found Dorothy Vann was going with me to the conference, I felt I should get the license before going out of state. Thus I stole time I should have used for preparation, correction of papers, etc. and went to Columbia. "Have you ever applied for a S.C. driver's license before?" I said not. "Why didn't you get it at Orangeburg?" I said, "To tell the truth, the clerk seemed to resent my address." "That is just what I'm thinking, too. Do you actually live at Claflin?" I admitted as much. He looked at me in amazement then said, "What is your room number?" I was fearful lest I disgrace Claflin by failing my test, but he didn't mark anything wrong so I assume all questions were correctly answered. The man who took me out for the driving was very, very nice—but, of course, he did not know my address.

We were shocked Thursday morning to learn that Dr. Tait had died in his sleep. He was one of the elderly white teachers. He had complained to me just the day before that it was so difficult for him to make any progress in his classes this year. He has looked tired and worn, but I supposed that was his natural look at this point in his life. Mrs. Tait is alone—no children. She teaches here too. Memorial services are in just one hour.

November 4, 1961

This evening one of my few A students met me going to the cafeteria. He said, "I hope you won't think I'm trying to polish the apple, but I think you're about the grandest person I know." He added that his buddy, equally good, says, "When you shake hands with Mrs. Campbell, you can know you're shaking hands with a great lady." While helping me wash my car tonight in preparation for our mission tomorrow, he volunteered, "The reason I admire you so is that you are a real Christian. You stand up for what you believe."

I feel like those Jesus referred to when he said they had their reward here so need not expect anything in the hereafter. Reading this letter, you can see just how selfish I really am—I do just what gives me most pleasure—what is most rewarding to me in this life—here and now.

My day started in high gear, too. While I was eating breakfast, Mr. Moody, a former Rust student now at an interdenominational school of theology in Atlanta as a grad student, walked in. We had a good visit. He said he might remember something about the history I taught him, but the thing he would always thank me most for was composition. At grad school he finds this so important and so many of the students have such trouble with their papers. When they ask him how he does it, he always answers, "At Rust I had a teacher—-etc." This pleased me because he used to get awfully upset with me for demanding re-writes and special sessions to work on his paragraphs. One-paragraph papers were all I ever tried for after the first month. I used to tell him I wouldn't ride him so if I didn't see possibilities in him. Certainly I wouldn't bother with someone who couldn't learn or who had nothing of value to say to the world if he did learn. He always tried to smile when I'd say something like that, but I could see he didn't really believe me.

Mrs. Tait and I have been to dinner twice this week. She is a wonderful person. I never became too well acquainted with her before because she and Dr. Tait lived off campus. Mrs. Tait received a letter from a member of St. Paul's Methodist Church (white). This lady couldn't openly be friendly as she would like because of where the Taits worked. She couldn't come to see Mrs. Tait because of where she lived (a Negro neighborhood—but a very nice area). She was sure though that Mrs. Tait would find strength to see her through this loss because she had found strength to live in hostile surroundings. There were three large pages written on both sides. Mrs. Tait says the woman's two sons are preparing to be missionaries.

Tomorrow I'm taking three students to St. Paul's Methodist on NAACP assignment. The five main churches in town will be visited. It wouldn't surprise me if we were accepted tomorrow. After all the publicity given to turning the two students away a month ago, I shouldn't think they'd want any more. Folks tell me I'm naive to think that way, though.

November 12 [1961]—Sunday p.m.

I met [my sister] Bobbie's equal today, another minister's wife. Mrs. Davis of the A.M.E. [African Methodist Episcopal] church was putting the finishing touches on two choirs when Mrs. Tait and I arrived at 10:30 this morning at the parsonage. Then she was in charge of the service, this being Women's Day. A couple of weeks ago, I was honored with an invitation to speak. It was a beautiful service and the congregation responded warmly to my efforts. After that Mrs. Tait and I were guests in the parsonage for dinner. At 3 Mrs. Davis brought us home and returned for a tea being given in the parsonage as a part of the Women's Day program. Then the women have the evening service. Besides all her church work she teaches 5th grade—only 51 children in her class! She was very charming through it all. I came home at 3 and went to bed. All I had done was to talk for 15–20 minutes. Otherwise I had been waited on all morning. I was even called for by a car so I wouldn't be bothered with parking problems, etc. I received my highest pay rate today: $25 for 20 minutes. I tried not to take it but it was in hard cash in an envelope and they wouldn't allow me to turn it back.

Perhaps I had better put it in an account for Rust. I made a rash offer of $2000 for a housemother for the men's dormitories. A letter from Nashville says President Smith is looking for one. I had a good two-page letter from Dr. [Ralph W.] Decker in Nashville about Rust. He had been down for four days along with several others making a study and I do believe things are going to happen there. Let us hope.

Did you catch the significance of the note on the outside of your envelopes last week—"I was naive"? My three students and I went to St. Paul's Methodist. Arrived too early for the ushers to be on guard. Thus we were able to go in and sit down—for about five minutes. Then two stern men walked up to the students and brusquely ordered them out. They stood. I stood. One man said, "Are you with them?" "Yes." "Then you can go too." I said of course I would go but I wondered if they realized these were Methodist students from their own Methodist college. "Yes. We know that, but they have their own church. You may come back anytime you want without them."

Sitting in is a disease. It hadn't run its course with us that morning yet and since we still had time to make another church we went to the Presbyterian. There we were met by five men outside. "Are you interested in worshipping?" "Yes." "Would you like us to direct you to the colored Presbyterian church?" "We'd rather worship here." "Churches abide by the customs of the community so that is impossible, but we'll be glad to show you the colored church." "Do you think I would be accepted in the colored church?" I couldn't resist asking. "Oh yes, we don't. . . ." The sentence was stumbled over and ended quite meaningless. Of course, he almost said we don't segregate. We allowed them to take us. When we arrived one got out of his car and came back to us to point out where we might park. I said, "I want to be sure I understand you correctly. Are you directing us here because you do not want us to worship with you or because you think we'd be happier here?" "Because I think you'll be happier here." With that he dashed back to his car. They were courteous throughout, I'll have to admit. I did needle him a bit too much, perhaps.

This week I made an appointment with Dr. Frampton, the pastor of the white Presbyterian Church. He was very nice. He thinks right, but like most people is afraid. He says the Session rules the church and for him to go against them would be to lose his job. (I didn't quote Rev. McCollom to him: "No place in the Bible does it say you must keep your job!") I told him I wasn't at all sure that sitting-in was the right way to proceed. It really wasn't the way I was used to. Always in my area if we had a grievance we went directly to the persons with whom we differed and tried to negotiate through conversations. But here, I said all channels for communication seem to be closed. He agreed that this was the pathetic part.

Dr. Frampton LOVES the Negro. His heart *bleeds* for him. His mother used to get on her knees and pray with every Negro who came to their plantation home. And today he is heading up a [campaign for a] $150,000 home for the Negro aged. He is, at the insistence of the high school principal and state college president (both Negroes), putting together an integrated board of trustees. One of his first meetings for this venture—money raising—will be Tuesday night.

Before I left he agreed to come to Claflin to talk or to take part in a small discussion group. I'm not sure he'll have the courage to follow through, but I have told Dr. Jackson, who is in charge of our vesper services and assemblies. He will give Dr. Frampton a chance to make good on his promise.

Charlotte, we are boycotting all stores except a few Negro stores. Thus I won't be able to shop for gloves. I can't even go to Columbia as those stores are boycotted by the Negroes too. I may get to Georgia before Christmas, but am not sure.

Did I tell you President Smith wrote me a very nice letter about many things? I think he likes me at a distance.

I liked [my daughter] Charlotte's closing on her personal note. "I never know whether to say 'Carry on the good work' or 'For Heaven's sake be careful' so just Love, Charlotte."

November 19, 1961

Charlotte worries about that statement, "Is the white man really your friend?" That floored me to begin with, but I understand the problem better now. Too many Negroes don't want to take any stand because their boss is so good to them; "Miss Sue gave me the dress I'm wearing," etc. There's always some white person who has done some nice paternal thing for them and so they don't feel they can demand the right to sit at the counter in Kress. "Miss Sue wouldn't like it." It's the modern version of the old slaves who had good masters so gave away the information about planned revolts because their masters would be hurt. The ethics involved get awfully confused.

Dr. Frampton, minister at the white Presbyterian Church whom I talked with after we were refused admission to his church, is pushing a home for Negro aged. He has all the dignitaries of the town in on the deal, the mayor, the judge, lawyers, ministers, etc. The planning meeting that Dr. Manning asked me to attend was, according to him, the first interracial meeting in seven years. There were some whites there whose position was secure enough for them to risk coming (my interpretation). Dr. Frampton has been disappointed that the Negroes have not shown more interest. The trouble is (again my interpretation) he has asked none of the [real] Negro leaders because they are too well known in the movement for desegregation. Dr. Manning and Mr. [Johnny] Walker, Claflin's public relations man, were the only two [blacks] that appeared to have any spunk.

But the interesting thing to me was a telephone call I received from Rosa Rush. She is *Mrs.* Rush but was never called that at the meeting, of course. She and her mother now run the crowded rest home which is so inadequate. She called to tell me how wonderful it was of me to come to the meeting, how much she loved Claflin—she graduated from high school at Claflin long years ago—how helpful Dr. Manning was in his remarks.

Then the purpose of the call was revealed. Would I use my influence to get the students to stop demonstrating with sit-ins, picket lines, etc., just for six weeks until we raise this money for the nursing home? The mayor is about to give a thousand dollars but he says he won't give it if these students get Orangeburg in the news again. She pleaded with me to pray over it before I refused. Tonight she called again to see what I had decided. I told her I thought such action would be a good illustration of selling one's birthright for a mess of pottage. These people are not really interested in the home if they put that kind of price tag on their deal.[4] I didn't tell her but I have my own theory. When they won't let a Negro sit beside them at school or church they have to do something nice for the "poor colored people"—in order to live with themselves. Of course, the nursing home is needed.

4. When a black leader in town was approached with the same kind of proposition, he asked if the mayor was making a gift or a "purchase."

[My nephew] Chuck wants information about segregated schools—advantages—disadvantages. Several of my students are writing him their ideas. I think the way they say it will indicate the problem more than what they say. All who are writing seem eager to do so.

Claflin, Orangeburg, S.C.
November 23, 1961

Today is Thanksgiving and I, by choice, am spending it quietly here at the dormitory ever conscious of the many things for which I, personally, am thankful. High on the list are you, my family and friends, and Claflin associates with whom I shall soon be eating turkey. Tomorrow evening I am invited to dinner in town and Saturday and Sunday I'll be in Augusta, Ga., with a friend from near Holly Springs, Ruby Berkley. In between I hope to get a number of odd jobs done.

Certainly life here is not dull. Dorothy Vann, president of the student chapter of NAACP, came to me with a plan minutely worked out for a modified sit-in at Kress. "It all depends on you," she said.

At 10:30 a student would pick me up at my dorm, drive me to within a couple of blocks of Kress. At 10:40 I would enter and order coffee, a hamburger, and a sundae. At 10:50 Dorothy and another student would enter and sit next to me. If they were not served, I would offer each of them one of my dishes. At 10:53 the photographers would arrive and snap our pictures. [With some trepidation, I agreed to cooperate.]

When the girls sat beside me, I greeted them. They were ignored by the waitress. They started to eat the food I offered them. The waitress bang-bang-banged on the bell and put up a sign "CLOSED." The lights of the store flashed on and off. Customers at the counter left. The manager ran the length of the building to the lunch counter. Police were called. The timing was off just a bit because the photographers were held up by the manager, but while one feigned interest in a purchase, the other got the pictures. As I left by the front door, the waitress glared at me saying, "And *you* ought to be strung up!" I said, "Oh, you can't mean that. Just because I shared food with my friends?" "Yes, I do," she said. The police arrived as I was picked up by the cruising, student-driven car. The two girls escaped out the side door and took refuge in the Catholic church until police left the scene and they were picked up by a cruising faculty car.

I was impressed by the detailed planning of the students and by the way we all sandwiched the mission into our regular day. The girls and I had 9:30 and 11:30 classes. We missed neither. In the cafeteria at noon an announcement was made of what had transpired. I was called up to receive a big applause from the students and faculty—which I little deserved as I had done none of the planning. Our pictures [see the front cover of this book] were in at least two papers and short notices made several more. Last year the students had waged a long campaign to integrate Kress with sit-ins, boycott, and picketing. This was the first Negroes had actually eaten there [if a few bites can be called eating].

Dr. Calhoun, one of the other white faculty members here, told me yesterday that he had followed my example and joined a colored church, St. Luke's Presbyterian. He calls the white churches the temples of Satan. In answer to you who have asked, so far as I know there are no other white members of either Trinity or St. Luke's.

Many of your letters express a continuing interest in Rust. Dr. Smith, president of Rust, writes me that the merger [with Mississippi Industrial College across the street] is not really dead as I reported to you before—shall we say it is just in a "coma"? There is a difference, of course. In the meantime the University Senate from Nashville has made a study of Rust and I understand is ready to move out strongly to make Rust the school it should be.

Your letters have been wonderfully inspiring. I love hearing from you and wish I could answer each of you individually. I like my cousin Arlene's quote from John Donne, "letters mingle souls."

[c. December 3, 1961]

Another new [Southern] experience. I was turned down on my application for a charge account at the leading large department store in Columbia. The store was wonderful to me before I applied. It cashed my checks, it sent me mail orders. Of course, since applying I have learned I am not supposed to patronize Columbia stores either so I've lost nothing. I suppose it is my residence that hurts [my credit].

Mrs. Tait would like me to live with her. I feel selfish in not doing so for I know what she is going through [with the loss of her husband]. Yet, I hate to give up my room here on campus. The convenience to classes means much to me. I spent $25 putting up my aerial for the TV and more on my brick-plank bookshelves and floor-to-ceiling lights, etc. But really what bothers me is that I'm not sure I always want to be with someone all the time. Having a room to go to—away from everyone—has its advantages. Her home is very nice. If I could entertain a few people—even try an interracial small—very small—group—it would be interesting. The food would be more to my liking, but we'd have to prepare it—which I don't have to here. And actually, this semester at least, I have no time to entertain or prepare food and clean. So I stay bothered.

At Augusta last weekend I had a good visit with Ruby. Mother would enjoy seeing her Bethlehem Center right in the heart of the worst Negro area. Who am I to say it is the worst? At least I'd feel the housing was pretty sorry if I had to live there. On the other hand they are individual houses—not tenements. Ruby and a young girl just out of college live at the Center. It is large and is well painted and gleams with polish. We were invited to dinner by some interesting young friends of hers. We visited Ruth Bartholomew at Paine College. She wrote me last year asking if I'd like to teach at Paine. She has had two sabbaticals on which she taught in Kenya. Ruth, Ruby and I ate at a hotel dining room. Ruth's housemate (they live on Paine campus) didn't join us. She, like Peg Montgomery whom I met at Talladega, does not go anyplace that colored people cannot go. This is a nice way to cut oneself off from all influence, it seems to me, but maybe I'm only rationalizing.

Last summer when I spoke at Claremont [College in California], I was asked for some concrete examples of students' lack of background. I don't know that these examples are fair, or not, because individuals here and there don't account for all, but this is interesting at least. Mrs. Young, my suitemate, teaches Family Problems. They had discussed at length the problems involved in intermarriage of Catholics and Protestants. It was a lively discussion. After a student took a test on which he had been asked to explain the problems which a marriage between a Catholic and a Protestant might involve, he handed her the paper and said, "Mrs. Young, what is a Protestant?" That was a low moment for her. I felt almost the same—though not quite, as I hadn't tried to teach a lesson on the subject—when none of my English D students knew what "discrimination" meant. I wouldn't have been surprised had they not been able to express it in accurate terms, but they actually didn't have the slightest idea what it meant. They even came up with some far-fetched ideas.

Mississippi, as I predicted last year, is moving. The situation looked pretty bad in McComb, but more hopeful now. I think the FBI's presence and the publicity had some effect. Around these parts we hear the John Birch line all the time—but not under that name. We have "Alerts" here. Every town has its Alert organizations. I see Thurmond[5] has invaded Los Angeles and other western parts with his ideas.

[Orangeburg, December 1961]

[To my cousin Esther:] You may wonder why I always say "young ladies" or "women"—"men" and never boys, girls. At Rust everything was "young ladies" and women. The president spoke in chapel one day about how necessary it was for them to command respect—study to improve themselves so that when they went home no one would ever call them *boys.*[6] It was a sensitive point with them.

Here it is so different. These matrons—really the dean and assistant dean—even call the girls *children* when they want to. *Girls* is quite proper as is also *boys.* This I believe merely reflects the greater security these people have. Also some of the faculty call each other by first name here. Not many though.

There are some ways in which Rust excels, in my opinion, over this college. I don't like to compare, but seeing these students impresses me again with the good grooming of Rust students, the quiet voices, the dignity. I'm not too sure whether I should rejoice in it. It may be that all that is a product of inhibitions suffered throughout their lives whereas [Claflin students] have been freer. I never heard the noise in the dormitories at Rust that I hear here. Which is better I wouldn't say, but Rust was more comfortable for us who were beyond enjoying noise.

December 11, 1961

We've been through Hell Week and it is appropriately named. I never saw such degradations inflicted on people. What fools people can be during those green years when to go against the crowd is felt to be social suicide! I've been a good girl ever since I arrived but will protest this. Several others with me.

5. U.S. Senator Strom Thurmond of South Carolina is still in office in 1996.
6. In the South it was not unusual to call a black man "boy" until possibly in his declining years he was given a term of more respect, "uncle."

December 17, 1961

Mr. [William C.] Carr wrote me and sent a copy of a letter he had sent Kress in New York. Some of you may not know Mr. Carr, original subdivider of all that San Rafael area of Pasadena. His letter began: "After a two-year boycott, this white American has just weakened and bought lights, wrappings, books and toys at Kress Pasadena. I'm sorry, for yesterday a white woman whom Mrs. Carr and I admire sent us a letter from Orangeburg, S.C., which read in part:" (here he quoted my story of the Kress episode) "This occurred in our America at Kress in 1961. Your spineless policy and practice of going along with local subversive activity violates the spirit of Christmas, the spirit of America and the spirit of decency. My stuff from Kress is tainted. The one-man boycott of Kress is on again. I hope it spreads, for anti-communism is not enough. It was Lincoln who warned that if we deny freedom to others we would one day find ourselves in our present mess. For money you help undermine our country. Yet you will expect black and white young men who are not acceptable together at your lunch counters to die for you in battle. Why not set them an example of supreme sacrifice—lose money for principle."

Mr. Carr did what he advocated—lost money for a principle. He sold four lots to Negroes in the San Rafael area; one lot was next door to his own home. Both he and his son have suffered considerable economic reprisals.

January 2, 1962

Last night a neighbor called and asked me to dinner. I had been in my room all day working so it was good to get out. Another friend [of hers] dropped in and said she was sure she had met me before. Finally it occurred to her why my face was so familiar. She has looked at me every day while doing her dishes—my Kress picture.

January 7, 1962

We've had a busy weekend. Anne Braden[7] spoke in chapel Friday morning. The rest of the day she spent in conferences or visiting classes. At 6 we invited

7. Anne and husband Carl, whites from Louisville, Kentucky, were field directors of the Southern Conference Educational Fund (SCEF), a civil rights organization.

students in for a question and discussion period in the lobby of the dorm. Then at 8 one of the faculty members, Mrs. Williams, and a local resident invited her to Mrs. Williams's home. There were others of the faculty and community there. I was glad to meet several people about whom I've heard but have not met before. One man, a trustee of the college, told me the next day that he was interested to see the two doctors going at each other so—Dr. Calhoun and Dr. Milley [both white professors]. It was as stimulating a discussion and with as much participation as I have heard and seen anywhere. Mainly the discussion stemmed from the idea of civil liberties. How far can you go with such liberties in the time of danger such as we are in now?

Did I mention that six of us signed a suggestion to the Administrative Council that we make an evaluation of Hell Week now that it is over and—well, I'll quote what we said: "Once more Claflin has concluded a week of Greek letter society initiations. We wonder if an evaluation of the week's activities would be in order. Perhaps this would be an appropriate and profitable subject for discussion in a faculty meeting. Respectfully submitted."

The answer came to each of us: "In reply to your letter of Dec. 12 we should like to request additional information from you individually. Answers to the following questions will be of great assistance to the committee: 1. Purpose of the evaluation 2. Method of procedure to be used 3. Instrument to be used for collecting data 4. Personnel to be included to carry out evaluation 5. Value or justification of the evaluation to the Claflin Community and the College in general 6. How results from the evaluation will be used. We would appreciate a written response from each member of the group."

I took Anne Braden in to meet the dean. As we were about to leave I said, "By the way, I received your memo, but I'm not biting. I know that little trick and have sometimes used it myself—when you want to stifle a suggestion or prevent any more suggestions you just throw it back at the suggester. What you've asked for would constitute a term paper—and I have all I can do with my classes." Of course I had him at a disadvantage with Anne there. He said, "Well, when someone wants to sweep he should bring a broom with him." We carried on a little more banter all in good nature—I think. One can never be sure.

Mr. [Kelley R.] White [black], however, blessings on him, wrote a thorough reply saying everything I would have loved to say only for the fact that I have sworn not to be a reformer this year. Then he took it in to the dean in person and added more words. The dean told him that I said the memo was a slap in the face. I didn't think I said that but maybe I did. At least it would have been true. The dean thinks I egged the others on to do this. I think it was Mrs. Davis's [black] idea—I can't be sure, though. At least I know I toned down her idea. She wanted to write everything that was wrong with the week and I said I would be no part of that—all I would do was to suggest an evaluation and/or a discussion. Mr. White told the dean—"You think I was incited to make this protest. I was not. It has been on my mind ever since I was a student here and went through the initiation myself." Of course it is much better for Mr. White to say all this than for me because he is a product of the school and he is practically indispensable. He is the French teacher; he is an EXCELLENT teacher; he has six classes, all overflowing.

January 8, 1962

Dear Mr. Carr:

Your letter to Kress's New York office was excellent. Many of my co-workers have read it and have been heartened. It also gave me a good opportunity to tell them about your role in this changing world.

The answer indicates an awareness of the problem; at least it was not a hasty brush-off. I am giving the answer to Rev. McCollom. I'd like to know just what the stand of the NAACP leaders is. He might have more direct knowledge of it.

The day after receiving your letter, I received a letter from Stella Mann, author of a number of books on personality problems. A whole page was devoted to reasons why all that I was doing was wrong. Happily she ended it, "Sincerely and forever your friend."

Such a letter helps me to keep my feet on the ground. I'm grateful to her for her honesty. I've had many responses from my letters and only two have been critical so I suppose I can't complain about the average.

Last year I almost went to New York in May to attend the Socony Mobil stockholders' meeting to present the case of John McFerren, who could not get any oil company to fill his gas pumps. When I asked for a spot on the agenda, I was told that I could bring the matter up in the general discussion period, but no vote could be taken. According to a federal ruling, a motion to be voted on had to be submitted by February to give the company time to notify the stockholders.

Although I had intended even then to make a broader plea than just for McFerren, I canceled my trip when he received gas a few weeks before the meeting. Now I am eager to try the venture this year, getting my request for a vote in by February. I'm writing you to ask your advice and, if the advice is favorable, to get your help in writing the motion since you are more familiar with the business world than I.

I have been reading the transcript of last year's meeting and am sending it to you for your perusal. I'd appreciate your returning it to me, though.

My thought is to make a positive motion to the effect that Socony Mobil should make every effort to encourage its dealers (most of whom are independent) to provide restroom and drinking facilities for all without discrimination: to do this because it would be good business—yes, but even more because it is right and American.

I doubt that many living in other areas even realize that numbers of our stations do not offer accommodations for Negroes or that if they do they have separate facilities—usually one for WHITE LADIES, another for WHITE MEN, and one more for COLORED. How this last designation irritates Negroes! "Colored what? Is a Negro sexless?" they ask.

I hope the New Year is off to a good start for you and Mrs. Carr. You'll never know how much I appreciate your letters. Your Christmas card was good even though lacking the little Negro child I've learned to expect.

January 13 [1962]—Saturday

I've been working on papers. My good class in World History was comparing the conditions that led to the fall of Rome with conditions in America today. I cringed when I read in several papers of the disunity in America where "black is against white." I've noticed this whenever there is a chance to bring in the subject—the idea that it is a war between black and white. I wish they could understand that some whites are working along side of them.

I don't wonder these students feel this way. Last night in talking with Rev. McCollom I asked him again if there were *any* contacts with whites. Absolutely none.

Tomorrow we will have open house to show off our beautiful new men's dormitory. [I thought this might be noncontroversial enough that a few white citizens of the town would feel able to attend. Thus] I called the ministers of the Presbyterian and Methodist churches asking them to come. They were both very courteous. Dr. Frampton of the Presbyterian [Church] thanked me profusely for my thoughtfulness but I noticed he didn't commit himself. I'll not give him up until 4 tomorrow. Dr. Jones has such a full day; amongst other things they are starting their school for missions. I told him it would appear that this open house was made to order to start that school off with a real mission experience. He agreed that it might be so.

Mrs. Manning, the president's wife, told me today that when she goes to a national meeting of W.S.C.S. [Women's Society of Christian Service, a Methodist organization], she becomes so enthused about inviting the women from the white churches, as the meetings always say they should, but after a few rebuffs she settles down each time to content herself with her own group.

Of course I don't think they should give up. I think this open house ought to have nice invitations sent to the mayor and all public officials and ministers. A $500,000 building is after all an asset to the community. I suppose if my skin were black my hide wouldn't be so thick and I couldn't take these rebuffs in stride, either. It is different when feeling and speaking from the sanctuary of a white skin.

It is too bad I've made no white contacts here. These two ministers are all I know—and I don't know them, really, except as I forced myself upon each once.

Ruby Berkley, the [Methodist] deaconess I visited at Bethlehem Center in Augusta Thanksgiving weekend, is in all sorts of trouble because she had Anne Braden meet with 20 friends at her home, in the center. The United Fund threatened to cut off her funds; the newspapers carried editorials about her; the superintendent of schools called in the four Negro teachers who attended and told them it must not happen again; the editorial, I should have said, called for an investigation of the center. On the hopeful side, the Methodist bishop asked ministers to write to the paper in support, call on the paper and members of the United Fund whom they know; the [white] president of Paine College [a black Methodist school] wrote a letter in her behalf; her own minister is standing by her; the W.S.C.S. wrote a fine letter to her which she had mimeographed and distributed. I told her I thought this latter part very encouraging. A few years ago I doubt such support would have rallied around her.

January 21, 1962

The Framptons of the white Presbyterian church did come to our open house. They met all the right people—the president, the chaplain and their wives, and several others. Dr. Manning announced in faculty meeting this week that the school had Mrs. Campbell to thank for the first show of interest—at least the first any white person from Orangeburg has shown interest by coming on campus since the '54 decision.[8] In '54 the local white members of the Claflin trustees resigned, and there has been no white local contact since.

This morning I went to a Baptist church to hear one of my freshman students preach. He is in my very good class, is a fine student, gave a message with many good thoughts. Considering he is only a freshman, he does show potential. He is evidently well liked by the students as they turned out en masse and crowded the church.

The NAACP met at 5 this evening. One of the problems discussed was registration of voters. Rev. McCollom asked one man if he could get the city employees under his supervision to register. He said they were afraid and he wouldn't dare ask them. There are about 75 of these men. Another man said they were not afraid but they were not eligible. To register one has to be able to read and write or show receipt for taxes on property assessed at $300 or more. He said most of these 75 men could not read or write, did not own anything but maybe an old car that wouldn't be worth $200. So the talk turned to the need for a [literacy] school.

The other exciting part of the program this evening was due to the announcement this week of an industry's coming here to locate. The Utica Drop Forge and Tool Division of the Kelsey-Hayes Co. is a multi-million-dollar metalworking plant employing between 450 and 500 skilled workers and providing an annual payroll of nearly $2½ million dollars. [White] Orangeburg is elated. Negroes are also elated because, having government contracts, the plant is forced to employ without discrimination. However, Rev. McCollom pointed out that if we didn't apply right off beginning tomorrow morning when the employment office opens, they may say they have all the skilled jobs filled and have only room for broom pushers now. A training school is being set up for employees. Orangeburg city has invested $30,000 in this training school.

January 29, 1962

I don't think I was cut out for a purely academic life. I feel so relieved to have but three preparations and five classes. I've already planned to use the time

8. The *Brown* v. *Board of Education* (of Topeka, Kansas) U.S. Supreme Court decision ordering public schools to integrate.

saved three times over. But surely I will get out into the community a bit more and meet some people with whom I can at least disagree! Have an appointment to see the white Methodist minister tomorrow at 3. Purely an exploratory talk—but I have a few ideas I hope I can bring up.

Marion Downs[9] wrote that she might be able to come here on the 27th of March. She is singing in Hawaii during February. We hope to use her afterward to attract a few white people to an after-concert party. Mrs. Williams [music professor] and I are planning the deal. We saw the president this morning and got his blessing.

We had some biscuits for dinner. Mrs. Young said, "These biscuits are good even though the cook did treat them like the Lord treated us—left them in the oven a little too long."

I'm going through the agony of writing a speech for a seminar on race relations. President Manning is eager to give people the idea that race relations means more than taking a collection for the college. The booklet the Lines sent gave me some help. I'll begin again on that inspiration.

February 4, 1962

I decided my hairdresser to whom I originally went out of town seven miles was giving me the brush-off. She was always busy when I called for appointments. Thus I called a nice little establishment in the better part of town out near the hospital. I said I didn't suppose there would be a chance to get an appointment that day, but would ask. Yes, I could have my hair cut one hour later—at 11:30. When I arrived I was treated very cordially. After the operator cut my hair she said, "If you have time, Mrs. Campbell, I'd be glad to shampoo and set your hair." I told her I'd be delighted. The only reason I hadn't asked originally was that I did need the cut and was afraid if I asked for too much on such short notice I'd be turned down for all. While she was working on me we got to talking about her family and mine. One of the other operators asked if I were new. I confessed to all on question: from California; arrived last September; leaving in June; teaching. "Where do you teach?" "At Claflin College." Dead silence. "Have you ever been to the college?" "Yes." This I knew to be untrue. Nobody [white] comes to Claflin. She meant she had driven by, I'm

9. Black concert soprano, widow of the minister of the Pasadena black Methodist church, who studied in Italy on a Fulbright scholarship.

sure. "Well, you should come again; we have a beautiful new men's dormitory. You should see it." Continued silence.

I had my hair dried in another room. Of course the driers would preclude my hearing what was said anyway. When my hair was combed out, I asked for an appointment a week from Friday. "I'm sorry, I'm all filled up for then." "Well, how about one of the other beauticians?" "They are filled up too. You see we have standing appointments that keep us booked up completely. We just happened to have a cancelation today." Of course I invited all this. I could have kept them from asking so many questions. I could have answered more vaguely, but I hadn't been out on the field of battle for so long, I just had to beg the question. So, now I'm looking for another hairdresser. I may have to go to Columbia, if I continue talking too much.

February 11, 1962

Our Race Relations Seminar is over and a good thing, as I had difficulty keeping up with classes when trying to get that talk to jell. I think there is no doubt but that Rev. McCollom and I carried the day. We were on together. When he finished we had reached such an exalted state that I felt we should stop right then. However, I know my part was needed too because we needed something real practical to go to work on, and that was my part as assigned. I felt pleased with the reception because I had said many of the things that I had been wanting to point up—ways in which Negroes could help themselves—little ways which are so important in human relations.

I started by saying that when I come to the end of life I doubt there will be many to mourn my passing; that this would be in part due to a perversity of mine that when I am with a predominantly white group I'm always stressing the inalienable aspects of rights and freedom—that they are not something we earned but are God-given. Thus I make few friends among the white group. Then when I am with a predominantly Negro group I stress the idea that for every right there is a responsibility—obligations and rights go hand in hand. Thus I make few friends among the Negroes. But all this is probably not too important. I only hope that in the process we can find ourselves thinking together—if at times we find ourselves disagreeing that we can disagree agreeably—and always think.

It was a good audience for response. I could feel them with me all the way.

In my classes I am forever insisting that a student's written work MUST BE HIS OWN—not copied from the book or—heaven forbid—another student's paper. Thus I smiled when one student asked me in somewhat awed tones, "Did you write that speech all yourself?"

Mrs. Stackhouse, a former dean of Limestone College (private white South Carolina school), came from Columbia. She was most effusive in her praise of my talk and said one could just see that I was a born teacher. I was happy to hear that she could see that—because I have often wondered if I was a *teacher*—let alone a born one. She also said that when she first met me she felt so sorry for me here at Claflin. But yesterday she made the discovery that I LOVED being here. She said my love for the work here just radiated through my every word and she would never again feel sorry for me.

Though I had invited Rev. Jones and some members from his Christian Social Concerns Commission, and Dr. Frampton from the Presbyterian church, and my doctor and dentist whom I have gone to while here, none came. But I'm glad I invited them. I also wrote a note to Mrs. Frampton and asked her if she could pull herself away from her husband's preaching for one Sunday to be my guest at Trinity today—Race Relations Sunday. She wrote me a very nice note declining. I'm sure she had to do considerable thinking, if not actual soul searching to write the note, and that too is probably all to the good. And she did leave the door open for me to ask her again. This I appreciate. As I said in my talk, "Ours is not the responsibility for their acceptance; ours, only the responsibility to invite."

February 22, 1962

My school board ought to be paying me for this year instead of having paid me for that year I took a sabbatical to get my master's. I've learned so much more this year—and I could add, I've studied harder, too.

This fall Claflin was accepted by the Southern Association of Colleges and Secondary Schools—the regional accrediting agency. There was great rejoicing. However, we are on a probationary arrangement for three years. This may have influenced the action taken at midyear—81 students were not allowed to register for the second semester because they did not make a grade average of .65. (A "C" average would be 1.) Though it is spelled out in the catalog, the practice, I am told, has not been so strictly adhered to. There was much wailing and gnashing of teeth. We all felt like crying, and my freshman English class that I had such high hopes for was almost a complete wash-out. Out of 16 members only two survived. (Not necessarily because of my teaching; these were at the bottom on the entrance exams at the beginning of the year.) Some faculty members are critical of the practice, saying that given another nine weeks some of these students could have made the grade—adjustment period is longer for some than others, etc. I may sound hard-hearted, but, sad as the experience was for us, I believe it all to the good. It has had a salutary effect on those who are left. They are studying much better, and of course there is not the drag of the laggards. Most of mine went home in tears but with a vow on their lips to come back next fall and make good. I tried to explain to them that this could be the making of them. Most of them could make good if they would realize they were here for business instead of play. I'm all for the procedure, but it is hard at the time. Some of these students actually won honors in high schools, indicating, I should think, something about the quality or lack of quality in their high schools.

I did have a very good conference with another of the local pastors. Ministers are in a difficult spot. I have very positive ideas on the role of a minister, but few ministers share those ideas with me and maybe if I were in their shoes, I'd feel more as they do. Anyway, I had to take what satisfaction I could from this minister's parting words, "Well, Mrs. Campbell, I won't say there haven't been painful moments, but I have enjoyed our conversation." Considering that three students and I had been put out of his church early in the fall, I was grateful for those words.

Our local radio station has a habit of giving editorials which are taped and run six times during the day. They condemn the United Nations, extol Strom Thurmond and General Walker, fuss about the Supreme Court, etc. I particularly liked Rev. McCollom's answer to one. To the credit of the station, it ran the answer as many times as the original statement.

The students have been admonished so many times of the importance of "marching" to the library and staging a "study-in" right here on campus that I do believe they have taken it to heart. At least there have been few demonstrations downtown. The leaders of the local nursing home project had their worry for nothing.

I particularly enjoyed the *Rust College Sentinel* for February. It revealed such a good, strong, vital spirit all the way through. It told of a number of achievements thus far this year. The science building seems to be a sure thing—certainly much needed. Improvements in the math department were noted, also a must for any adequate science program. The Theater Guild is presenting an ambitious program; its first play was "Antigone," and "A Raisin in the Sun" and "The Glass Menagerie" are coming up. There were many features in the paper which evidenced a widening interest. I hope to see a couple of Rust graduates, now studying at Atlanta University, next week.

10:00 p.m., February 23, 1962

I'm developing into a character, I think. Anna Morsey [vice principal at Washington Junior High] once told me every *good* teacher was something of a character. I hope I'm also good. These students chew gum so much. It embarrasses me to tell college students to spit out their gum but I detest standing up and looking at them. Besides I always think of the trouble they had at Lincoln Avenue [Church] getting young people to usher—they were so apt to lead someone down the aisle chawing all the while. Then I remember one of the teas at the Line home where a sister of one of my Washington students appeared. I had never met her before but knew she was of that family because she chewed in the same manner—and at this lovely tea. So I feel a bit of responsibility to let them know, at least, that gum chewing and the best society are not compatible. In the talk I gave at the Race Relations Seminar I had a paragraph [on gum chewing] in the section telling the need for financial independence. I brought in a bit about how Rockefeller saved on 50¢ a day and thus started himself on the road to his millions. Of course some may feel more concern for the Wrigley [gum] fortune—etc.

In the midst of class this week I said, "Miss Haywood, there is a paper on reserve in the library I want you to read. After you have read it write me a note, please, and tell me why you think I asked you to read it. I know it's good because I wrote it myself." After class several asked me if they could read it too! One of these extra readers told me as our paths crossed on campus that he read it. I said, "And do you know why I asked Miss Haywood to read it?" He didn't, so I said, "Well, if enough read it someone will catch the point." Today I received the letter from Miss Haywood and she was all chuckles as she handed it to me. It was well written for which I was glad as she was in my English class last semester. "I think you had me read that article on 'Race Relations' because I was chewing gum in class on Monday. I have enjoyed reading it very much. Most of all, it made me stop and ask myself what am I doing to help promote civil rights." Now wasn't that nice? I think maybe she will remember not to chew gum in my class and perhaps she has learned even more, for that was such a small part of the speech.

One student is forever hitting me for a loan. He has always paid me back. Today he handed me a note which told of his present plight and need for a loan until his mother's letter arrived—hopefully tomorrow. I accommodated him then handed him his note and said, "Now correct the grammatical errors you have made in this note and return it to me. You need to know your grammar if you are going to be a success at anything."

Someday I must write you of their determination to hold on to their religion. Even if the Crusaders slashed off the heads of the infidels, piled the arms and legs up in a heap, waded in blood up to their knees—yet it was God's will and the Crusades were divinely inspired. The Christians were better than Saladin who was chivalrous, merciful, and magnanimous. Because *he* was a Muslim—an infidel—not divinely inspired!

February 26, 1962

You may have guessed that I have an admirer [white]. He is so sweet; I never really realize how sarcastic and catty I have become until I am with him. He is a food "purist." Today he left three fancy pound boxes of dried fruits from California—figs, prunes, and dates—on my office desk. On Valentine's Day there was a candy box of what appeared to be the most luscious chocolates—but there isn't a smidgin of chocolate in them—molasses or something treated to look like it. That is one box of "candy" on which I have had no difficulty exercising self-control. I love the apples he keeps me supplied with. And the stone-ground flour fruit cake. Nothing is ordinary. Everything comes from afar and has never been poisoned with insecticides. Only organic fertilizer is used. Also he takes me out to dinner at least once a week.

[March 1962]

Mr. White says a student came to him complaining, "Lord, I've never been in such a predicament. I come directly from Mrs. Campbell's class to you." I know Mr. White works his students hard in French. I suppose that means I work mine hard, too. They really are doing more in history than I ever dreamed they could. And the teacher is racing along, trying to keep at least one step ahead of them.[10]

Saturday afternoon Mrs. Tait, Dr. Calhoun and I drove to Atlanta. We saw Agnes Scott College, a real gem; Georgia Tech, which is a city school but has pretty new buildings; Oglethorpe, a gray stoned architecture; University of Georgia, where the two Negro students were finally accepted after much ado about nothing last year; and of course we went to Atlanta University to see Rev. Burley whom I had in class last year. He is now in graduate school and working *very* hard he thinks. He says at one point he could understand a person's desire to seek the tallest bridge. Also said one of his profs told him he had voted against his admittance to grad school—not because he had anything against him personally—he didn't even know him then—but because he came from Rust and he couldn't imagine his making good. Burley says when he looks back on those classes, he is astounded at what could pass for a college course. He is still in an English remedial class in Atlanta.

Mrs. Burley had intended coming to Atlanta from Louisville next weekend but when she learned I would be there she came this weekend instead. We all had dinner at a quiet, well-ordered and -appointed restaurant run by Negroes. There were other white people there. It looked like the kind of place where you'd pay $2.95 for a dinner—it was 95¢ plus dessert! We heard Rev. [Ralph] Abernathy preach to a capacity audience. He is one who was associated with King in the Montgomery boycott of buses.

Marion Downs is coming on the 27th. We are trying to get some white townspeople here. Have donations coming in to pay Marion's fee of $100. We won't charge any admission. We plan an informal gathering afterward to meet Marion.

Isn't Mother a world's wonder? Imagine doing all that she does [at 77] and now giving music lessons to three girls! I wish I could keep up with her. Just being away this weekend threw me.

March 11, 1962

Learning that Rust students haven't forgotten me always sets me aglow. Rev. Newman (I think he is state president of NAACP) and I were talking after the

10. My 1958 master's degree was in school administration. Later I took four years off teaching to earn a doctorate in history.

seminar on Christian Social Concerns Friday night. He said he learned that I didn't only talk about concerns but acted on them. He had seen some Rust students at Jackson. Said they were decrying my failure to return to Rust. Rev. McCollom had already given me a note from a Rust student received at the same meeting in Mississippi. The students apparently still have administration limitations on their activities. At least they have an NAACP chapter now.

Food is a problem, I suppose, in any institution. We have plenty to eat, but variety is so limited. Wienies and bologna must be traditional in the South—but if so, many have not reconciled themselves to it. There are two kinds of grace said at our faculty table in the interest of an honest approach to the Lord: "We thank you for this food . . ." and "Lord, make us thankful for this food."

We had a good seminar Friday night and Saturday morning. There were three sections. I took the one on alcohol education not only because of interest but because we had a local Methodist minister—white—to lead it. He is from a new church on the edge of town. A young man. The fact that he helped in this program is encouraging. I have an appointment to talk with him tomorrow morning. After sitting through two-and-a-half hours of discussion on what we could do to discourage college drinking, etc., I met Mrs. Williams, head of the music department. She said she had two ads for the Marion Downs program sheet. I asked from whom. A shoe shop and a *liquor dealer.* You can imagine my response! She backed down, saying she didn't know if we should use it.

Saturday, March 17, 1962

I hope everyone is well and happy now; otherwise I'd feel guilty enjoying life so much. Sometimes I wonder if I'm not using teaching as a stage for ham acting.

After class today a student asked me for the loan of a dollar. He has done this quite often. This morning I turned on him with my gruffest manner. "You don't need a dollar. You smoke too much." He disputed this. "Yes, you do. You reek so of tobacco I can hardly stand being near you." "I've got a job, but I need a dollar to get to it." "You could easily have transportation money if you didn't spend it all on cigarettes—wrecking your health and your independence at the same time. No matter how successful you are in getting civil rights, you'll be a slave so long as you don't have a dollar in your pocket." I handed him the dollar. He said, "Can I be your chauffeur to California this summer?"

"No, you smoke too much and you don't talk well enough. I'm not going to introduce you to my friends." "You *know* I'm working on my English." Then I melted and said sweetly, "I know, and I'm real proud of your progress."

When I think of how I used to plead and wheedle students—I can't believe I am hearing my own voice now. But they seem to like me this way. It's exhilarating to *feel* students with you. (Take this all with a grain of salt. Next time I write I'll probably be in the depth of depression concerning relationships with students or faculty or both.)

[My daughter] Camie used to say I had the worst case of an inferiority *complex* she had ever known. She was dead wrong. I WAS *inferior.* But I'm not now and don't mind saying so. No teacher here has students working any harder or better for him than do mine. It's really great.

Three classes did not do well in the midterm tests. These tests are hard for them. We are going at college pace (I never did last year—nor even last semester, though that was better than last year). There is lots of reading and understanding involved. I give 50% objective and 50% essay. They find it hard to learn specifics and then to use them in their thinking. They are fond of writing something and when they get through I say, "Yes, but you could have told me all this without ever having sat in this class." Or they give you such faulty thinking based on absolute contradiction of facts. One class did *very* well. Dr. Calhoun helped me correct their essays and was amazed at the work. (It is a help, though, when they come to you smart—as they did in this class.)

When I turned the papers back to the other classes, they were so depressed. So I told them about how glad I was that no one had valued a mere grade so much as to try to get it by hook and by crook. After all it was only a grade and not to be compared with the worth of one's integrity. They could take pride in a C or D honestly obtained if it represented their best work. "I think most of you *are* working hard; perhaps a few are trying to get by." Then I paused and said, "You know, last night I had a peeping Tom. I heard a scuffle and whispering outside my window. I raised up in bed to look out and there was a face pressed against my window. When he saw me he said to his companion in a loud whisper 'Jeepers! She saw me,' and they both ran like mad. At first I thought maybe I should feel flattered—that any young man should be interested in peeking in at me—at my age." I got a big laugh out of them at this turn of thought. "But my second thought was—why aren't those men in their rooms studying for their midterms?!" At this the students really laughed. One of the fellows said, "What time was this?" I guessed it was about 9:45. "So early! If I were going to do anything like that I'd pick a later hour." I said,

"Shall I expect you—later?" The kids seemed to get a kick out of all this though some were distressed that this should have happened. Of course there is no assurance they were our college students. Could have been outsiders. I ended by saying I knew none of them were wasting their time peeping, but if they were wasting their time in any way at all, they might consider settling down to hard work from now till the end of the semester.

Some were so disappointed in their grades and I do know they have worked hard. So I agreed to give them an hour's review on their own time and another midterm exam a different day, again on their own time. The American history class came yesterday for the review. All but one were there and he had told me ahead of time it would be impossible at that hour for him.

Students asked me to speak at the Power Hour Wednesday evening. You remember how concerned I was over Hell Week. The machinations and the competition of the Greeks on campus is most unwholesome, I'd say. I've talked to the chaplain. He doesn't feel he can do anything because he is not a frat man. Rev. McCollom is a member of a frat on campus and so feels he can do nothing. All he can think of is to abolish them anyway. We had our rebuff from administration when we wrote the letter asking that we discuss the matter at faculty meeting.

So—I decided maybe I was in the best position to speak out. Thus I hit it straight and hard in this 15-minute talk to about 200 students. I'm sure the speech was a bit corny—but the meaning was clear and my position was made clear. Sometimes something a bit corny gets over better than the scholarly approach. Woven in the talk, I said sometimes I agreed with Hollywood—that the worst thing that can happen to us is to be ignored—that is an indication that we are nobodies. "For instance, it won't bother me a bit if you get real mad about something I say tonight—but if you really want to upset me, just ignore what I say—never think about it again."

So far there is no indication they are ignoring what I said. Immediately after the talk many students came up to shake hands and tell me they enjoyed the talk. I discounted all that as form. But I appreciated the ones who said, "I was so glad to hear you say all that." Or, "It was time someone came out on that subject." "Someone should have said that long ago."

Dr. Jackson, the chaplain, came up, shook my hand, held my hand a few seconds looking right in my eyes, his lips parted as though to speak, he finally said nothing. I take it that he agreed but felt he couldn't say or express himself.

Well, back to the student reaction: Mr. White, French teacher, told me the students in the dorm were talking about it. Several told Mrs. McNeil here that she missed a good talk. Students are still stopping me to talk about it. I walked into class yesterday and found them discussing it. You can see the position the students were in. Everyone is supposedly desirous of being pledged. All these stupid things go on. No one says anything against them. They naturally suppose the administration approves—that this is what one aspires to do when he is educated. Coming from country towns they are ripe to learn the ways of the world—this they assumed was what they were supposed to learn and want. I say no one says anything. Not quite true. Dr. Calhoun told his class it seemed odd they were so dead set against one kind of segregation and working so hard for another kind. Mrs. Tait has talked to her classes and the student body president who is in one of them, asking him to bring it up in student council and the Pan-Hellenic Council. Dr. Milley (white) told his class all that initiation stuff was for the birds. So there has been something done but I fear mostly by us whites.

I had a good visit with a minister again yesterday. He actually appears to enjoy our talks—and says he does. Still full of his rationalization—I was there to ask him to come to Marion's concert—he thinks this might do more harm than good—he sees no need to make announcement of it in the bulletin of the church if it will be in the newspaper—anyone interested will learn about it there—then he stopped and said, "I suppose this all sounds like rationalization to you." I think what he meant was that it sounded that way to him. At one point he said, "You are doing what we all should do; you take your stand openly." He became interested in my future—would I come back? Did I have children? Don, his son wants to be a designing engineer. He asked me if you had need of a foreign language in your work. His son doesn't do well in languages and he wonders if it's worthwhile to keep him struggling. So if you have any thoughts on that subject it might be the opening for another talk with him.

March 24, 1962

We had three days off for the spring break. Mrs. McNeil, Mrs. Tait, Dr. Calhoun, and I took a two-day tour of South Carolina colleges. Before leaving, several of the faculty asked me what we would do with Mrs. McNeil (light colored) when it came time to eat and sleep. I said we'd put her in the middle and walk in with heads up. One of faculty said we couldn't get away with it in her home area, she'd guarantee.

Our first meal happened to be in her hometown—a city of about 30,000.

We walked through the lobby of the best hotel and into the dining room. I asked for a table for four. We were seated very courteously. After we ordered, the manager approached me and asked if this were a missionary group. I said no, but it was flattering to think we might look like missionaries. After we were served with the greatest solicitation, the manager again came to us and said to Dr. Calhoun, "I keep thinking I've seen you before. Were you ever at Erskine College?" He admitted he was there from '33-'36 and they chatted about the various people living and dead whom they had known in common. She said, "We must have an article in the paper about your visit here." She thrust pencil and paper before him and asked for all our names, where we were from and where we were going. Dr. Calhoun complied. She was so excited and said she wished we could stay overnight. At least we could make use of the lobby if we would like to relax a while before going on. As we paid our bill, she said, "We really were expecting a group of missionaries. When I saw this lady (looking at Mrs. McNeil) with the dark complexion, I just assumed you were that group." We smiled sweetly and asked for the restroom. While we were gone she asked Dr. Calhoun what nationality the dark-complexioned lady was. He said, "Oh, she's American."

In the ladies' lounge a very skeptical lady, I presume an employee of the hotel, came in. She stared at each of us in turn. When we returned, the manager of the dining room beamed, "You all come again now," but the woman who had followed us to the restroom, now standing at the side of the manager, just continued to glare at us.

Night found us in Greenville. Being tired we didn't attempt to push our luck. Dr. Calhoun and I went into the Holiday Inn. He signed for his room and I signed for the two rooms for the three of us women. We were able to go to our rooms without going through the lobby, so there was no chance for detection. We ate at a drive-in. But the next morning we walked into the Holiday dining room looking out over the pool—a lovely setting. From two doors we were intermittently stared at by the help. None of the other breakfasters seemed to pay us any attention. When we paid our bill, there were stares, but that didn't bother us.

For the noon meal we stopped at the best hotel in the little metropolis (about 3,500) of Rock Hill. We feel safer always in a place of quality where they are likely to have good manners. If we are to be thrown out, we want it to be done with dignity. Again we received the best of service. Mrs. McNeil was treating at this meal and kept looking right up at the waitress to make requests for more cream, etc. At the end, Mrs. Tait pantomimed to me that I should pay the bill so Mrs. McNeil wouldn't have to approach the cashier. I said to Mrs. McNeil, "Do you want any help?" She answered emphatically, "No." I wish you could have seen her. She walked up to that cashier and with all the dignity of a queen said, "We enjoyed our lunch so much. Everything was delicious." The cashier thanked her and gave the usual response, "You all come back real soon." Then Mrs. McNeil walked across the room to the waitress and, placing a dollar bill in her hand, looking her straight in the eye, said we had appreciated the good service. She was really superb. No one stared noticeably while we were in the room, but as we walked to our car I turned around to see heads peering out the parted draperies. And as we continued past the kitchen to our car in the parking lot, a black face was peering out the kitchen window.

I was happy all turned out so well because neither Dr. Calhoun nor Mrs. Tait would have chosen to do all this. They were a bit perturbed when I told them I had asked Mrs. McNeil to go with us. Now I think they'd be willing to do it again. I think it all helps to make people understand that nothing much happens. The customers didn't make a mass exit. Perhaps we give too much to the opposition by default. We should use the rights we have and not assume always that we don't have any privileges.

April 7, 1962

Did you miss my letter last week? I took four students to a South Carolina Council on Human Relations (student chapters) retreat at Penn Center near Beaufort on the coast. About 60 were there. Many of the white students came without the knowledge of their schools or parents. Had a good experience but returned exhausted and if anyone had visited my Monday classes he'd have recommended I be fired. On top of returning exhausted, I had essay tests done in my absence to correct. I'm trying to develop the honor system in my tests. Not all are mature enough for it yet. They can't understand how I know when they open their books and peek. In other words they haven't learned to be clever about it and don't realize that they don't usually use the kind of construction that the authors use—to say nothing of the exact phrases and organization. Usually questions I give can't be answered directly out of the book, but as a third alternative I said if they couldn't write on either question given, they could write on a subject of their own choosing. This was a mistake. I discovered a number enjoy being "parrots." But it was a learning process. We understand each other better now. One doesn't learn by copying, and it's not honest, etc. Many need this kind of learning more than history. I recall Keith's question: When do we teach honesty? Too often we don't; we just expect them to have it.

Anne Braden asked me to be a consultant for a conference in Birmingham next Friday and Saturday. I don't believe in neglecting my classes, as education is basic to civil rights, but the temptation was too great. I succumbed. Birmingham is a hot place right now. Latest is the cutting of all Negroes from the relief rolls until Negro leaders call off the boycott. It was in Birmingham that the policeman put Miss Jackson and me out of the train station last year.

You remember the student who asked to borrow a dollar and I told him he smoked too much? He was chewing gum in class this week. (All the South chews gum and many never learned to keep their mouths closed in the process.) After class I asked him to present a portion of the lesson next time. "And don't chew gum while you're talking. We want to understand you." "Ah, Mrs. Campbell, I just forgot this once—and I did stop smoking." "Bless you," I said. "You and I are going to get along yet." "Well, you told me I shouldn't waste my money and I decided that made sense." And as he left I realized that he hadn't reeked with tobacco as the previous week.

Another student approached me asking "a personal favor" (not one of my students). "My buddy is going in the dog house tonight and has to have $5. Could you loan it to me for him?" I said, "Do you mean THAT kind of dog house?" pointing to the "graves" marked "Here lies Dog so and so"—one for each of the present members of Omega Psi Phi. He said he did. I proceeded to deliver to him a portion of my Power Hour talk that dealt with these ridiculous pledging activities. I added a few extra flourishes such as "He knew he would need $5 tonight. Why didn't he prepare for it? What makes him think he can earn it any easier after he is initiated than before? I'd only be encouraging him to live beyond his income. Anyone who lives beyond his income is a slave." "Well, if you feel that way about lending to him, won't you lend to me and forget him?" I suggested he see one of the faculty who has more sympathy for the cause. "I know there are a number who do, for I registered my dissatisfaction after the last Hell Week and was criticized for my pains."

Later I was told by one of the faculty that another, having been told by this student of my denial of his request, was peeved at me. I said as far as I could learn someone was peeved at somebody all the time so it was no more than fair that I should have my turn. Too bad, though, because this person (one peeved at me allegedly) has been a staunch friend—I thought.

Yesterday a student asked if I would help the pledges of Alpha Phi Alpha work out a chapel program. They thought they might give a skit or something to dramatize what I was saying about Hell Week. I asked him if he and the other pledges were willing to take the consequences. I said it was like working for civil rights—might boomerang. He said he was willing to take that chance. Today the entire group of seven met with me. I think we've worked out something pretty good. It will remain to be seen how it goes over. The serious part is to be in the form of a short debate: Hell Week is a discredit to Claflin.

Do you think I'm a troublemaker? I *did* want to make good this year!

I stopped writing at this point to go to supper. I didn't get there. Had to take in the death march. The pledges of Omega Psi Phi were carrying with one hand their tombstones (heavy cement blocks) to their plots. They were accompanied by all their brothers and all were singing the dirge: something like, Nothing can stop me, Going to make Omega Psi Phi, Only the righteous can make it. Over and over clear across campus. No sooner had this procession ended with a return to the gym, a good block or more away, goose stepping all the way, than the Alpha Phi Alphas started. With a fancy step such as a baton twirler might use, they came all the way around the drive saying, "Next time you see me, I may be an Alpha." This chanted over and over again. Am I out of date? Do most colleges do these things? They seem so absolutely juvenile to me. What they do where we can see them is only a fraction, I am told.

Guess I haven't written since Marion was here. She made a real hit. We had a good crowd. One white person came—a Catholic priest who has a Negro school in town.

When I was at the retreat, one of the men told me that a friend of his used to be at the Baptist church and he said if he hadn't lived here he never could have believed that people could live under such tenseness. He said he had been all over Virginia, Georgia and South Carolina but had never been any place as tense as Orangeburg.

April 21—Saturday—1962

I've just returned from planning and practicing for the pledges' program next Friday. I hope it goes over well, for these fellows are really sticking their necks out. It is fun working with them.

Mrs. Brown [black] from Trinity Methodist rode on the bus with me as far as Atlanta a week ago. We ate together at the Greyhound station in Athens—the town of the University of Georgia where the registration of two Negro students caused so much disturbance last year. I saw one colored man in the waiting room at Birmingham where Miss Jackson and I were asked to leave 18 months ago. In Augusta there were four Negroes in the main waiting room. Other than for these few, racial segregation continued though there were no signs on the doors. I suppose this is all right. The important thing is that those who want to enter the mainstream of life in a bus station may.

Dr. Jim Dombrowski [Director of SCEF] wrote the mayor of Birmingham asking if we would be breaking any city ordinances by having an integrated meeting. The city attorney answered that there was no *enforceable* ordinance prohibiting integrated meetings in a church. We would not be allowed to integrate in other private places. Strictly speaking we decided we were breaking the law by sleeping and eating at Gaston's, a motel owned by Negroes. A car filled with white men slowly paraded through the grounds of this motel after we returned to it Friday night.

My roommate (white) from Scarritt College and I walked to the evening meeting. Two [white] policemen were standing at the entrance of the church. As we walked up the steps, a photographer stepped out and, taking careful aim, snapped our picture. Reaching the top of the steps, another photographer got us. When, after two hours of the meeting, we were all walking around the room laying our collection on the table (colored style), I decided to step outside ostensibly for a bit of fresh air—really, I must admit, I wanted to see if the "guard" was still there. It was, though augmented in numbers. And—I had my picture taken again. Only the white were so honored. It was all a matter of intimidation as there was a complete blackout in the news—no mention whatever of this meeting or the conference the next day. When the service was over, the area literally swarmed with police, on foot and on motorcycle. Just before leaving, Rev. [Fred] Shuttlesworth [black, president of SCEF] cautioned everyone to remember, "These are tense times; drive carefully; don't speed; if you are stopped, answer courteously."

The workshops were held late Saturday. I was the last on the program so was in a rush to make the bus to Talladega. I asked the motel office to get me a cab. After about 10 minutes, one arrived. The driver got out and said, "You white, ain't you?" I admitted as much. "I can't take you." Another colored driver came by. I hailed him. He stopped, looked at me and shook his head. I asked the office to call a white cab and was told a white cab wouldn't come to that address. A Negro, who was whiter in coloring than I, saw my predicament and took me to the station. Had it not been that the bus driver was involved in a conversation, I would have missed my bus.

The conference itself was one of the best I've ever attended. So many had been in jail that I almost felt outside the "fraternity." A number of Talladegans got out of jail after the meeting started and came over to the meeting. This meeting was intended to encourage the people in Birmingham who are on the fighting front. I'm sure it did that. A lawyer, Mr. Rosenfeld, was there from Los Angeles, having been sent by the Lawyers' Guild, an organization of attorneys from all over the nation who are pledged to donate up to 40 hours a year to assist Southern attorneys who feel incompetent or at a disadvantage in other ways. All in all I was glad I went. And I think my students grew by the experience of taking tests on their own. Still had a few bookish paragraphs. I'm unabashed in refusing their bookish work now—not accusing them of copying from the book in a test but merely stressing that I don't want any parrots in the room; if they are memorizing the book, they are wasting their time.

April 27, 1962

The Alpha Phi Alpha pledges' program just ended. By the frequent round of applause that was spontaneous and long, I gathered the students were more than glad to have this whole thing aired. Now they will not be so afraid to talk about it. And I will have to *hope* that some reforms will be made.

They started with a little skit just to make everyone sit up and take notice. The pledge dean came out and gave the pledges a pep talk congratulating them on having come this far. But he said they hadn't seen anything yet. They were about to go through the final week of initiation to Iddy Biddy Pi. "When do I get that pie?" called out one pledge. Another said, "Make mine pumpkin!" Another, "Make mine lemon!" etc. They were duly reprimanded for being so materialistic—always thinking of the good things in life—like pie. "And you have an unforgivable fault—you THINK. We can't have anyone in Iddy Biddy Pi who *thinks.* Here you do as you are told. Now line up for classes. You will always march to classes stepping high. And you will sing our Iddy Biddy Pi motto." Holding it up for all to see, it read, "O-wa ta goo si am." Mention had already been made of the fact that Iddy Biddy Pi was Siamese for a *noble* name they couldn't even know until they had been initiated. "Now we never never say this motto. We only sing it. Hold up your Iddy Biddy emblems.

Ready, go!" They started goose stepping and singing, "Oh what a goose I am" as they marched across the stage. Then they let out a "honk" as they ended.

Thus being awakened, the MC said we were going to have a panel discussion of a problem on our campus. We would do this with malice toward *some* and charity for *none.* And any resemblance to organizations living or dead would be purely *intentional.*

They had to change to a panel rather than the debate originally intended because no one would defend the present practice. One teacher, Mr. White, one independent student, and Rev. McCollom were the panelists. Afterward there were many questions from the audience. We ran late because the enthusiasm was so great. No student dared get in the act after the bell rang, but the teachers exercised their prerogative to continue it a bit. I was asked to be on the panel but I told the boys it would be stronger if they could get new people to take a stand. Everyone had heard me. However, I'm getting many congratulations—even from pledges. I keep telling the Alphas I think they are tops to let their pledges put on such a program. About half a dozen of them sat in on the practice last night and the pledge advisor sat in a week ago. This is, I understand, one of the more civilized fraternities on campus.

I asked two questions near the end to give a boost to the independents. First, "Do you think some people are so insecure within themselves that they need the support of a secret organization?" And second, "Do you think there is danger that the Greeks may control campus activities too much?" After both were tossed around, I stood and said I agreed with the answers. I really wanted to point up the fact that a person could feel pride in being an independent. Many people are opposed to organizations that they feel are undemocratic. They can hold their heads high and say, "I am an independent." I ended with the cowardly remark, "I say this as a sorority woman." This latter brought another round of applause. (Guess I better pay my dues.)

People are still knocking on my door to hug me for my final remark. This airing of the problem is good. Poor students! They have been given the idea that unless they're Greek they are nothing. And this ridiculous, degrading, and unscholarly procedure, they accept as college.

April 29—Sunday—1962

We just returned from a visit to the home for the aged (colored). Twenty-nine persons in it. A ramshackle building. Well cared for, though. This is the institution that Dr. Frampton (white), Presbyterian minister, was moved to improve and now has the campaign far enough along to be assured of Hill-Burton funds to build a $200,000 nursing home. Mrs. Rush, one of the garrulous owners, is thoroughly disgusted with her people—the whites give—great numbers of them—some in large amounts—but her own colored people do so little.

Mrs. [Gloria] Rackley, a member of Trinity and a public school teacher (a lovely woman in appearance and character—about 32 I should say), was in court last Tuesday to witness in an accident case. It so happens Dr. Milley of the faculty was there on a traffic citation (he's white) so I got his side of the story too and it jibes with hers. She was asked by a policeman to move. She asked why. He went to the judge who ordered her below. She was escorted to a jail. What incensed her so was the filthy condition of the jail. That any human being should be asked to be in it she felt was incredible. The same description was given by one of my students who was in the Jackson, Mississippi, jail last summer—probably when Don and I were trying to get in. As visitors, of course. How to tell them that we believe in cleanliness or in doing our work well? Fortunately she was left there only a half hour. She has had no further explanation about reason for putting her there at all. There was no sign indicating the courtroom was to be segregated, but of course it was obvious that was the attempt. There is a mass meeting next Tuesday night at Trinity concerning the whole affair.

On Easter Sunday the same four—Mrs. McNeil (light colored), Mrs. Tait, Dr. Calhoun, and I—had a smorgasbord dinner at the Hotel Jefferson in Columbia. We were well treated. Nothing worse than very obvious stares. One woman could twist her neck as far as I am accused of doing when my curiosity overcomes my good behavior. But the cashier asked if everything was satisfactory. I wish the two were willing to try the same with some other more obviously colored person. I think it might be done but they are fearful. In fact I have to push a bit to get them to do it with Mrs. McNeil. Then when we make the grade they are pleased as punch.

May 6, 1962

This has been a "meeting" week. Monday night I attended a candidates' meeting. Wouldn't have missed it for the world! About 20 candidates spoke—those for lesser offices only two minutes. About seven minutes for gubernatorial candidates and perhaps 10 for the hopeful senators. The courtroom was crowded, with people standing. However, some standing could have sat, as there were seats near Negroes left vacant. About 40 Negroes were there. It was a shock to me to hear those candidates come out without a blush for what they would do to maintain white supremacy. "If we had a situation similar to that in the University of Georgia (two Negroes applied and now attend) I would close the university. I have six children and they shall *never* attend a mixed school. I say to my *Nigra* friends here tonight that I would give them equal schools but never integrated" and on and on. Senator Johnston said he would be catching the 12 o'clock train (or was it plane?) back to Washington so he could keep his commitment to filibuster the next day against that bill making a 6th grade education the only possible kind of literacy test. He would speak two hours against that bill. It was very obvious all the way through that their talks were leveled at a low educational level. This seemed odd because everyone or at least most in the room seemed to be the upper crust of the town and I would have supposed they would want something a little more sophisticated. There were two candidates for governor whom I would term the comedy features. They were a scream. One appeared so illiterate he could scarcely read his speech. He is running on a platform to legalize all kinds of races—horse, dog, cock, etc., and to open cocktail bars. Following him was the other "comedian" running on a prohibition plank. He is a revival—tent-style—minister and made the most of his opportunity to play on the emotions of the audience before him. He had no program. He would just call in all the teachers and say now tell me your problems. Likewise with labor, business, and all areas of our state. He ended by saying, "You cain't say I didn't keep my promises, if you elect me, because I ain't making you any." Oh yes, he hadn't had much education but he knew enough about education to know "we need it." Most of the candidates bragged on how little education they had had—that they had come up from the masses—were self-made.

The next night I took my class in South Carolina History—only three girls—to the city council. We were allowed to sit together, which some faculty bet we wouldn't be. We were the only guests which was probably why. The people don't mind being decent if they won't be "caught" at it. We were given the agenda. All the things we were interested in hearing were skipped over. The meeting was adjourned in a half hour. No one moved very far from the room so I imagine they resumed their meeting after we left.

Yesterday Dr. Calhoun and I were invited to attend an executive meeting of the South Carolina Council on Human Relations—the most "respectable" group in the state working to these ends. Again, what waste motion. It is needed—but it meets with little action before meeting again.

The foregoing may give you the idea I am unhappy. Not true. But, I'm certainly not sold on methods being used to better the world. However as long as we have to rely on people I suppose we'll have to expect them to be human and make human errors. As for me, I'm tending to be a lone wolf. I'm sold on teaching. My classroom is my kingdom and in it I find my greatest encouragement. I am optimistic about the ideas I have been able to get across to my students. I *think*.

Yesterday the pledges came to me again and asked if they could do something for me. Said they could never repay me for my ideas and help on their program. I said, "Oh yes you can—and I hope you spend a lifetime doing it. Just speak out when you see problems. Do something about them yourself. Don't wait for the other fellow to do it." Then I told them many people had done nice things for me. I can never repay *them*, but if I can do something for someone else, that will be their best reward. And so if I have done anything for you, I'm glad. What seems to make them so happy is that their program was so well accepted by their own fraternity. This was more than I had hoped for, too. Dr. Calhoun says it may be an indication that the abuses were becoming burdensome to the abusers, even.

I will be through here on the 23rd. Mrs. McNeil and I may do something for a few days so that I won't leave here until June 1. Then I'll begin a summer session of study at the University of Mississippi. July 13th I hope Mother and I will be starting for home; we may take about a week or 10 days.[11]

P.S. to Mother: I'll not send money for bonds again until next school year. Overexpended myself and have to keep enough in bank for excessive bail should I need it! A *must* around here!

May 9, 1962

Dear Mr. [Cong. H. Allen] Smith:

From where I stand there is real need for some way to measure literacy other than the biased subjective judgment of a registrar. When college professors and medical doctors are failed in the test on reading and explaining the

11. Mother accompanied me on most of my trips between California and the South.

state constitution, something is wrong. A 6th grade education should suffice. Are you supporting this bill?

Have you heard of the treatment of Mrs. Gloria Rackley [black public school teacher] here in Orangeburg about two weeks ago? Because she asked why the officer wanted her to move in court where she was appearing as a witness in a traffic accident case, she was jailed without any explanation given. She remained in the indescribably filthy jail for thirty minutes, at which time she was called back to the courtroom to testify regarding the accident. No opportunity was given her to see the judge who ordered her to the jail. Mrs. Rackley is a lovely young mother of two daughters; she is quiet and well mannered, but not one to be pushed around. Her case is typical of injustices that are common around here. Yesterday I visited a student in the local county hospital. If the South prefers "separate but equal" it might begin by making some facilities equal, such as the hospital.

Don't be taken in by all the arguments of our illustrious senators—Strom Thurmond and Olin Johnston. You can't live here among Negroes without weeping for America.

My best wishes to you and Mrs. Smith.

[In a May 14 letter, Cong. Smith said, "The situation you mentioned regarding the treatment given Mrs. Gloria Rackley seems almost unbelievable in this great country of ours."]

May 12, 1962

Last Monday I took my girls from the South Carolina History class to the municipal court. Had a little difficulty making the arrangement but the chief finally said it was open to the public so we went. When we entered there were two white women sitting on the far side; we sat on the other side. I purposely sat in the midst of the girls. Fifteen minutes late a man came in and told the women to move to our side; told us to move to their side; a couple of white men came in and sat on the women's side. Then the man in authority motioned to "us" or perhaps he meant it to be just to "me" saying, "You sit over there." I said, "You want us to move back?" He repeated, "You move up here" but he was pointing to the obviously "white" side for the seats farther up. I said, "We can't stay very long so we'd prefer to remain back here." "This won't take long," he said, but he did not insist further. Either the court had learned a lesson from the Rackley case or he gave in because I was white sitting with colored whereas she was colored sitting with white.

Yesterday we went to the county courthouse and visited several offices unannounced. We also visited the restrooms just because I was curious to see how equal they were. Everyone in the South believes in "EQUAL" facilities so they say. There was no comparison—the white was spacious and clean (by Southern standards) with a huge mirror. The "colored" signs directed us down in the basement, out through the utility room, clear outdoors and back through an outside entrance. The doors were all rusted. The bowls hadn't been cleaned in a long time.

One of my students has a vein infection in his leg. He is a huge football player and quite an intelligent one. This seems to be a serious ailment he has. The pain was excruciating and his temperature high. He took ill over the weekend and a white doctor of the city hospitalized him as our nurse and the school doctor were both away. I went to visit him. He is in the basement. There are beds all down the hall. One man there was in an oxygen tent; another was so sick he had lost all control of his bodily functions. We continued into the room where my student is. Six beds are as close together as they can be and still allow for walking between. The place was most uncomfortably warm and the odor was offensive. Again, it appears to be a beautiful hospital—certainly the facilities are not equal.

I received a most interesting Mother's Day card from two boys in one of my classes. Very fine chaps. The card interested me. "From Your Secret Pal Happy Mother's Day." Inside the verse read, "This card is from your SECRET PAL, So I can't tell my name, But I can hope your Mother's Day Is happy, just the same!" It was signed by the two.

Last Sunday afternoon a carful of boys from (white) Clemson College—about 150 miles north—came for a discussion of the books *Black Like Me* and *To Kill a Mockingbird.* It was suggested at our interracial student conference that I attended at Beaufort that we all read these. We wanted the Clemson boys to read *Black Like Me* so they could understand better how the Negroes feel and our students would read *Mockingbird,* but the Clemson team couldn't get *Black Like Me* at any of their book stores. We had a delightful time and the students were so happy over the experience. I was very proud of our students.

May 23, 1962

After correcting the objective part of my finals—100 questions (constituting 50% of the exam)—I posted in the two dorms a list of students to be congratulated on high scores. There were 8 A's and 25 B's out of 78. That sounds good, but the sad part was the 17 F's. Anyway, the point is that the list disappeared from the men's bulletin board. The dean traced it to one of the rooms and asked the student why he walked off with it. He said he wanted to send it to his mother; it was the first time he had ever had his name posted for outstanding work! I was really touched. I told the dean to give it back to him and let him send it to his mother. Camie and Keith are always so insistent on giving recognition for scholastic achievements—and I wondered if more of us shouldn't follow their example. This student is a football player so he is not without his laurels. He is and has been from the beginning of the year a steady B student—a nice chap. Freshman.

We have had several difficult experiences at the end of school. A group of boys broke into a professor's house and changed exam papers, for one. There are so many problems in a school. Last year I was still living under the motto of Father Kelly—YOU CAN CHANGE THE WORLD. Even this year I made an assembly talk on the subject. But now, I'm operating under the philosophy, "It is better to light a candle than curse the darkness."

Next address
Gen. Del., University of Miss., University, Miss.
May 26, 1962

The year at Claflin ended with the usual pageantry of college commencements. I'll not elaborate on it except to say this is a warm climate for traditional robes! From here I'll go to the University of Mississippi for the first summer session.

At the moment we are thrilled that Robert Kennedy's office has requested Mrs. Gloria Rackley's presence in Washington. We presume it is in response to all the letters the community has written regarding her being jailed for 30 minutes without explanation beyond "judge's orders" and an earlier similar case [before my Orangeburg days] when she was ordered out of the hospital waiting room while her daughter was receiving treatment. There were no signs indicating the waiting room was segregated. She didn't leave and was taken in a police car to the station. (At the first hearing her attorney, Mr. Perry, was put in jail for a few minutes because of some offense taken by the judge.) The hospital case is still pending.

Mrs. Rackley has just been awarded her [state] teaching contract for next year. It was long past due and there was talk of carrying an organized protest through channels. Her finally receiving this contract is a long cry from the many dismissals of a few years ago merely for belonging to the NAACP or for signing a petition. So—even South Carolina is moving ahead.

May 29—Tuesday—1962

Yesterday I took Mrs. McNeil to Morrison's cafeteria. It is a very busy, well known, and good cafeteria in Columbia and in many of the larger Southland cities. The first lady who served us from behind the counter neglected her next customers to stare at Mrs. McNeil. At the last end of the counter a young colored girl helping behind the counter stared a hole through her, then catching my eye she and I both broke into a big smile. I'm sure she understood and appreciated the "joke." As we were seated at a table very close to another, the lady next to Mrs. McNeil had a few puzzling glances for Mrs. McNeil. Other than that we got by without incident. I would so like to try these places with someone a little darker. With her they think she's colored but don't quite dare to accuse her of such a "crime."

I'm about to take my car to the garage for a last-minute check-up before leaving. While my car is there, Mrs. Bythewood, a Negro as white as I, and her daughter are taking Mrs. McNeil and me to Charleston to "do the town"—since I have only been there twice and then on special missions—always in a hurry.

University of Mississippi, Summer 1962

[Oxford, Mississippi—Ole Miss summer session]
June 17, 1962

Just returned from Holly Springs [about 30 miles north of Oxford].

[At Rust,] all the civil rights [workers] have so much to tell me. These young people have been busy. They proudly wear their NAACP pins. They have formed a credit union so that if any of them need bail there will be a means of credit.

Dell Webb's city near Mother sounds fabulous. But as for me, no. I'd rather retire in a more normal community. Say Holly Springs. This is the most beautiful country right now that anyone could imagine.

While my car was being washed yesterday at a service station in Oxford, I asked if there were a drinking fountain. I was directed to it. A good refrigerated one. Returning I said, "Do you allow Negroes to drink from that fountain?" "I should say not!" and he started toward the fountain. "Did you see one drinking out of it?" I said no, I was just wondering. "One day I caught one at it and I sure told him off." I asked how they were to know they weren't supposed to drink out of it. There is no sign or anything. "Don't worry. They all know." Then I pressed him a bit further, asking what the objection was since by the very construction of the fountain one could not touch it with his lips. No satisfactory answer. I recalled Rev. Burley telling of being bawled out for drinking from a fountain in a service station that had no prohibiting sign. Maybe those stations with signs were doing the Negroes a favor. They at least knew the score.

[Oxford] June 20, 1962

Just returned from Rust [again]. Everyone welcomed me with open arms. President was wonderful. It does seem many improvements have been made. New life on the trustee board—including Rev. [G. H.] Holloman. President and Mrs. Smith have forgotten my part in interesting Rev. Holloman in Rust—which is the highest compliment. Miss Couche says many of our [Grievance Committee] suggestions have been acted upon. Mrs. Smith had ice cream and had saved some of the president's fruitcake for me. She remembered my fondness for it. She is still a darling.

Last year I had some sympathetic professors [of history at Ole Miss]—they let me off easy. One of the two [this summer] expects me to read four books and present critical reviews on them besides a stiff test. And on top of that I have to read a basic text to get the background I've forgotten, if I ever had it.

Interlude: Pasadena, CA, 1962–63

Pasadena, California
October 1, 1962

If [Mississippi's arch-segregationist] Gov. Ross Barnett desired to occupy the center of the national stage, he has today succeeded. I recall the individuals at the University of Mississippi who expressed to me their willingness to see James Meredith enrolled. If only those people would speak a little louder now. What a man this Meredith must be! I doubt any experience in the air force required more courage.[1]

My days in Mississippi and South Carolina seem to belong to another world—a world to which I hope to return one of these days. But life moves on and I am here in the crowded but beautiful new Pasadena High School. Every nook and cranny is used as a classroom to accommodate the 3700-plus students. As one of the last teachers assigned, I have no room of my own but must, in the seven minutes passing time, make a get-away from one class and arrive at another—sometimes buildings apart. My first act of preparation was to invest in several pairs of low-heeled shoes hoping they'd contribute to some fast footwork. Because of housing practices, there are comparatively few minority students in this school. However, the few we have take an active part in student affairs and we have several Negroes and Orientals on the faculty. This is saying the obvious to most of you but may be of interest to my associates of the past two years.

Immediately upon my arrival home, I met up with several situations which reminded me that the South has no monopoly on racial problems. An Occidental College student [black], his wife [white], and baby stayed with me until they could find a place to rent. A deposit had been made on a house before they

1. Denied admission by Governor Barnett, James Meredith was ordered by a federal court to be enrolled as the first black student at the University of Mississippi. President John F. Kennedy sent 300 federal marshals to protect his entry on Sunday, September 30, 1962. Though Meredith was safe in a dormitory, hundreds of whites rioted on campus, resulting in the shooting deaths of French journalist Paul Guihard and Ray Gunter (white), 28 marshals and 130 others wounded, nearly 200 arrests and dozens of weapons confiscated. Soon 20,000 federal troops were in Oxford to maintain calm.

moved down from their home near San Francisco, but when the husband arrived, the landlord explained he couldn't have non-Caucasians in the court.

I even learned of a sit-in in a nearby community which broke down discrimination in a barber shop. It had a couple of unusual facets: first, it was engaged in by tough young [black] teenagers from a mission church who were well acquainted with law forces and who usually fight at the drop of a hat. They discovered as they endured rebuffs and physical abuse that nonviolent techniques take more courage than using fists. Second, after the proprietor called the sheriff's office, two NEGRO deputy sheriffs arrived, and upon hearing the story, told the proprietor he had violated the law. The sheriffs suggested the young men go with them to file charges against the proprietor. They did. Later they learned this was not in accordance with the principles of nonviolence which they were trying to use. When the case came up, they withdrew the charges. This so impressed the proprietor that he changed his policy and now cuts hair without any qualifying adjective. A real success story!

I recently met an outstanding realtor (white) who sells on a nondiscriminatory basis. He not only helps Negroes to find homes in previously all-white neighborhoods, but he visits the surrounding homes and attempts, with some success, to sell them on the advantages of an integrated community. Then, too, he tries to interest Caucasians in a neighborhood such as mine where the balance has become weighted on the side of Negroes. We feel this is as attractive a neighborhood as can be found, but it still shouldn't become a segregated community. Segregation in itself keeps people of different groups from knowing each other and results in distrust and misunderstandings. Thus I was happy to list my place with Mr. Culwell. Of course, this is no assurance that the place won't be sold to a minority family as nondiscrimination is his policy. After living happily for two years in a single room, I am determined to reduce my worldly possessions to fit a small apartment.

Now to give an account of my last Southern experiences. The night before leaving South Carolina, Dorothy Vann, president of Claflin student chapter of NAACP, and I attended the first session of a weekend NAACP conference in Columbia. When the secretary read the names of colored motels where we might room, Dorothy and I said we preferred going to a white motel. The secretary said perhaps when we come to the next conference in '63 we could, but as yet motel segregation had not been cracked. We said we would try anyway. Then everyone volunteered bits of advice and insisted we write down two numbers to call in case we needed bail. First we made reservations by phone for the Downtowner. The colored porter met us with a questioning expression.

We made ourselves known at the desk. The embarrassed clerk stammered something about this being the Deep South. We thanked him and left. The porter followed us out. I said, "Well, it was a good try." He smiled broadly and said, "*Yes, ma'am.*" After two more refusals we came to the Tremont—a very nice motel. Dorothy suggested we try it even without a reservation. I asked for a room for two. The clerk asked, "Is this the other party?" looking at Dorothy. We confirmed his assumption. He, without any hesitation, pushed the registration pad toward me and I recovered from the shock sufficiently to sign my name. We were shown a beautiful room.

We went back to the NAACP meeting. Persons there were jubilant though they warned us not to be too confident. The clerk on duty might be overruled and when we returned we might find our suitcases in the hall. But we returned to enjoy a good night's sleep. The next morning we had fruit juice, coffee and donuts on the house in the snack room with the other guests. As we drove away, Dorothy said, "I wonder how many privileges we do not avail ourselves of merely because we think we can't." Here I think she put her finger on something very important.

[En route to California I stopped in Atlanta and ran into Mrs. Brown.] She is from Orangeburg and has three boys in Morehouse College.[2] She showed me around with the help of one of the boys. A Morehouse College student drove with me from Atlanta to Mississippi. We stopped at a hotel in Gadsden to eat. A Negro waiter told us we could not be served. I asked to see the manager and was told he was out. I said, "Was that he who left as we came in?" It was.

We approached him as he was trying to get lost in the lobby and asked if we could have a table for two. Again the same embarrassed stuttering pattern as he tried to explain that this sort of thing couldn't be done in Alabama. I said, "All through the South we have found it possible to be served in the better hotels. This looked like a good hotel. I'm disappointed." We thanked him and left.

In the Greyhound station across the street, however, we used the unsegregated restrooms and lunched together in the cafe. Some hard glances came our way but nothing more. This, I think, would have been possible no place like Alabama before the Freedom Rides.

After my summer session in the University of Mississippi, Mrs. McNeil of Claflin and Mother from California met me at Memphis for the trip to Califor-

2. A highly regarded Atlanta college traditionally for black men.

nia. With Mrs. McNeil along, our trip home was a continuation of social experiment. In Memphis, where two motels turned us down, we had our only reverses. After a breakfast in Arkansas, the cashier asked me, "What nationality is she?" I answered, "Oh, she's American." Outside Mother asked what I'd have said had she asked what race. I said I didn't know but hoped I'd have said, "Human."

Actually we had no more difficulty in restaurants or motels. This is a measure of the change taking place in our South, for Arkansas and Texas certainly have not always been so tolerant—nor even New Mexico and Arizona—nor, for that matter, California.

[After leaving Mother at her home in Winchester, California, Mrs. McNeil and I continued another 60 miles to my daughter Camie's home.] My three grandchildren in San Bernardino had been looking forward to the arrival of Grandma Campbell. The middle one, not quite three, had seen me only as a baby and a few days last summer. Entering their home I made the rounds of greeting then settled down to catch up on talk with my daughter. Mrs. McNeil in the meantime gave her undivided attention to the children. Little Clarice climbed all over her lap, was intrigued by Mrs. McNeil's hair rolled into a bun on top of her head, produced all her special toys for Mrs. McNeil's approval, etc. After we left Clarice said something which made her folks wonder if she had properly identified her grandmother. They asked where Grandma had sat, and Clarice ran to the chair which Mrs. McNeil had occupied. I fear it was a traumatic experience for the child to learn that the very nice lady who took a grandmotherly interest in her (while that other lady merely talked with her mother) was not her grandmother. At least, it is obvious that I should stay home if I want to maintain my position in the family.

While at the university I visited friends at Rust College. I'm sure some of you have caught my past discouragement over the almost insurmountable problems at Rust. However, I was encouraged this summer. President Smith is excited over plans for academic improvements. There is a new spirit of hope and expectancy throughout. The University Senate from Nashville (headquarters) made a study of the college last fall and came up with a report which emphatically declares there is real need for this college, but it must be brought up to standard for accreditation. It continues with specifics needed for the academic program, faculty qualifications, for library, etc. But the first step, it says, must be housing. In this I agree. I have no patience with those who tell me the dormitories are as good as the homes from which some students come. If some students come from inadequate homes, it is even more imperative that they have four years of good living conditions to establish the habit. One dormitory for women and all men's dormitories are still in bad condition. Two new dormitories are expected to be built this year with federal aid.

Last year a minister spoke in the chapel service and spent the entire day visiting all buildings and departments. A few weeks later he returned bringing a friend. This summer I learned that the dormitory conditions so concerned the friend that before he left he wrote a check for a thousand dollars to be applied toward renovation of the E. L. Rust Hall for women. Later, learning there was need of more money to finish the job, he sent another thousand.

If I could paint a picture as vivid as a real live visit to Rust would produce, I'm sure there would be many persons reaching for their checkbooks. Words, however, can never be as vivid as seeing. The South is a beautiful area rich in history; the people, in most respects, are charming—in all respects, interesting. I wish more people would plan vacations in the South and while there visit their own church institutions. Isolation in itself is the cause of some of our neglect.

In the meantime, like most colleges, Negro colleges need money. There is no doubt in my mind but that Negroes will get their rights. The walls are tumbling daily. The problem now will be to advance the educational program rapidly and thoroughly enough for them to assume their responsibilities. We need colleges to graduate teachers that will permeate the elementary and secondary schools, not only to disseminate knowledge but to imbue the youth with a sense of responsibility and purpose.

You remember I promised you that one day you'd get an appeal from me for money. This is it. If any of you feel so inclined, checks may be sent to Rust College, Holly Springs, Miss.; or Claflin College, Orangeburg, S.C.; or any college in which you have a personal interest. There are also three funds which I have set up: one based on minimum standards for diet; one on standards of sanitation; and one for faculty summer scholarships to enable some of the present faculty to study while guest instructors, we hope to send, take over their classes.[3]

These past two years have been most rewarding to me personally. I heartily recommend such experiences. If you cannot consider a full year, do think in terms of a summer. And now, I thank you all for your many letters while I was away. How I loved mail time! You are the best of friends.

3. A University of California professor and his wife taught one summer and a Los Angeles State College professor gave a workshop another summer at Rust, all at their own expense.

Pasadena, California
January 18, 1963

Dear Mr. [James] Meredith,

You have more friends all over the nation than you can ever know. As we talk of you with great admiration, we always marvel at your calm poise and dignity.

I have several units from Ole Miss, myself, and I taught two years ago at Rust College. Believe me, I know what you are going through is not easy. Your remark as reported in *Newsweek*, "The price of freedom sure is high," struck a familiar note with me. In all my history classes I point out that every freedom we have has been paid for with blood and long persecution. Religious freedom, freedom of the press (John Peter Zenger), the right of labor to organize—you name it—study its history, and you'll find the price has been very high indeed.

Today the scene has shifted to freedom for persons of color, but it is a fight which is important to all of us. Denying you your freedom degrades us. You are a very important person at this juncture in history. I hope you can and will continue.

But, if continuing is impossible, do not be downcast or discouraged. You have opened the way. You have performed a mission few could and none did. We are still indebted to you.

[Influenced by the Grievance Committee's visit to one of Rust's men's dorms, I had given a "Sanitation Scholarship" to Mr. A. He was to be responsible for clean lavatory facilities in his hall, inspire others to take pride in keeping it clean, and be a serious student.]

[Teaching at Pasadena High School] Pasadena, California
April 20, 1963

Dear Mr. A,

Your letter telling of the cooperation you receive in keeping the lavatory and washrooms in good condition was encouraging and gratifying. Of all the gifts I have made, none ever gave me more satisfaction than your scholarship. This is because you have caught the spirit of the project. Through your efforts, the scholarship has benefitted more than yourself—it has helped all your dormitory, and any improvement in the dormitory advances the entire school. Because of your attitude and performance, it is easy for me to believe that your entire education is not a selfish effort on your part merely to insure that you will have the comforts in life that one usually associates with the educated; rather, through your education, I feel that all around you—always—will benefit.

I'm pleased to learn that your grades are improved. My only concern here is that you do your BEST. Grades are tricky things. I'm sure every teacher would like to do away with them, but, human nature being what it is, few students will study and put forth their best without them. There are many fallacies and pitfalls in grades, beginning with the difficulty of making an accurate evaluation. Sometimes grades can be made merely by studying the professor and doing what pleased *him* (and I do not discount the value of being diplomatic); sometimes there are less than honorable ways of getting grades. When you leave college, grades will be the simplest way for others to check on your ability, but after that, it will be what you know and what you understand that count. You seem to have the right attitude toward grades—work to understand and learn (within the framework outlined by the professor, of course) and trust the grades will be to your liking.

I noticed Willie Peacock[4] mentioned in the *New York Times* as being active in the demonstrations at Greenwood. I'm proud of him. The suffering of many people merely to claim what is guaranteed them as citizens is disheartening. But, I'm sure things will be much better in the near future because a few are willing to take a stand now and pay the high price of such a stand.

We are having our problems here, too, though on a different level. Our present concern is for a recommendation of a citizens committee appointed by the superintendent of schools and made up of some of the most outstanding citizens of the community. These recommendations included gerrymandering our high school zones to equalize the Negro enrollment. This would require additional busing. There is real opposition to all this. At best it is not the perfect plan, but the alternatives have serious defects, too. Actually, the problem is one of housing discrimination. California is working on this statewide with a bill in the legislature now. If there were an efficient policy for housing guaranteeing open occupancy, there would be no school problems of unbalanced racial enrollment.

Thank you for writing me even when I have not held up my end of the correspondence. I shall try to improve on that score.

4. Now called Wazir Peacock, he interrupted his Rust studies to work for civil rights and tour as a Freedom Singer.

Pasadena, California
May 18, 1963

Dear Mr. [Cong.] Smith:

It is difficult for one protected by a white skin to know the hazards of being black in America. I expect I came as close to knowing as anyone by living with Negroes for two school years.

Traveling miles—as a faculty member and I once did in Tennessee—looking for a gas station that would allow her to use the restroom, being turned away from restaurants, being put out of the Greyhound station in Birmingham by a policeman, being confronted with two drinking fountains, one for me and one of lesser quality for my companion (or one fountain with a sign above, "for white only—colored use cup" and the cup a dirty plastic one), having my car insurance canceled because I lived on a Negro campus (and hearing my colored friends tell of their difficulty getting insurance at all), being ordered out of a Methodist church because I had three of my students with me, being asked to segregate myself from my students when visiting court and knowing that my school teacher friend, a Negro, was jailed a week earlier for not moving to the colored side when asked—these experiences, to mention but a few, leave me thinking something is wrong in our great country.

Add to these some which I did not personally experience but knew at close hand: My doctor in Mississippi, an M.D., a graduate of Howard Medical School, was thrice denied registration on the ground that he could not satisfactorily read and interpret a section of the Mississippi constitution. Several of my friends lost their teaching positions quite obviously as a result of having taken part in a conference on civil rights. I have talked with Negroes in one of the tent cities who were put off their farms which they had sharecropped upward of 14 years—ostensibly because mechanization was taking over, but curiously, only those Negroes who registered were dislodged from their farms. I talked with John McFerren several times when he could get no gasoline for his gas station—again obviously because he was encouraging Negroes to vote.

Does it ever strike you as ironical that, though we glorify our forefathers who fought and killed for the right to tax themselves, we condemn loyal Americans who in nonviolent demonstrations are reminding us that they still do not have the right to elect the officials who tax them?

For a hundred years these people have relied on us as Christians to give them their fair share of the goodness of American life; they have followed the time-honored American tradition of going through the courts and, though they won decision after decision, they still found themselves unable to get adequate education in many of our states; those few who were fortunate enough to get the education found employment, housing, voting, traveling, and creature comforts still circumscribed. Now through direct nonviolent action, in which they willingly suffer but try not to inflict suffering, they are making gains even though much too slowly.

I hold no brief for Adam Clayton Powell [flamboyant black Congressman from Harlem, NY] (though I agree with much that he said in the enclosed which you were kind enough to send me) as, in my opinion, he lacks integrity. Neither do I hold any brief for the Black Muslims. But if we fail to support the good Christian American leaders such as Dr. King and the Rev. Shuttlesworth, then we are asking for the leadership of the Powells and the Malcolm X's. Not even Dr. King can keep these people on their knees much longer unless the results begin to come faster than they have so far. The masses of Negroes will follow what appears to them stronger leadership. Such leadership will usher in a sad day for America in which I believe not only Washington, D.C., but all our big cities will see riots.

I have often wondered if there weren't more that could be done through legislation to implement the decisions of the Supreme Court. On this you know more than I, of course. The Democrats are handicapped by the Southern members of Congress, but it would seem the Republicans and Northern Democrats could combine to put over some good legislation which would enable the country to make this transition to full civil rights for all in a smooth and peaceful manner. That the transition will be made is no longer debatable. The only question now is how it will be made.

As I have written you before, there is a difference between states' rights and the denial by states of basic constitutional rights guaranteed every citizen. I don't think one has to be a lawyer to understand this.

A few more points I would reiterate though I presume we could both agree on them: Negroes are not responsible for every Negro spokesman any more than whites are responsible for every white spokesman. (I'd hate to be judged by Barnett or Wallace[5].) All Negroes are not equally good or equally bad, any more than are all whites. If a larger percent of Negroes seem to be problems today than whites, it is because we have made them so. I hesitate to think what I would be were I a Negro! Because Negroes in this fight for freedom

5. Arch-segregationist Alabama Governor George Wallace.

may make mistakes in matters of discretion and timing, we cannot excuse our greater mistakes of principle.

I appreciated your letter and I always look forward to your reports. My faith in democracy is the greater for having the conscientious and hard-working Congressman I have. Believe me, I know your position is not an easy one.

May 21, 1963

Republican National Committee
Washington, D.C.

Dear Sirs:

"Battle Line" was just delivered in my morning mail.

Is it possible that the Grand Old Party—founded in part as a protest of slavery—should not even *mention* the present racial strife as even *one* of the many critical issues of the day?

Though I have always been a Republican; though I have worked on the precinct level organizing, ringing door bells, and hosting coffee hours; though I have contributed through Republican clubs and dinners—even the $100 a plate kind; I cannot much longer tolerate a party that speaks so softly, if at all, about human rights in Birmingham, Greenwood, Oxford, and, indeed, throughout the nation.

Pasadena, California
June 18, 1963

Dear Dr. [James] Silver [History Dept., U. of Miss.],

A long overdue thanks is due you for your letter to the Peace Corps on my behalf and for your note to me. I am now on the treadmill that should lead me to St. Lucia in the West Indies for two years of teaching.

With our own country in such turmoil I'm not sure I want to leave. Having cleared everything here for the Peace Corps, I could just as well move to Mississippi to make it my home. This has real appeal to me and if some college would say "We need you" as convincingly as does Mr. Shriver, I'd scuttle the Peace Corps even at this late date.

Your description of Mississippi as a police state parallels the word I get from Dr. Smith of Rust. These are difficult days for both races, but I believe the tensions will resolve into something better than either race has known so far. An interesting point is that the entire nation is swept by this movement for complete freedom—L.A. and Pasadena are hit hard by the impact though here the law is on the side of freedom.

All our human relations organizations are in full swing trying to bring the realization of the American dream into focus with a minimum of discord. It appears that de facto school segregation will go—at considerable cost—for shuttling children around by buses has many disadvantages.

I'm glad you are getting to know personally the Negro leaders. Mississippi is fortunate to have you. I wish she had more like you.

[Mississippi NAACP Field Secretary Medgar Wiley Evers was assassinated in Jackson on June 12, 1963. Prosecution of the only suspect, Byron De La Beckwith, resulted in mistrials before white juries in 1964. After a 15-day trial in Jackson by an interracial jury of Panola County residents, Beckwith was convicted on February 5, 1994, and given a life sentence.]

[June 15, 1963]

Dear Dr. [President] Smith,

Your letter just arrived. As you foresaw, more violence was to come. Tragic about Mr. Evers. My heart aches, not only for the Negroes, but for the soul-sick whites who have "lost their way."

I'm sure in my own mind that the laws will soon be changed to conform with our democratic ideals, though there may be more violence and bloodshed between now and then. But even with the law on our side, there will be need for conciliation and understanding between the two races. This will require person-to-person relationships—knowing each other. People are what their experiences make them. Most white Southerners have never had any personal acquaintance with Negroes of education and culture. This was even true of Dr. Silver at the time he spoke to our student body the year I was there.

It is in bringing little groups together here in Pasadena that I have had my greatest satisfaction in the field of human relations. I am thinking of what opportunities might be open to me if I made Mississippi my permanent home and attempted the same sort of work there. If I were to have a couple of classes at a college, I would have a bona-fide *reason* (necessary to white Southerners) for moving to the state. This would leave the rest of my time free to cultivate friends in the church, at Ole Miss, and anywhere I could gain acceptance.

These are difficult days. I know the tensions with which you live may seem at times unbearable, but I believe they are necessary to progress. Peace without justice was a false peace unworthy of either race. I agree with Dr. King, who said words to the effect that those who love order more than justice are more to be feared than the Ku Klux Klan and White Citizens Councils. These days will usher in a better tomorrow—if we are true to our responsibilities today. Of this I have no doubt. Blessings on all of you who stand on the cutting edge of social and spiritual change. You are the real heroes of America.

Danville, VA, Summer 1963

Danville (VA) [on a short SCEF assignment]
August 10, 1963

Dear Jim [Dombrowski],

Thursday (August 8) Dr. Newman and I conferred for nearly two hours. He feels his influence in Danville was lost when Carl [Braden] introduced him as a board member of SCEF. He feels Carl's appearance—his greetings—were unnecessary—did no good—did much damage to the cause. At the end of our conversation I tried to impress him with the thought that a lifetime of service such as he had given (he has plaques, awards, letters, all over his walls) could not be forgotten so easily and he surely continues to have influence. What has really been damaged is only his *confidence* in his influence.

That man is an ardent researcher. He has a folder (looseleaf binder) a couple of inches thick of letters written and received, photocopics of articles, etc., pertaining to the possibility that SCEF might be communist in orientation.

Before he permitted his name to be put up for board membership he wrote Un-American Activities Committee and Attorney General and FBI. He submitted what newspapers had said about SCEF and Carl and asked if these had validity. He explained his own complete opposition to anything remotely communist. His answers received were always verbose, but none said either the organization or Carl were communist.

He believes there should be a mimeographed sheet or pamphlet to refute the charges that are made by irresponsible papers. When such an article as was printed in *Register* July 17 is run, SCEF should demand printing of the true story.

Dr. Newman is willing to write such a pamphlet but would like you to send him such history of SCEF as you have—also the names of board members past and present—anything you have on them. He will continue the research on his own. He wants to tell the fine things they are known for.

He is *very* eager to do this. I would say it would be worth your while to visit with him to discuss such a plan personally. Perhaps a personal talk would not be as important if you agree to the idea, as if you do not. If he is thwarted, it will crush his enthusiasm and confidence—the latter being already damaged.

I do believe the man has much influence and his strong voice is needed in the community. (The article he would write would, of course, have wider usage than just in Danville.)

He feels never to clear Carl's name is to abandon him and this would be doing the same thing that we criticize our foes for doing.

If the paper is well written—I should think it might be used not only to refute false innuendos but also as a story about SCEF before one of its representatives speaks or enters a community. Soft-pedaling breeds further suspicion. (Just one woman's view for what it's worth.) There would have to be a more positive story for this latter use, I suppose.

I'm winding up my work here, as I see no more I can do. The experience has been good for me—it has convinced me that I prefer to *teach.* I'll ask no expense money as I doubt I was worth that much—but I cling to the hope that more may have been accomplished than one can see now.

Thursday I also talked with five Negro women in Mrs. Harvey's home. These were professional women or wives of men in the professions. We discussed their applying for membership in League of Women Voters, claiming victories won by using the library more, especially the children's story hour on Fridays (beginning October 1st), sitting in previously white sections at Trailways cafe, etc., methods of helping the Negro students who would be going to previously white schools, and Project Friendship—similar to what was done at Knoxville. Some were afraid to initiate this lest the whites accuse them of trying for *social* equality. On leaving, Mrs. Harris told me she felt she could start it with a white friend of hers—others felt they'd have to build up to it.

In writing the Rev. Webster to thank him for giving me his time, I suggested the possibility of a few of his church members starting such a project explaining the fear the Negro women had of being misunderstood. This was the type of discussion we would have had, had the gathering materialized which Mrs. Bourne and I were laying plans for.

Also suggested to Mr. Webster that it might be well to have *observers* at the court trials. Also told him of a couple of methods churches in other cities had used to let Negroes know they were welcome in the churches. All or several churches acting together, etc. (Details I'll omit here. Miss my typewriter.) I tried to word it so as not to seem presumptuous and of course all was an outgrowth of our talk.

Yesterday I had barely been admitted to the DCPA office when there was a knock on the door. Three police and two cameramen entered and stalked through the place much as I would picture the gestapo having done. All the while they were looking for Daniel Foss, white SNCC worker, the Negro group somewhere in the back of the office—unseen by me—was singing one of the new integration folk songs. It was a new experience for me.

I stood in front of the office awaiting the taxi which I had phoned for. Mr. Meadowbrook came out and advised me to wait up on the step in the recessed part lest the police—then across the street—arrest me for blocking the walk. This I refused to do, saying if it were unlawful for a visitor in Danville to wait on the sidewalk—the sooner the country knew it the better.

The police are everywhere. Editorials complain of the cost of having so many extra police and indeed it must be a terrible financial strain—partially offset, I presume, by fines.

I was impressed by [National Lawyers' Guild attorney] Len Holt's post-meeting (after court trial). He gave a good buildup including, "Remember, this is not a struggle between black and white. In every case where we have suffered some white people have suffered with us. When blood has been shed, some has been white blood."

I feel Danville has made more gains than most admit. The situation appears more hopeful to me than either Orangeburg, S.C., or Holly Springs, Miss.

Here, there are numbers of individuals who in some way have gone on record as being for a change. Thirteen ministers signed petition, 45 women of League of Women Voters made a statement and signed their names. The Council on Human Relations is started, still very new, and is made up, of course, of both races. The United Church Women is integrated. YW board is integrated. Some eating places are open to all. No obvious signs for colored or white are seen. Some of the stores have upgraded Negro help. School integration begins with 11 in September. There are colored "Parking Maids" as well as white. I can ride in either white or Negro taxis, which I couldn't do in Birmingham. And, *very important*, the Dan River Mills have quietly desegregated. I'm sure there must be more that could be mentioned, but this much I've seen in nine days. Oh yes, the library is desegregated—*individual* desks are in the formerly white library rather than tables for several. Several churches accepted Negroes on their kneel-ins. Voting is merely a matter of convincing the Negro. I see no opposition such as in Mississippi.

Yet to be: Advisory Committee which includes the Negro *leaders*, not just those the white community likes to think of as leaders. More jobs—I don't even see Negro postmen. Am told there are a couple. This I should think would be easier to correct because of the federal nature. Theaters don't even have a

Negro section—just *no* Negroes allowed. Hospitals are segregated. Housing is a problem.

So much has been accomplished the nation over by demonstrations and nonviolent resistance that I hesitate to throw in my conservative ideas at this point but—it does seem to me the Negroes have reached the point in Danville of diminishing returns. They evidently feel they must keep the movement alive by doing something to irritate the community. So they lie down in front of traffic, sing on street in violation of injunction, keep city phones tied up, etc.

Personally I wish they could concentrate more on self-improvement or run a parallel program aimed at preparing themselves for the first-class citizenship which is now virtually assured them.

Voting registration must be continued, of course. Literacy classes I think are being considered by SCLC—which is good. If something could be done to improve *skills*, they'd be prepared to fill the positions being opened up. Even in California this has been a problem—finding Negroes qualified to fill openings which government contracts require. Better scholarship could well be stressed. As a public school teacher, I'd say home and church influence here is most important—even getting to meetings on time at night. English improvement would certainly help. Home management, saving, etc.

The problem of keeping the morale up would be more difficult while working on these positive fronts. A certain amount of demonstration will probably always be necessary for morale.

If you've read this far, please remember Dr. Newman's concern and offer. He hopes to hear from you.

Danville, 8–24–1963

Dear Jim,

For my own satisfaction, stopping here en route to Mississippi has been well worth the trouble. I left a week ago with a sense of defeat but have returned to find some ideas taking root. Even the League of Women Voters has accepted a Negro into its membership—so perhaps my fear of irreparable damage was ill-founded.

In talking with Rev. Chase yesterday and again with Rev. Campbell, I heard some of the very words I had used when talking with Mr. Womack repeated—those about the inevitability of the Negro group's ill-timing of demonstrations if they did not know what Womack and the white group were attempting. Now Womack has been to see Chase and Campbell. They are trying to coordinate their efforts more.

Immediately upon arrival I stopped at Dr. Newman's. Found him in a much better frame of mind. Gave him the two pamphlets Carl [Braden] had sent me. He said he, too, had heard from Carl. We ended up agreeing that the established policy of SCEF—ignoring the charges of communism—was good. He is continuing his letter writing which is his forte. He writes to individuals and sends copies to about 150 key people. This he thoroughly enjoys doing and I'm sure his influence must be felt. He had just given $10 postage money to Rev. Thomas for NAACP distribution of the editorials of Richmond *News-Leader* and Danville *Register*. I hope you have seen them. I gave my original copies to Mr. Karro, who wanted to make copies for distribution at their meetings in the neighborhood.

Dr. Newman brought me out to Mother Teresa's.[1] Was so pleased to see the place here and said he would return with Mrs. Newman in the near future. It is something if like-minded people can just get to know each other.

Rev. Taylor, ousted minister of Disciples of Christ Church, came here to see me yesterday. He remained for 3 hours and might have stayed longer had I not had the 12 o'clock appointment with Rev. Chase. He was pleased to have the opportunity of meeting Mother Teresa and later Rev. Chase. He took me to High Street Church to meet that appointment. Rev. Taylor appears to be a very fine person. This is the second time he has lost his position because of his stand on race. He says it is hardest on his children—two boys in high school and one just starting college. However, he hopes he is giving them a heritage greater than the security they might have were he to keep silent. He is still looking for a pulpit. Thinks he may have to change denominations as there aren't many openings in Disciples of Christ. The membership is even declining sharply. Maybe you can keep him in mind—as you did me.

In Washington I talked with my California Congressman at some length. He set up an appointment for me with my Mississippi Congressman, John Bell Williams. *Very interesting* discussion followed.[2] Saw Mr. Flannery of Justice Department re Danville situation. He suggested I see Mrs. Stendig of Holiday Inn. Also saw Mr. Stern of Justice re Tougaloo situation.

1. This Mother Teresa was a white American, head of a small group of women religious who served the poor.

2. When told I was on my way to teach at Tougaloo College, John Bell Williams said he hoped I would not become a Communist like them. I asked, "Are they *really* communists?" "Well, they act like they are," said Williams.

Mrs. Karro made appointment for me with Miss Toitsch, Congressman Ryan of New York's secretary. She was very interested in Danville as is the Congressman.

Mrs. Karro—the white woman who was jailed here 11 days—has so inspired her neighborhood that it is housing two busloads—about 80—Danvillians—for the March on Washington. The neighbors have a community swimming pool which the guests will use. The guests will put on a program the evening of the 27th explaining the problems in Danville, etc. The neighbors expect to finance one busload for the trip.

I regret missing the March on Washington but feel the need to get settled in Tougaloo and to learn what courses I will have, to get acquainted with the texts, etc. Sally Harper, one of the young girls who was jailed here, is going for me under my sponsorship.

August 25, 1963

Dear Camie and Keith,

It was not difficult to know when we approached Tuscaloosa—the home of the University of Alabama, where Mother and I were one summer (1957). The odor of paper mills was unmistakable. Now our bus is changing a tire at the station, one of the very worst. I thought that in 1956 and I still think it. In Alabama the segregation signs have been removed, but segregation is mostly a fact except for a few brave souls. Just one Negro in main room here. Others are huddled in a little dark room. Notable exception: Birmingham—where policeman put Miss Jackson and me out in '60. Many Negroes using cafeteria—main facilities there.

Tougaloo College, MS, 1963–64

September 14, 1963

Tougaloo College! A 20-minute ride from the heart of Jackson. For you who have envisaged me on a picturesque island in the Caribbean, I'll explain that I just couldn't pull myself away from America at this critical time in history.[1] So I set out from Pasadena not knowing where I'd land. It was my good fortune to arrive here just as one of the social science professors resigned to become a field secretary for the Southern Conference Educational Fund.

For several years Tougaloo was the only regionally accredited four-year Negro college in Mississippi. The college is sponsored by the United Church of Christ and the Disciples of Christ. Ole Miss and Tougaloo have one thing in common: They are the only institutions of higher learning in Mississippi that have integrated student bodies! We have about seven Caucasians. Ole Miss has Meredith.

Beginning this year we have four unusual grants from foundations. Three are for those whose schooling is interrupted by their civil rights activities. The grants enable the school to keep contact with these students while in the field and offer scholarships upon their return to school. The grant that will affect my work most gives the social science division two tutors. Both have just received their degrees—one an MA from Duke and the other a PhD from Southern Illinois. These young men will work with our better students to prepare them for graduate study. This is an experimental effort to overcome the deficient public school background against which most of our students struggle.

[The August 28 March on] Washington was a real morale builder for the Negroes in this area. They saw the many friends they had and were cheered by the respect shown the Mississippi delegation. One incident marred the occasion: At the Meridian Trailways station white hoodlums beat up three young Negro men as they were returning to Tougaloo. I could well understand this happening in Meridian. When I was there one week earlier waiting to change buses, a white man said to me, "Was that a nigger who just came out of the restroom?" I answered that I hadn't noticed and he struck off after the woman

1. The final straw for me was the murder of Medgar Evers on June 12. I gave up all thoughts of the Peace Corps, wanting only to return to Mississippi.

for a closer look. His companion moved over to sit next to me. He said, "Once a nigger sat on that stool at the end of the counter. I went over and sat down next to him and said 'Nigger, take your God damn drink and get behind that wall where you belong.' " I commented that I thought discrimination in bus stations was prohibited by ICC ruling. "Hell, yes! The clerk can't do nothing about it now. But nobody can stop me."

He asked me if I'd like my daughters to attend a mixed school. When I told him they had, he said, "Lady, I thought you was white. You look white, but maybe you ain't." His companion, now returned, asked me my name. I decided the Hotel Lamar a better place to pass the next three hours. This, I gather, is not an unusual method of extralegal control.

Sunday, another white faculty member and I accompanied by a Nigerian Baptist ministerial student attempted to worship at Galloway Methodist Church [in downtown Jackson]. As we walked across the street toward the church we could feel all eyes on us. Three men standing at the corner were obviously not ushers. There were several doors opening into the church. The men blocked the first; we moved on—they moved on; we continued to the last door—they continued. Finally we had to turn toward the door and face them. Without apparent embarrassment, one said, looking at Mr. Odu, "You can't enter here." Mr. Davison said, "This gentleman is a clergyman from Nigeria" and further explained our desire to worship together. The men were unimpressed; we expressed our disappointment and left.[2]

Two encouraging notes: The Unitarians were very hospitable to us though one young man suggested we not talk in Jackson about being there as the police were always watching them since Unitarianism is not a popularly accepted religion in this region. Second, a Presbyterian minister called our chaplain asking that several students attend his church Sunday. This minister met the students on the steps and, waving the half dozen policemen on, ushered the students into the church. (At first I couldn't understand the need for policemen to direct traffic in front of churches. One learns.)

I arrived in Jackson in time to observe the gubernatorial primary campaign. The Kennedys really took a beating. All candidates lambasted them for interfering with "our way of life." But what amused me was the blast against

2. Sixties Galloway minister Dr. W. J. Cunningham wrote to me October 6, 1993: "Galloway closed its doors to worship by black people June 12, 1961. The Official Board voted for the policy, 184 to 13. Dr. [W. B.] Selah, senior minister at the time, opposed the policy. I also opposed it when I came. Everyone knew of my opposition."

candidate [James P.] Coleman, who as a former governor had allowed Senator John Kennedy *to sleep in Bilbo's*[3] *bed*! The paper even carried a picture of Bilbo's bed—canopy and all—with a caption below asking if we wanted this to happen again. I thought this ludicrous, but was sobered by Mrs. Karro's comment, "I can understand that; I know how I would feel if someone had allowed Bilbo to sleep in Lincoln's bed!"

Mrs. Karro and her husband, a lawyer in the Department of Labor in Washington, had lived in Europe during the period when Hitler was coming into power. She was alarmed at the similarity between the silence of the people of goodwill in Germany then and the present silence of such people here. Determined at least to make her own position known, she went to Danville, Va., and marched with the demonstrators, carrying a sign, "Segregation Must Go." She was booked on a half dozen charges and jailed. While in jail her husband and son came to see her. Her son, an Oberlin senior, kissed her and said, "Mom, I'm so PROUD of you." Mrs. Karro remarked to me that the expression of the matron standing by was most interesting. The day after Mrs. Karro was released from her ten days' confinement, I met her at the farm known as the Society of Christ the King, where we both enjoyed the hospitality of the sisters while in Danville. I was on assignment for SCEF then.

The Danville struggle which has been in the news considerably is a tough one. Undaunted by the past police brutality, the Negroes and a few white friends continue to demonstrate though an injunction has been issued against all demonstrations and gatherings to discuss demonstrations. Strictly interpreted we were violating the injunction when we attended civil rights meetings in a black church—or even discussed plans together in a home. I was interested in many new folk songs coming out of the Danville struggle. Matthew Jones, a former teacher in Tennessee who lost his position for his civil rights views, is the prolific writer and composer of many [songs]. Word just came of his arrest again—no appeal permitted.[4]

You probably saw the three-hour NBC program on the civil rights movement. Two sentences in the summarization I thought worth the whole program: The same states that refuse to obey the Supreme Court decision of 1954 never obeyed the decision of 1896—separate but equal. 2. The Revolution of '63 is occurring for the same reason an earthquake occurs along a fault line.

3. Theodore G. Bilbo, often called a demagogue and a race-baiter, was twice Mississippi's governor and its U.S. Senator 1934–1947.

4. One of the Freedom Singers in the early 1960s, Matt Jones continues to write and sing songs about human rights struggles.

Five of us from the faculty attended an open meeting of the Mississippi Advisory Committee to the U.S. Commission on Civil Rights. Dr. [A. D. "Dan"] Beittel [white], president of Tougaloo, is the secretary of the Committee. Persons who felt they had a grievance were invited to testify. The stories of police brutality we heard directly from the Negroes involved were absolutely incredible. No wonder Americans don't get excited about what's happening. I'm sure they just can't believe it. After hearing over and over again of kickings and beatings with blackjacks and pistols by the police for no real offense, one's sensitivity even becomes dulled—a protective mechanism built within us, I suppose. One incident: A boy walked down the street wearing a T-shirt he had worn in the Washington march. On the back was printed "Freedom Now." He was arrested for parading without a permit. As is customary, other charges were added including in this instance vagrancy and resisting arrest. The latter is a complete fabrication so often resorted to. Negroes in Mississippi just don't resist arrest—the penalty is too high. This boy was cursed and kicked, the police declaring he didn't say "Sir." In the end he was released on $400 bond.

At the close Charles Evers, the NAACP leader here since the murder of his brother, Medgar Evers, asked how long Negroes were expected to take all this; how long could America endure as a nation with so many of its citizens denied simple justice and freedom to enjoy their homes, their jobs, their very physical safety. "We've cared for your children, nursed your sick, served you in every possible way." At this point his voice broke and he walked to his seat daubing at his eyes with his handkerchief.

I wept too.

Again we are promised a filibuster when the Civil Rights Bill is presented to the Senate.

In the past a filibuster by Southern Senators supported by Western and Midwestern Senators has killed civil rights legislation. The last such occurrence was on February 7, 1963, when out of 96 votes, 54 were cast for cloture (to end debate)—10 votes short of the 2/3 required to win—and 42 in favor of the filibuster.

The 20 Senators who voted with [Mississippi's] Senator [James O.] Eastland and the South against cloture, and thus against civil rights, were:

Arizona, Goldwater—Hayden
Iowa, Hickenlooper—Miller
Nebraska, Curtis—Hruska
Alaska, Gruening
Nevada, Bible—Cannon
Wyoming, McGee—Simpson
New Hampshire, Cotton

Hawaii, Inouye	New Mexico, Mechem
Idaho, Jordan	North Dakota, Young
Illinois, Dirksen	South Dakota, Mundt
Kansas, Carlson	Utah, Bennett

If you know anyone who lives in one of these states you may wish to ask him to write his Senator requesting that he vote for cloture (against the filibuster).

Anyone interested in receiving the REPORT ON MISSISSIPPI giving actual cases of police abuse may write Dr. A. D. Beittel, Sec., Mississippi Advisory Committee to the United States Commission on Civil Rights, Tougaloo College, Tougaloo, Mississippi.

Sunday, September 22 [1963]

It is still an early morning hour and perhaps I should be studying while my brain is fresh from a good night's sleep. Did student ever study as hard as teacher?! But, on the other hand, it has been a full week since I've written any of you and longer for some—and joy of joys! I now have a typewriter.

I am now doing more work in my office—a full room to myself for the first time in my collegiate life! It is in the same building as my living quarters but upstairs and in the other wing.

At first my rooms were discouraging to me. I concentrated on trying to make what I have livable. At least my two rooms in one of the oldest buildings on campus were clean. The floors of asphalt tile were polished to a real shine. I gather the radiators will heat well in the winter. The main drawback is a community bathroom, but as you get to know the persons who use it, you don't mind so much—though it is still inconvenient.

I found a prize in my little GE TV set. Perfect for my small living room. From one to six faculty members squeeze into my limited quarters to see Huntley-Brinkley right after dinner every evening. Some of them have their own TVs but this is good and it's more fun viewing anything with company. I haven't tried to compete with Dr. [Ernst] Borinski, who also serves coffee when we occasionally go there. Thought I'd let him keep this added inducement since his TV is not nearly as dependable as mine! We are in a good-natured competition in our hosting for Huntley-Brinkley.

I'm fast becoming accustomed to the luxury of having my two rooms cleaned twice a week. Also, I like having my laundry done, hotel linen service.

September 29 [1963]—Sunday p.m.

Every night when I lay me down to sleep I wonder how I happened to be so fortunate as to get this position. I can't think of another place in the entire world I'd rather work. Administration sets the pattern for quality education with a purpose. Dr. and Mrs. Beittel are not above being a part of every college function. They attend chapel services. When the chapel was so poor at Rust in program and attendance, I used to wonder why the president and dean did not attend. Here they do and the services are good enough so they are not wasting their time.

The general conversation at meals is a real treat. I can't keep up with it. The topics range far and wide, religion, philosophy, economics, politics, music, art, literature—you name it and it's discussed with fervor.

Exciting experiments are going on all the time. I have been asked to lead two weeks of the seminar on the freedom struggle. The outline covers everything in the past 187 years that has a bearing on the situation we find ourselves in today. A young law school graduate from Yale is setting it up. He is waiting for his service call—I think he has it but has about six months to wait. About 10 of these voter education young people who are working in Jackson and Vicksburg will come out four times a week for the seminars—no credit. It seems a wonderful idea, for I saw at Danville how imbalanced these workers get in their thinking when they become so involved with jails and police. This seminar is part of the program for which we have been given the foundation money.

Faculty seminars begin this week in the Beittel home. Dr. Sewell, better known as Elizabeth, will lead the first discussion. She has published several novels and books of poetry. She is a remarkable person—so typically English. She teaches a year then writes a year.

The social science seminar Wednesday night features the chapel speaker for Thursday—a woman from the State Department who deals with Latin American affairs. I am one of the few invited by Dr. Borinski to supper first. He runs the social science lab—a large area in the basement of this old building given over to his books, his classes, and his kitchen! He is the most energetic and remarkable person. A short stocky German [who escaped Germany in time to avoid the Holocaust] with the best interest of the students always uppermost in his mind and heart.

This morning I drove Elizabeth and Charlie Rowell (Negro) to the Catholic Cathedral. Charlie even took communion up in front. No stares. No police.

Afterward we drove by three Protestant churches and saw the bouncers out in front—fully a dozen men in front of the Baptist church. Church had started about 15 minutes before we made this little tour. The Christian church had no men out but two policemen were sitting across the street in a car. (One policeman was at the Baptist.) At the Methodist we saw no one at first. We slowed down. A man opened the church door and stood on the steps staring at us until we were completely out of sight.

The White Citizens Council announced this week that it was developing a plan to eliminate integration in local churches. "A few all-white churches have admitted Negroes to their services in recent weeks. We feel that it is time to come forward with a positive plan of action to save these churches from integration. Experienced lay leaders will conduct a series of meetings on the situation. From these meetings will come an overall plan designed to eliminate church integration entirely."

When I first came to Jackson last summer I took the guided tour through the governor's mansion. This morning I went alone to the door to ask if the mansion was open on Sunday. The butler said not as a rule but he'd be happy to show me through. I said I had a couple of friends in the car and would go back for them. He asked where I was from—I said California and one of my friends was from England. The other was a local resident. As I write this I can see that the *local resident* was probably what tipped him off. It would be normal, I suppose, for the local resident to be making the inquiry. Anyway, when we returned from the car, the butler was out in front waiting for us. As soon as he saw us he went inside. When we rang the bell a policeman answered. He said the mansion was not open today. We'd have to call the hostess tomorrow morning after 8:30 for an appointment. I'll try to do that. I'm wondering what tactic the hostess will use to learn who we are. When I went before, I just walked up and in at the suggestion of the bus driver (local bus). I saw the $10,000 gold bathroom just recently completed and Bilbo's four-postered bed.

We have all been disturbed by the McDowell[5] pistol at Ole Miss. We can't condone his carrying a pistol, of course, but the frightening part is that so many in this area do carry pistols. I have been told that the Ole Miss students have arms in their rooms. This together with all the traffic accidents makes me think I'm in the most dangerous place. Mississippi, according to the newspaper, has the second highest death rate on the highways.

5. Cleve McDowell, studying at the law school, was the second black student admitted to Ole Miss.

Dr. Smith of Rust came into my classroom last Wednesday. He was his usual ebullient self. He urged me then to come up while [Miss Dorothea Fry[6]] was there or any other time. He spoke highly of the Schuilings'[7] contribution to the life of the college. Dr. Smith conducted a good discussion with students about the Ole Miss situation since that was uppermost in everyone's mind just then.

October 6, 1963

Tuesday a student reported he had attempted to get some books on states' rights from the Freedom Bookstore in Jackson. He was refused the right to purchase anything. Because he was preparing for a panel on the inter-relationship of the U.S. and Mississippi constitutions, he asked me if I'd buy for him. I did, with some interesting verbal exchanges—each speaking in dead earnest and yet each trying to follow the rules of conduct expected of true ladies.

When I entered what looked like a real bookstore, I was asked why I had stopped. "I enjoy browsing through bookstores." I was told this was a patriotic bookstore and asked if I were interested in patriotic books. "Of course! Who isn't these days?" The inquisition continued with my answers being recorded in a notebook. "Are you a teacher? Where do you teach? How long there? Where are you from? California has gone completely to the left." etc.

"A couple of students from Tougaloo were here today."

"Really? I wonder who they were."

"One was in a wheelchair."

"Mr. Carter! I'm delighted he's taking his assignment on states' rights seriously."

"Did you say MR. Carter? We don't say MR. for them."

"Well, Mr. Carter fought in the defense of our country, was wounded, and is now in school under the Veterans Rehabilitation program. I doubt anyone would object to calling him *Mr.*"

"You have communists at Tougaloo." She had already told me that she never made any statement unless she could document it. I asked for documenta-

6. Miss Fry, a Los Angeles State College professor, was giving a workshop for the professors, as she did regularly in California.

7. Dr. Schuiling, from the University of California at Riverside, and his wife donated their teaching for a summer session at Rust. Their young son made friends with children of Rust professors.

tion here. "Mr. Salter."[8] He is the one whose resignation made room for me. I asked for further evidence. "I could give it but I won't."

She marvelled that anyone could read the literature available and still persist in social mixing which could only lead to miscegenation which in turn would lead to the downfall of our civilization. I said we might be surprised if we knew how many of our finest leaders had some Negro blood in them. "For all I know I could have Negro blood in me. I certainly don't know all my ancestors." She said I should know; she knew of a certainty she had none such blood. This I questioned in all good nature. Etc. etc. ad infinitum. We parted friends on the surface. Mrs. Beittel says this is a Citizens Council bookstore.

As your news media probably informed you, we now have a "safety tank" [called "Thompson's Tank," after Mayor Allen C. Thompson] to plow through any demonstration, turning on tear gas or guns as needed without any danger to the police who will be completely protected inside. Jimmy Ward, editor of the local paper, explained that, though Jackson is quiet now, at any moment Martin Luther King may get visions of sugar plums in the form of fat collection plates and start a movement here. If he does, our tank is waiting for him and his kind.

The paper gives large space to letters from the people but they all reinforce the editorial line. I wrote yesterday asking how this came about. Do only those who agree with you write letters or do you print only those letters that strengthen your editorial policy? I doubt I'll get an answer because my address is Tougaloo if not because of the question itself. Other local people dare not write or speak out unless they are prepared to be tracked down by police in their every act, lose contracts, have mortgages withdrawn, credit ended, or some kind of harassment. It would seem to me good if more persons from outside the state—beyond the pale of the Citizens Council—would write letters to the state governors and local newspapers. This paper is the *Jackson Daily News.* Letters from California, New York, Minnesota, and all parts of the nation are printed—but they always express views that out-Barnett Barnett and out-Wallace Wallace.[9] I'd be interested to see if other letters that I knew were written were published. If not, this fact alone might be used as the basis for a letter or article in a nation-wide publication. Subjects of popular interest here are the civil rights bill, power of Department of Defense to declare off-limits segregated

8. Tougaloo sociology professor John Salter was a chief strategist of the "selective buying" campaign in Jackson in the early 1960s.

9. Mississippi's and Alabama's governors.

areas surrounding camps, the Citizens Council plan to save our churches from integration, and always the schools—and demonstrations.

Rev. Kleen [of San Bernardino's First Methodist Church] wrote me such a good letter in response to his copy. He frets that he can do so little but actually he seems to be doing much. The work in North and West may not be as exciting, but it is as important if not more important. The South cannot move far without the rest of the nation; I believe the greatest danger now is from areas outside the South where, being faced for the first time with the realities of discrimination, they are unwilling to change. This is giving great strength to the arguments of the Southern leaders of segregation and I fear will defeat some important parts of the civil rights bill.

Tomorrow Dr. Beittel has invited the faculty and staff to a dessert to meet the Board of Trustees. Did I mention before that the Beittels always eat with the faculty on Sundays? In the dining room. A nice custom.

There are so many things going on all the time here—all good—that it is increasingly hard to get time to prepare lessons and read sufficiently and do the correction of papers which these students need. High schoolish you say—but still so needed by them. However, it is the best possible college for me. I find it more to my liking every day. It has faults, but no one is afraid to mention them and everyone is eager to tackle their solution. Sometimes the attempts at solution bring more problems.

October 13, 1963

Last Sunday three of our Tougaloo students—two Negro and one white—attempted to worship at the Capitol Street Methodist Church. They were met by a church usher and a policeman. Upon being given two minutes to leave, the students asked if they could at least remain on the steps in silent prayer during the service. This request was denied them and they started to leave; but by then two policemen who had been in a car across the street grabbed them saying they had waited too long and were now under arrest.

Interestingly enough, the three students were released on bail money sent our chaplain by the national office of the Methodist Church, which was most embarrassed and apologetic over the situation. And—more money was promised for any eventuality which might occur another Sunday! This might suggest an interesting pattern whereby every denomination would assume responsibility for raising bail to release persons who find themselves in jail for having tried to worship in its particular denomination.

Today, one week later, the Caucasian student, Julie Zaugg [an exchange student] (from Oberlin), attended on invitation a Sunday School class of college students at the same Capitol Street Methodist Church. She was asked to discuss with them what happened to the girls. Julie concluded the discussion by inviting any who would like to join with the same three at 11:00. Two of the Sunday School class did so even though they believed they would be jailed for it. However, though the area was swarming with police, the girls were not arrested. They remained on the steps [talking to the ushers and letting as many church people as possible see them].

Also, today, several of our students were admitted to one of the Lutheran churches where they found in the order of service a written apology to the students who had been turned away the week before. An Episcopal church accepted Tougaloo students today, too.

Not so, the St. Luke's Methodist where one of the several men "on guard" in front stepped up to us and looking directly at the two Negroes with me said, "We prefer that you go to another church." I said we'd like to worship here today. He said they wanted no trouble and I assured him we had no intention of causing trouble. He said he didn't want to discuss it, and after I informed him I was a Methodist and would like my friends to worship with me, he said he would not discuss it further. Expressing regrets, we left with none of the police observing, doing or saying anything.

The gains here, though small, are significant. The much-touted campaign of the Citizens Council to prevent any integration of the churches was given a bit of a setback. Had nothing been done today, it would have been assumed the treatment of the girls last week had been effective in intimidating others. However, the point is far from won. We drove by several churches. All had police in evidence. In front of the Christian church was the "paddywagon" ready for business. The Baptist church had fourteen men, by actual count, standing guard plus police sitting in a car across the street. As we drove by another Methodist church, one of the men in front wrote something which I assume was my license number. A car having integrated riders is always suspect, especially on Sunday morning.

Sunday, October 20, 1963

You were so good in remembering my birthday that I should write a real letter, but the hour is late so will mainly write a note to let you know I'm not in jail as I might have been. The chaplain, Ed King, had asked me to take a Methodist minister from Chicago and a Negro student to the same St. Luke's Methodist that we were turned away from last Sunday. This is a different Chicago Methodist minister from last Sunday's man who went to Capitol Methodist. There are three (maybe more) ministers from Chicago and one lawyer layman with them. It seems Julie Zaugg, the Oberlin exchange student who went to jail two weeks ago with the two Negro students, has wide influence in Chicago. Her family's friends, mainly church people, are carrying on the crusade. Two ministers went with Julie and her same two friends today. All five are in jail now.[10] Before I left this morning, Ed King came over and said another faculty member, Mr. [John B.] Garner (white), was in jail along with two Negro students. He is a member of Galloway Methodist, has been a regular attendant and an active member of the Sunday School. He was asked by the class to bring two students with him this morning for a Sunday School class discussion. They no more than got inside than they were arrested by police. Thus, Ed King felt it better that I not try to go inside the church at St. Luke's but merely act as chauffeur. He said the college couldn't afford to do without too many of its staff at once. But, my minister passenger and student were not arrested. They followed my line of retreating after some conversation. Had they insisted on standing on the steps, I'm sure they would also have been arrested. Mr. Reed, the minister, is a bit disappointed, I think. There were no police at this church this morning. I wonder if the St. Luke's members asked them to stay away or if there weren't enough police to go around to all the churches. One success was at the Presbyterian church across the street from St. Luke's. That is where the students were requested to visit several weeks ago, but the church has been closed to us since. Now they were asked again, and an usher met them and took them in with him.

I gave a test in Western Civilization this week. The papers were for the most part so poor that I feel more than ever obligated to stay on the job if possible without curtailing too many of my impulsive desires. These students can never be truly free until they get a [good] education.

10. Julie Zaugg, now practicing law in Wisconsin, wrote October 14, 1993: "We were in jail that time for five days because it took longer to raise $11,000.00, in those days a tremendous sum. In addition, William Kunstler and his partner Arthur Kinoy journeyed down from New York City to defend us. They succeeded in unearthing an old provision which allowed for removal of our case from the state court to the federal branch. The feds had generally more sympathetic judges, or at least more just judges." Nationally known for defending controversial cases, Kunstler died in September 1995.

We did have a treat last Friday night. The airport [largely financed by federal funds] is the one place that we can eat with our friends—any of them. Six of us went—one faculty Negro, one faculty member from Pakistan, one from England, and three of us plain white Americans. The dining room—very nice (a new jet airport just dedicated) was all partitioned off [by green plants] so that we almost had a private room. Dr. Borinski, our sociologist, says he likes that because it is an intelligent solution to the problem! We had a delightful time.

Last evening the Pakistani and the Nationalist Chinese faculty members entertained three of us from faculty and two couples from Jackson with a dinner of their native foods in their house here on campus. That too was most interesting. This is still a wonderful place to be. Stimulating.

October 29, 1963

A note lest you worry about me. A meeting of the American Association of University Professors kept me occupied every spare moment Saturday. We have just formed a chapter and I am on the board so was obligated to spend the day aside from class at this state meeting—held here as the only school in Mississippi where all members could meet. Such other schools as could have us have no chapters—some like Rust because of ineligibility—not accredited.

Sunday I expected to hole in and get some work done but was asked to drive two ministers from Chicago and a student to Galloway Methodist. I packed my briefcase again with toothbrush and bedroom slippers—wore a warm suit, though the day was warm, as the veteran jail-birds say the nights are cold in jail. My orders this time were to park in view of the church front and wait for the others. We made the whole hour o.k. Those who did the same thing at Capitol Street Methodist were jailed—the two ministers, not the student who returned to the car as did our student.

One of my minister passengers just spoke at [our] chapel. His theme was the reformation which this revolution is causing in the church. Scripture dealt with making your sacrifice at the altar—leave it there and go to your brother asking forgiveness—not necessarily for what you have done but for what you have not done. Our sins are more of omission than commission—standing aside while a brother is abused. He thanked the audience for his own renewal—seeing how wrong he had been remaining silent too long. He was not a dynamic speaker—is young—but was terribly moved himself so that I think he closed sooner than he expected—almost breaking.

I forgot to say that Friday afternoon was entirely devoted to sitting in court where our eight students and four ministers were having a hearing. Their bails were reduced (in federal court) to $500 each instead of $1000 each so they felt repaid for having stayed in jail the six days.

Two nights ago the bells of the church rang for about a half hour at 12:15. It seems our chaplain had been warned by the Jackson police that there was a raid on us in the making. The young men organized for two-hour shifts around the campus. Nothing happened. The Jackson police being what they are, I wonder if their call was more of a threat than the actual danger, but I am told there have been several town incidents that would indicate not. Steve Rutledge, our perfectly wonderful [white] student body president, tells me everything is well organized; they have been through all this before as they had a long siege of it last year.

November 3, 1963—Sunday p.m.

Most admirable is the use of intelligence and ingenuity to attack the civil rights problem in this area.

This week the British Royal Philharmonic Orchestra performed. Mr. [Henry] Briggs and Dr. Elizabeth Sewell, our faculty member from England, saw the manager of the series asking that the performance be open to all. Being refused, Mr. Briggs wired Sir Malcolm Sargent asking him to intervene. When he arrived Mr. Briggs and Elizabeth saw him. His position was that he takes no sides in local matters. He is a musician; as such he has played to audiences in South Africa and will play here. Dr. Sewell used the argument that his orchestra is subsidized by British taxes and the British would not approve denial of admission to anyone on basis of color. She has written several officials in England along this line.

Friday night one of our music majors and an Englishman, a Yale student who is presently in Mississippi working on the Freedom Vote, took their places in line at the entrance to the auditorium. Dr. Sewell stood at a discreet distance to act as observer. Police immediately stepped up to the men and said, "You can't go in there." Our student said, "We have tickets." Policeman answered, "I'm not going to argue with you; you're under arrest." The students went off to jail. Elizabeth came right to my room when she reached campus and asked for a cup of coffee. She was shaken up. Said of course our students have been going to jail all year, but this was her first experience to see it, and it really got her.

Elizabeth called the English consul in New Orleans who in turn called Mr. Thompson, mayor of Jackson. Last evening both our student and the English Yale student were out on $500 bail each. After dinner here with us, I drove the English student back to his Yale team at the Freedom Vote office downtown.

Next week a Bulgarian group of artists will be here. Efforts are under way through the Washington embassy to have the program either open to all or canceled.

You probably have had news in papers of the Freedom Vote. Aaron Henry [a black] druggist in Clarksdale, is running for governor and our chaplain, Rev. Edwin King [white] for lieutenant governor. It is an unofficial ballot but they go through all the motions—making speeches around the state, etc. as a demonstration to the world that Negroes want to vote and cannot.[11] They will announce the result of the election—hopefully having around 200,000 votes.

Last Tuesday two plainclothesmen marched up to the platform in chapel and attempted to serve Ed King (chaplain) with papers to appear in court to show why the injunction against Tougaloo and himself should not be made permanent (against demonstrations). Ed refused to accept it, saying this was a religious service. Such matters could wait until chapel was over. Then he prayed a very pointed prayer about the whole subject. The men left at the conclusion of the prayer with the papers on the pulpit. Ed and Dr. Beittel have been in court much of this week though.

The W.S.C.S. [Women's Society of Christian Service] of Boling Street Methodist Church here has voted to send no more funds to the National Mission Board because it used some of its money to bail students out of jail—students who had defied the laws of Mississippi in an attempt to attend Capitol Street Methodist Church.

Yesterday several ministers arrived from Wisconsin and Illinois. They repeated the performance of last Sunday—two white ministers with one Negro student try to go to church. Refused admission, they take the student back to car (it's exam time and students can't afford to be in jail) to wait in full sight of the dozen ushers on the steps. The men return and stand throughout the

11. Ordinary cardboard boxes were placed in black stores, gas stations, etc., for voters to drop their ballots.

service on the steps. The funny thing this morning was that they made a mistake: meaning to go to Galloway Methodist, they actually were at the Baptist which looks the most formidable of any because there are usually at least 14 men standing in front and several police. About half way through the service—still in front and having conversation with those formidable appearing men, they discovered they were at the wrong church. Then they went down the street a block to the Methodist but had to admit the Baptists treated them better than the Methodists. All of yesterday was spent in visiting the [local] ministers again. This I feel is about the most valuable part of the ministers' participation. No one was jailed today.

I stayed here in my office all day working on my exams and lesson preparations as I am going to Asheville, N.C., on Wednesday to the meeting of the Southern Historical Association. Dr. Silver of Ole Miss is president and is reading a part of his new book soon to be published on some such title as *Mississippi: The Closed Society.* This I must hear. The college is eager that we take as much part as possible in our professional organizations.

I was surprised last Tuesday with a phone call from Chase Page.[12] He wanted to know whether or not a carful of Garrett students could give effective witness. He was very thoughtful in wanting to work with Ed King and not be off on a tangent of their own. Ed said he would call Chase today. I hope he doesn't forget. He has so many things on his mind all the time. I really don't see how he keeps going. Ed said to me, however, that he didn't think the seminary students would be as effective at this point. They wouldn't carry the weight with the ministers here that full-fledged ministers do. But Ed continued, they are considering what can be done using seminary students during the Thanksgiving vacation. It's encouraging that people from all over are so interested in doing something to help. Mississippi will never move without outside help. Of this I am convinced.

The election is almost upon us. There is a last-ditch fight against the Republican renascence. The candidate Rubel Phillips is making a good campaign and has the Democrats really scared. They unashamedly say that a two-party system would end their segregated way of life—two parties would be sure to give the Negroes the balance of power. Politics are as low as they come here. In fact, the reason it is so hard to get anywhere with the race issue is because politics are so corrupt.

12. Mother's student pastor for several years at Winchester, California.

Yesterday Ed King our chaplain came into dinner with his few survivors and announced 10 in jail as a result of their visits to four different churches—all Methodists. Two were our students, two were Negro ministers from Michigan and the others either visiting laymen or ministers from Michigan (white). One retired minister among them says he'll not take bond—that this is as good a way as any to use his retirement.

Ed also told us he heard that a white woman shook hands first with the Negro minister and then with the white on the steps of Galloway. The first time this had happened! Later during dinner a young [photographer] came in and when he was introduced to me said, "I wish you would reenact that scene at Galloway. I was so shocked I failed to get a picture of you."

Too bad I lost my anonymity as it was so encouraging to think some "normal" woman had dared to shake hands with these two men. Actually I had hoped I might be a decoy—maybe others would follow my example, but the only followers I had were policemen. When I arrived two were watching from across the street. I'm told I had no more than disappeared inside the church than our two men were arrested.[13]

The minister gave an extensive welcome to all visitors and asked us to sign our names and drop cards in collection plate. I did, adding, "As a visitor I am impressed with your welcome. Does the Negro whom I met on the steps know he is welcome?"

Now that I've had my relaxation I can get back to work. There's no end to the work here but everything I *have* to do is what I *want* to do anyway. What have I ever done to deserve this delightful place? I can't wait to see you to tell you about all the exceptionally fine people here.

While I was in Asheville hearing Dr. Silver and other historians, a cross was burned on our campus.

13. In *Mississippi: The View from Tougaloo* (p. 206) I wrote of myself: "a white faculty member who was also a member of Galloway Methodist Church dressed up in her best finery and without consulting anyone went to church to welcome the visiting men she knew would be on the church steps. She broke through the ring of ushers surrounding the black and white ministers, extended a gloved hand, and said, 'Welcome to our church. I hope you enjoy the service.'

"Leaving the startled group, she escaped to the balcony where she removed her feathered hat and mink stole. Out of the corner of her eye, she saw two men enter the balcony and look the worshippers over carefully before leaving. The Jackson newspapers carried the story," saying an "unidentified white lady" welcomed the visitors.

Everyone has been so good to send me clippings. The minister from Encino, Calif., is certainly doing his part to arouse churchmen to our plight. He learned a lot in the 24 hours he was here. Eugene Carson Blake's[14] speech in Pasadena was certainly direct and to the point. Beloved as he is, there ought to be some effect. Idaho's Lewiston paper had an excellent editorial, on Silver and other Southern heroes. We were especially heartened by the Methodist bishops' statement including "to move to arrest any persons attempting to worship is to us an outrage. We affirm the legality and right of those minorities who are oppressed anywhere in the world to protest, to assemble in public, and to agitate 'for the redress of grievances'." Some of the ministers wanted to pass out the bishops' statement on the church steps but Ed advised against it as he knew they'd be arrested immediately on the "litter law."

While some of us are in jail it's "business as usual" with the Greeks on campus. I'm getting very anti-Greek as I've seen it here and at Claflin. Such tomfoolery—such exhibitionism—such a slump in scholarship during pledging period and especially Hell Week. It all adds up to one word for me—DISGUSTING.

December 8, 1963

We have just heard Mozart's "Requiem in D Minor" sung by our choir as a memorial to [President John F.] Kennedy [assassinated in Dallas November 22]. It was beautifully done. The church was full, including the balcony. Many were from Jackson—white and Negro.

It was great being with so many of you Thanksgiving. What a grand family we have—and what singers! I'm firmly convinced the value of a trip is in quality of the days rather than quantity. Once I arrived, everything went so perfectly.[15]

Monday's teaching suffered somewhat from my weariness but aside from that things have moved steadily and intensely all week. We are nearing the end of term—only four weeks before exams. I've been correcting library papers (using three references). The results are heart-breaking. We've reached the point where we can write answers to simple questions but to integrate three references

14. Former pastor of Pasadena Presbyterian Church; later General Secretary of the World Council of Churches.

15. Several planes had been canceled going out of Jackson because of President Kennedy's death.

and make sense is still to be learned. When I get discouraged, I remind myself that we are covering the work twice as fast as in either of my other two years and even so the papers and tests are better than those except possibly in the one superior class at Claflin.

Today I've been preparing for tomorrow's Mississippi History class, reading about the 1890 Mississippi Constitution under which we still operate. The text is the state-authorized one so that what I write here is not my biased statement nor do I have to read between the lines. One of the main purposes in writing the new 1890 Constitution was to disfranchise the Negro.[16] When the white dirt farmers opposed the literacy clause there was a "gentlemen's agreement" that the tests would not be used against the whites. Mississippi never made the mistake of some Southern states, says the text; she had a good lawyer in Senator [J. Z.] George, who made the provisions which resulted in making the disfranchisement constitutional and they were so declared by the Supreme Court in 1898. However, the voting qualifications other than literacy did limit the white vote—so much so that whereas in 1890 there were 120,000 white voters, in 1892 there were only 68,000.

In the 1890s the state was again broke (it had happened before) and issued paper money. This being in violation of the U.S. Constitution the governor, auditor, and treasurer were arrested, but the local jury refused to indict them. Federal juries, today as then, are still local people. This week the federal court jury found officers innocent of beating and kicking the Negro civil rights workers arrested in the sit-in demonstrations at Winona. But as our Mr. [Oscar] Chase from Yale law school says, he (white) and several Negroes had to stop at Winona two weeks ago, and they were not beaten this time, so even without a conviction there is progress of sorts. (You may recall Winona is the place I wrote had removed all eating facilities from the depot rather than integrate on court order. When I went through in July we had to go without breakfast. When I returned in September there were six food-vending machines.)

December 15, 1963

A note under my door this morning asked me to drive two N.Y. ministers to Galloway Church. I packed my briefcase with the usual toothbrush, slippers,

16. The 1868 Constitution written during the Reconstruction government in Mississippi gave all male citizens the right to vote.

etc., just in case. We met with the chaplain, Ed King, for a few well-chosen scripture verses, prayer, and, time running out, we did the singing in the car. For the first time I actually saw the arrests which took place less than 10 minutes after the two—one white and one Negro—ministers started up the church steps. At least before they were taken away by the police, they talked to a few people, and Mr. Garner, white faculty member, and his wife [Margrit] who are members of Galloway, shook hands with the visiting ministers and the ushers with them. It was all over so fast.

Ed King was surprised at the arrests, as yesterday the visiting ministers had met with four laymen of Galloway (a mark of progress that the meeting was interracial) who assured the ministers there would be no arrests today. When the ministers asked if one of the laymen would stand on the steps to wave on the police, they were told the police would not be there. Interesting for two points: the laymen felt in control of police action indicating possible past collusion, and 2, the police acted contrary to the wishes of the church members.

Encouraging note: These ministers were officially sent by the New York Methodist Conference Social Concerns Committee, their way and bonds being paid by the conference. Bond will probably be set at the usual $1000 each. However, these men expect to stay in six days.

Being officially sent by the N.Y. conference should assure them of publicity. The lack of publicity for the many things that have been happening here is of major concern to me—and I'm sure to others. Without publicity, the conscience of America is untouched. Then what purpose do these jail sentences and heavy bond investments serve?

Miss Lois Chaffee (white), Oberlin graduate who was on the Tougaloo faculty last year, is in jail. She stated under oath that she saw the police beat a demonstrator after Medgar Evers's death. The police insist they did not beat a demonstrator. Lois is in on perjury. Bond has been set at $5000—not cash, but property located within the city limits of Jackson. This rules out help from Tougaloo as our property is outside the city limits. The penalty if convicted, and it is feared she will be, is ten years in prison.

It is one thing to flirt with a jail sentence of a week or less—quite another to flirt with a ten-year sentence. Already I can see that the charge is effective for I find myself planning to be more circumspect in my own operations.

"If this be 1789—as it may well be" begins many a discussion around here. Everything seems set and moving inexorably to a point of no return short of military force—which, however it developed, would be tragic. For instance, the Negro civil rights organizations have decreed a black Christmas as a symbol of their mourning for Medgar Evers and John Kennedy. No lighted trees in Negro homes. Some Negroes have threatened to break windows where trees are seen. Mayor Thompson took to TV to offer prizes of $100 down to numerous baskets of groceries to "our Nigroes" having the prettiest Christmas decorations. Or again, some Negroes were reported to have threatened Negroes who bought on Capitol Street [downtown], which is under boycott. The mayor on TV announced the city has 275 police officers and would hire as many more as needed to assure every one of "our Nigroes" the right to buy on Capitol Street.

It has been repeatedly denied over TV that there was cheering in the local schools upon learning of Kennedy's death. Teachers have "sworn under oath" that this rumor was a malicious lie, we are told. But I talked with a teacher who said the students were hilarious in the hall—Kennedy is dead, he was shot in the head, etc. She went to the principal and reported it to him whereupon he chuckled. At that point this teacher said she burst into tears, and then the principal went out and tried to quiet the kids.

Sunday, January 12, 1964

It hardly seems possible I have been back here only 10 days and on the job only seven.

The train travel was a vacation in itself. I was on long enough to settle down to some reading and even to relax a bit.

We had a delightful Christmas in Moscow [Idaho] with four excited children reveling in the magic of the Christmas tree and all the packages under it. The children had made gifts themselves and even put on a musical show of piano and singing.

One evening Charlotte and Laird had some university friends in—chosen for their possible interest in the Mississippi story. We also had opportunity to stir up a little interest for Mississippi at the dean's reception. Lois Chaffee, Oberlin graduate from Idaho, who was still in jail when I left, offered a bit of common interest. She is now out on bail. Her trial is set for next month.

Dr. Zaugg, father of Julie Zaugg, is on campus working with our chemistry department. Dr. Beittel says he is considering joining our faculty. This would be something as he is a research chemist who has been with the same industrial company for 19 years. Dr. Zaugg went with Elizabeth, Roy, Charlie and me to the airport for dinner. We always get a royal welcome there from the maitre d'hotel and the waiter. Were it not for them, the experience wouldn't be half as much fun. It's always interesting to note the white stares we get. Of course the tables are set off by modern screens and planters—very elegant—but we always manage to seat Charlie where he can't be escaped by all coming in the room. One woman gave us a prolonged hate stare that made her anything but pleasant to look upon.

Our wonderful Elizabeth may be at Los Angeles State beginning in '66. She has offers from so many places—and rightfully so. She has a sharp mind, is well educated, and is a superb teacher. I notice the Beittels never miss a chance to exhibit her to all the guests of importance on campus. Yet she never loses the common touch. Her primary interest is in writing. Every other year she takes off to write. L.A. State has agreed to all her peculiar requirements by way of time off, and has offered her what she considers a fantastic salary—better than anyplace else. Also she says she has fewer friends in L.A. so could spend more time working.

Expect to attend church this morning. Five are here from Iowa to go.

Sunday, January 19, 1964

The entire week I have slept at the Beittel home. Dr. Beittel is returning tonight. In one way it has been a nuisance—not so much for having to pack my clothes around, and never having the right thing at the right place, but because she has difficulty understanding my need to work.

She said she'd like to do something Saturday night and suggested my asking a few to come in for Scrabble or other games. Elizabeth thought that would be ghastly—said she refused to play games with anyone but herself—solitaire! She suggested reading a play. Thus five of us gathered to read—each taking parts as necessary meaning sometimes we had several. The play was "A Man for All Seasons," a recent Broadway hit about Sir Thomas More. It was an excellent play and we had a delightful time. I commend it to those of you who would like to spend an enjoyable evening with friends. Read a good play.

Today Mrs. Beittel and I went to Galloway church. So far as I know, there were no planned visits today. Perhaps we are moving out on a different tack, which would seem to me good. Robert Raines, son of Bishop Raines, preached. The church was full. He preached a good sermon ending up very straight forward on race. He has been with about 40 of the church members for the past three days having special meetings. Should have said he is from Philadelphia. Evidently the pastor, Dr. [W. J.] Cunningham helped engineer the whole thing.

He must have known what was coming. The three days were probably for the purpose of getting rapport with some 40 leaders of the church.[17] The Raines family is an interesting one. The father a bishop who, as was said in the pulpit today, signed the bishops' statement on race; one son came through Mississippi with the first wave of Freedom Riders[18] in '61; another son was here about six weeks ago and attempted to visit a church with a Negro student, ending in jail. All three of the sons are ministers.

After church we drove beyond Piney Woods Country Life School[19] for dinner at an old-time hotel in Mendenhall where dinner is served on a revolving round table. We could have as much of anything as we could eat except the dessert which was passed to us. It was a delicious home-made coconut pie. The whole experience was good and different.

January 27, 1964

Saturday near midnight I heard several shots and learned at breakfast yesterday they were fired into the air from a car passing by our campus. All night our students kept watch at assigned posts (second time this year) armed with their *whistles.* The reason this time: Saturday evening after a crowd of 4,000 had waited 40 minutes to hear the jazz musician, Al Hirt, in a March of Dimes benefit, the announcement was made that Mr. Hirt refused to appear before a segregated audience. A telegram sent to Mr. Hirt by a Tougaloo student was read to the gathering. Here at the college a telephone call was received from a reporter friendly to us saying there were angry mutterings among the crowd to the effect that they'd get Tougaloo for this. The radio made mention of the situation every half hour on its short news broadcasts. One announcer said his

17. I learned later in Dr. Cunningham's book (*Agony at Galloway*, University Press of Mississippi, 1980, pps. 21–22) that Rev. Raines had agreed not to bring up the racial question, as Dr. Cunningham said he was yet new to the church and needed time to "build a good pastoral relationship" with the members.

18. Groups of blacks with a few whites exercised their federal rights, while deliberately violating Southern state laws, by riding interstate buses and using "white" facilities at the stations. They were beaten, especially in Alabama, and were jailed in several places, including Jackson, Mississippi.

19. Probably the best-known Mississippi private school for African Americans, founded in 1910 by Laurence C. Jones, a black Missourian who graduated from the University of Iowa.

station would never play an Al Hirt record again. Then no more mention was made of it at all. Even the newspaper Sunday morning went out of its way to lay all blame on his New York agent, and only at the very end did it mention that Tougaloo students had protested. We wonder if there was fear that the whole reaction would get out of hand or if our new Governor Paul Johnson is trying to play down some of the events that have given Mississippi such a bad image.

Hirt's cancelation was a blow to the state pride as it was the third cancelation within the past few weeks. First the Hootenanny Singers canceled and performed here at the college without charge to us; then the *Bonanza* stars canceled; and now this. The mayor of Jackson appealed to all Mississippians to turn the dial when the *Bonanza* program comes on. Yesterday's paper carried another suggestion: Go to church on Sunday nights!

Oscar Chase (white) with whom I worked in the seminar for voter registration workers, a graduate of Yale law school, was in Hattiesburg with the SNCC group. He was arrested for entering a colored section of a bus station. Later he was dismissed. Then he was arrested for having locked bumpers with another car. After getting out and finding no damage done he went on, but someone swore he left the scene of accident, etc. and he was again thrown in jail. This time the other inmates were told he was a "nigger lover" and they beat him up but good.

Last evening we heard in the Beittel home a firsthand report from Mr. Clark, dean of the chapel at Beloit College in Wisconsin. Fifty ministers of various denominations had joined SNCC in their efforts to crack the registration barrier in Hattiesburg. Mr. Clark said the ministers came assured they would be arrested during the first 15 minutes. They had the customary small change in their socks but little other money, expecting to be the guests of the city! Instead, the police were called out in numbers to clear the streets and keep hecklers away. For the first time in recent civil rights history, the police protected the demonstrators. Mr. Clark said when they discovered what was happening, they realigned their forces and marched and picketed in shifts to save their poor blisters. And the rains came as you may have seen on television. The police were lined up in rain coats but the ministers were drenched. All the while, prospective voters were admitted four at a time into the courthouse to fill out their registration forms which takes 20 to 30 minutes each. Those waiting were also drenched, of course. The ministers felt their greatest achievements were in the conferences they had with local ministers and a few city officials and in the new insights they, themselves, received. All ministers who come express their new or renewed dedication to finding solutions to the problems *in their own areas.*

The Presbyterians, at least, are committed to send new minister recruits for each of the next few weeks, about 12 each week.

I decided I should join a church so have chosen Galloway, the most influential [Methodist] church in the state probably. I signed a card a week ago indicating my desire to affiliate. My Tougaloo address didn't deter the office from calling me to say that though the ministers were out of the city this past week, one of them would call on me soon. I'm hoping this will be done. Just getting a minister out here will be good. So few of our detractors have ever been out. Of course we have one [white] faculty member and his wife who are members of that church. They joined when Dr. [W. B.] Selah was there. He left because Negroes were turned away from the church and he couldn't make his board take a stand which would prevent recurrence of such an event.

Yesterday I went to Sunday School—business women's class. A good lesson skirted the problems, but I felt everyone knew what was meant and if so some of the opinions expressed were quite liberal. I was warmly welcomed. My address wasn't generally known, but the three women who took me in tow for the coffee period asked me where I was from. They made no comment and my address or what I did here was not again referred to. At least they continued to be very friendly. I sat with them in church.

February 2, 1964

We just returned from a showing in the colored theater of the English film, "Lord of the Flies." This was a sequel to our venture last night when Hamid Kizilbash, Pakistani on the faculty, with three of his Negro students, Dr. [Madabusi] Savithri, new Indian on faculty complete with sari, Roy Davison, and I went to the Capri theater. The ticket sales were made inside the lobby. We got that far and were eyed carefully by all while Hamid tried to buy tickets. He was referred to the manager whom he told of the students' having studied the book in his seminar and of their desire now to see the film. The manager was most regretful but this being a white theater he couldn't possibly let us in. He did offer to run the film in the colored theater at 6:00 today for us—free of charge. Hamid asked if he couldn't run it in the Capri which would be so much nearer school, but the manager said that would be impossible. Thus we took two school busloads of students to the Alamo in Jackson. Our seven swelled considerably! The manager seemed very pleased with us and I imagine congratulates himself that he avoided a scene with police, etc. At least he made some money from the concession stand.

At the airport where we went for dinner Friday night, the restaurant was out of Sanka. This is the only place where we may take our Negro friends to eat. The waiter there and the maitre d' are such affable pleasant persons and as I was leaving I said, "Next time please have that Sanka for me!" The waiter said, "Let's see, who advertises Sanka on the radio and TV? Maybe it's taboo now!" Referring of course to all the people Mississippians are mad at and thus not buying from or looking at or listening to. Because the *Bonanza* stars canceled their scheduled entertainment before a segregated audience, we are told not to watch *Bonanza*; we are admonished to boycott the Chevrolet dealers because Chevrolet sponsors *Bonanza*. Our radio won't play Al Hirt's records and the papers' editorials are vehement in their criticism of him. Even Mr. Webb of the government space program canceled when the civil rights organizations wrote him that he would be speaking before a segregated audience. One editorial said we should welcome the secession of the United States from Mississippi. We'd be better off going it alone. (Shades of 1860!)

This morning I took two ministers from Pittsburgh to Galloway Methodist. They had talked previously to the pastor of Galloway and had his assurance he would not call the police if they passed out copies of the bishops' statement on race—though he did not approve of their passing them out. We were spotted as we were sitting in the back seat; the collars are sure identity. One of the Galloway men sat with us, introduced himself as a member of the Pastoral Relations Committee. After the service he and another tried to keep us penned up in our pew—a tactic I've run into before. We finally pushed our way out to the foyer and I watched from afar, as our chaplain was afraid there might be violence when the people realized there were no police taking over. However, everyone was well mannered. The worst anyone did was to return with the paper after he discovered what he had and throw it on the floor with an expression of his disapproval. The men had a chance to talk with several at some length. This was all encouraging. If we had time on our side we might yet make a breakthrough—but the problem is to work fast enough.

I forget how inured we become to our dangerous way of life but was reminded of it today when one of my ministers lost his breakfast just as we were ready to leave. He had his small coins in his socks for use of the phone, and had just written the chaplain's telephone number on his arm—all in case they were arrested. That did it; his stomach just couldn't take it. He said this was always his reaction to tension.

One of my students, a veteran in a wheelchair, received a letter from his Congressman [Jamie L. Whitten] in answer to a request he made for his newsletter. The envelope was addressed *Eugene Carter.* Inside it read *Dear Eugene.* Mr. Carter had written this same Congressman previously from Chicago regarding a matter pertaining to his disability and received an answer which began *Dear Mr. Carter. This* letter was sent from Tougaloo which of course gave his race away. Such a little thing, but it signifies so much.

February 9, 1964

Just attending Tougaloo has its penalty. One of our exchange students, desiring to see Mississippi from a white point of view, applied for admission to Millsaps, a good Methodist school in Jackson. To the credit of the college, the answer was forthright, if regrettable: His scholastic record was excellent, but the college couldn't accept one from Tougaloo. No doubt Millsaps is under great pressure not only from the state but also from the Methodist church in Mississippi. Then, I understand there is a problem with finances for the school as many foundations require non-segregation policies, meaning that more and more such schools as Millsaps must depend upon local support.

This has been a week of tension. Numbers, especially visitors, attended sessions of the Beckwith trial. Difficult to believe, but I have it from the school doctor and the chaplain, that the prosecuting attorney referred to "the nigger Medgar Evers" and "this gentleman, Mr. Byron De La Beckwith." He may not even have been aware of the slant of his terms—they being the natural expressions of many Mississippians.

Ed King, chaplain, drove into Jackson with a Negro student in the front seat and a white student in the back. The police followed them all the way into town; other motorcycle police were stationed at various corners with their guns mounted on their motorcycle handles. Finally Ed was stopped. Several police debated about 10 minutes what to charge him with, eventually coming up with failure to signal a turn. Ed says he'd rather they'd come out and say you have a colored girl with you. Ed was taken to the jail and with the effort of Mr. Charles Evers was allowed to come home. He now has the choice of paying a $17 fine or contesting the charge. If the latter, he will tie up $200 in bond and the cost and time of the case. If the former, he puts himself in good position to have his license to drive withdrawn as this is his third "violation." One more and he's had it.

The mayor took to the radio and TV again this week asking for emergency powers to issue $1,000,000 bonds to finance the fight against integration. These bonds will be "an investment in the future of the state." He also asked permission to make a compound for the detention of demonstrators and permission to send them to Parchman—the state work farm. Obviously, he was fearful of what would happen when the verdict on the Beckwith case was received.

During the week, a white driver hit a Jackson State (Negro) College student at an intersection where the students had been trying to get a traffic light installed. The student suffered a broken leg and the driver got out to wipe the blood from the fender of his car. The students surrounded the car, rocked it, scaring the man half to death. The police arrived with Thompson's Tank. Tear gas was turned on the students—but something went wrong with the equipment on the tank's initial engagement and the tear bomb exploded also on the inside of the tank! Students rioted; bricks, bottles, and rocks were thrown. Police used their clubs to crack heads and their guns to shoot. Three students ended up in the hospital from gun wounds. Jackson State students called our chaplain for recruits to help them continue with a demonstration. Of course, Ed is a staunch nonviolent advocate. He spoke to us in assembly of the need to keep our heads and to be in control of any demonstration we make rather than to react to a situation we cannot defend. Ed explained the Jackson [State] students had received no training in nonviolent techniques, they had no outlet for their pent-up emotions, no freedom of speech on campus, were not allowed to sing freedom songs and could not attend freedom meetings in churches off campus. One could understand their rioting, but we should find better ways to express our needs.

Dr. Silver sent a form letter to the 600-plus persons who have written him since his speech on *Mississippi: The Closed Society* last November. Generally they have written in support of the contents of his speech though some have attacked him personally. He says he feels less pessimistic than he did two months ago about the future of Mississippi. "Regrettably, there has been a decided exaggeration in the press of the plight of 'Old Silver' and his family. We do not walk alone, we are not ostracized. I am not the 'most hated man in Mississippi,' I do not practice with my shotgun on afternoons off, and Claude Sitton's quote 'Hell, I like it here,' still applies. I'm not one to go out on a limb but Mississippi is our home and we intend to stay."

I took Savithri to Capitol Street Methodist church this morning. She managed to engage one man in conversation for 40 minutes afterward—the same one who denied her admittance last Sunday. He said, "If you had come alone we would have opened our hearts and homes to you. But you came with those agitators (two ministers from Pittsburgh). That is why no one spoke to you today. Everybody knows the Indian lady came with outside agitators and is at Tougaloo." (I should have said Savithri went in alone. We went our separate ways.) The church must not be very friendly as no one spoke to me except when I spoke first. I am not known there either.

[March 1964]

Some of you have expressed concern that the civil rights movement is getting out of hand. If it hasn't already, I can assure you it will unless justice is done and that soon. The patient Negro is fast becoming the historical Negro. Today's Negro wants his rights now—during *his* lifetime. Laws on education, housing, employment, and public accommodations will impose some hardships as it is utterly impossible to legislate and administer every detail adequately, but we have been asking for these laws every time we denied an otherwise qualified person access to our neighborhood, our school, or our place of employment merely because of his color. Under law the burden of proof as to a man's undesirable character, his lack of skill, etc. will be on the other foot and we will not like it, but, as I said, we asked for it.

Teaching here is like teaching just behind the "front lines." Students are forever having to leave classes to testify in court, or even to serve time in jail. This past week one of our white faculty members [T. William Hutchinson, Jr.] was driving home from a meeting in Jackson. Because he had some Negro students in his car, he was followed by police. Then the police disappeared and two cars pushed our Tougaloo people entirely off the road. When the occupants of the cars strode toward Mr. Hutchinson's car, he stepped on the gas and got away. All in a day's work here.

Presently Tougaloo is being attacked by the members of the state legislature. As "rabble rousers and a nest of communists" we must be investigated, they say, and perhaps our charter should be revoked. Dr. Beittel, our very able president, told a newsman who called for his comment that we would welcome an honest investigation by a responsible committee, but he doubted the State Sovereignty Commission would qualify. Dr. Beittel also called the president of the Exchange Club where Lt. Gov. [Carroll] Gartin initiated the present blast against Tougaloo to tell him that he, Dr. Beittel, would be happy to speak to the club if they were interested in Tougaloo. I doubt he gets the invitation.

However, sometimes we have little surprises. It is encouraging, for instance, that the following was even printed in our local paper. "Editor: Another drab week has passed without *Bonanza*. Tell me again now, just what is the difference between white and Negro boycotts?"

March 9, 1964

Our current success story took place last Thursday night. In response to a "Cleopatra" ad, "No seats reserved—All ticket holders guaranteed a seat," Mr. Kizilbash and I asked Dr. Savithri (always striking in her beautiful saris) and a Negro student to go with us to the Paramount. Having previously purchased our tickets, we walked resolutely in the door with the student leading; our tickets were accepted in a routine manner; a man, presumably the manager, walked over to the side of the ticket man. After we were seated the two couples in front of us moved. Some in back also moved. Then all seats filled up again. There were curious glances but no bitter hard stares such as we get when we attempt to go to church. We thought hoodlums might be awaiting us when we left or neared our car parked on a dark street, but there were none. Not even police were evident as at church. We can't believe all this yet. We wonder if Dr. Savithri, so obviously foreign, was the acceptance factor. The next step is to go without her.

Mr. and Mrs. Hutchinson of the faculty had a repeat experience with hoodlums as they were going to church—this time with their baby and Eli, a white student, but no Negroes in the car. "A car followed them from the gate down the Old Highway. About a mile from the campus they were surrounded by five cars (four approached them head on, driving two abreast and completely blocking the road) holding about 20 white men. A man with a stocking over his face and a pipe in his hand tried to smash the windshield of Mr. Hutchinson's car. Another man approached from behind carrying a heavy mallet. For some reason, one car pulled over too far and Mr. Hutchinson was able to continue to church—just as the pipe hit the chrome above the windshield. Again, a red VW was involved. That afternoon a call came to Rev. King's house threatening to kill him if he brought a baby with him again." (From the Tougaloo student paper)

These calls continue day and night to the King and the Hutchinson homes always threatening dire happenings to the baby girl. Actually the Kings were not involved except as they are associated in the minds of everyone in Jackson with the work here.

Some persons in the Presbyterian church where the Hutchinsons worship were concerned enough to want to do something. They arranged with Ed King to escort a group to their church the following Sunday. Ed suggested that since only whites were involved the Sunday they were attacked, we should send only white adults with the escorts. The church representatives agreed this would simplify the matter for them. Because we didn't want to risk sending the Hutchinsons and baby again, Ed asked me and several other white adults to go. However, the other faction of the church got wind of the plan. It called church members practically all Saturday night asking them to choose between segregation and their pastor. It seems the pastor was blamed for the overtures which these few members were making to bring us in. The ones who wanted to escort us were the staunch supporters of the pastor and now they felt their doing this would work against him. The Citizens Council has boasted there were certain ministers they would get out of town. The first three on the list have left under pressure or resigned. This pastor was the fourth on the list. So Ed and the church persons involved decided the whole plan of escorting us should be given up. I said I'd be willing to go alone, but Ed thought this too dangerous and I didn't want to go against his advice as he carries a big enough load without his friends fouling things up.

During the past weekend I attended the Mississippi Historical Society annual meeting in Meridian. The president of the University of Southern Mississippi [Dr. William D. McCain] was dominating the dinner conversation around us with his account of John Frazier who is attempting to get admitted to Mississippi Southern. He declared this "Nigra" never made proper application; this was the reason he was turned down. (Tonight's TV news said Frazier stated he thought having filled out certain forms when he applied last quarter he need not fill them out again.) Dr. McCain said Mississippi Southern is "integrated" already so that question is not involved here. I asked if any Negroes had ever been admitted. "Hundreds," he replied. I asked if they were foreign Negroes or American Negroes. He admitted they were from Panama, etc. attending special institutes for short periods. Then he started to tell about Tougaloo's agitators. At this point the lady next to me interrupted to inform him I was from Tougaloo. I told him I'd be interested to know what he was about to say about our college so he continued unabashed: That Methodist minister—whose name he couldn't remember—was recognized as a troublemaker and a communist even when he was in school. Others at the table felt this was most convincing and I assured them "Ed King is no communist." Then the sparks did begin to fly across the table from me. I was nudged by my neighbor and everyone became alarmed. I asked one for the source of her information and she gave the newspaper. I said if she must label Ed she probably could call him a pacifist and be correct. She saw no difference between a pacifist and a communist. I decided I better call a halt before I received a harder nudge.

One of my mature students who is in the army informed me that he told his wife he was learning more history now than he had ever learned before in his entire life. This really set me up and I was riding high on those encouraging words—until the first examination. A very low F. More than ever evidently is not much.

March 12, 1964

Dear Bobbie Lee [my niece],

Your letter telling of the interest in your class for the civil rights movement was encouraging. Here we see so many flagrant acts against law, human justice, and human dignity. However, the problems are not just here in the South, as I'm sure you and your class are aware.

The whole problem is made more difficult because our educational system has never been equal. The ignorance and the unawareness of this ignorance is disheartening. As the NAACP president in South Carolina said to our students at Claflin, "What we need are more marchers—students who will march every day TO THE LIBRARY." This is something needed the nation over, for America was never intended to be governed by functionally illiterate people. Self-government demands enlightened citizens. Your integrated school in San Diego, by keeping academic standards high, can contribute immeasurably to convincing others that they need not fear integrated schools. And without integrated schools, good education for all—the basis of good government—is well nigh impossible. I'd like to see every student start the day saying, "As my contribution to the civil rights movement I will march today—to the library."

Success to you and to your class!

April 12, 1964

Don't worry about my safety in Mississippi. The police give generously of their time for our "protection." Last night the paddywagon followed us from the center of Jackson to the city limits, a distance of about 8 miles. Reason: Four of us faculty members—two white Americans, one Negro American, and one Indian walked together on Capitol Street. We couldn't have collected more stares and glares had we literally been the devils people apparently perceived us to be. One car of white women turned to follow us as we walked and continued following as we drove. They hurled insulting remarks at us and just before leaving us for good, made out to spit on our car. An ugly sight from representatives of white Southern womanhood.

Back to our stroll down Capitol Street. As we were about to cross a street on the WALK signal, two police stepped up on the opposite side as though to stop us. As we neared they stepped back and looked away. We were apprehensive about crossing as two weeks ago a couple of our Northern college visitors in company with one of our Negro students were arrested for "jaywalking." On these WALK signals there is only time to get half way across the street before the signal changes. This has the obvious purpose of forcing everyone to start at once. However, the police used it as an excuse to take the three students to headquarters. When the white male student was asked a question and answered "yes" one of the policemen slapped his face: "Say 'sir' when you address me." The one young lady of the group was asked if her parents knew she was going around with a "nigger." As the three left, one of the police said jaywalking was only a minor infraction, but the young lady knew what the real offense was. (For the uninitiated—mixed company.)

We started last night by a visit to Dennery's, a popular and good eating place. Probably it had never had a Negro attempt to eat there as we apparently took everyone by surprise. The waitress asked me how many and I answered, "Four, please." She led us to a table. All hands, including the cooks who are plainly visible in this place, stopped work. All eyes were glued on us. A man behind us said, "I never before saw anything like this here." We were about to celebrate the occasion with steak orders when Roy Davison was quietly approached by the waitress and asked to step out. He did and the question was put to him: "Is the gentleman colored?" Roy answered him politely, "Quite obviously, yes." "I'm sorry but we cannot serve him." Returning to us, Roy quietly announced the airport was awaiting us. (The one place we can all eat, it having been built with federal aid.) At least Charlie Rowell can say he has been to Dennery's.

Night before last a cross was burned at the campus gate. Two students found it, put the fire out, and eventually brought it to Ed King's house. We viewed it there last night on the screened porch. Crosses were also burned in front of the Negro Masonic Temple and the Negro church where mass meetings are frequently held. We assume the increased tempo of expressed antipathy is due to the presence of Mr. Eichelberger, president of the AAUN [American Association for the United Nations], on campus last Monday, and the folk singer, Joan Baez on Sunday. On both occasions there were numerous whites present—especially Sunday for Miss Baez when at least half the audience was white [and all joined hands at the end to sing the Movement anthem, "We Shall Overcome"]. Mainly they were students from Ole Miss, Millsaps, and Mississippi College. Newspaper editorials and Letters to the Editor have been rabid in their denunciation of the white attendance.

Dr. Sewell has a guest here this week whom she wanted to see the guards in front of the Protestant churches. I went to the Catholic church first with them and Charlie Rowell (Negro). Then we started walking in the rain. It was amusing to see no one standing in front until we approached the churches. Then they all came out. Six from the shelter of the Methodist church; nine from the Baptist.

April 25, 1964

Yesterday after our fancy dinner with the Board of Trustees, Dr. Beittel asked the faculty to meet him in the conference room. There he announced with a too serious and flat expression his retirement as of this summer.

This stunned most of us, though a few seem to have been forewarned. One said she learned of it from students who got it from Ford Foundation and Brown University men on campus. Today, Dr. Beittel told a few of us gathered around him that it came as a shock to him. He had been given to understand that he could stay for five more years if he wanted. He said the board wanted him to say it was his desire to resign but he couldn't honestly say that.

The board members with whom I ate this noon said the school was in for a great development program which would make Tougaloo a very different place. That's fine, but it hardly explains why the man who has laid the plans for such a development is suddenly out. We have been conjecturing that a Brown University man will be sent to us. It is Brown that has been interceding with the Ford Foundation to get big funds for us to launch out on the developmental program. Brown was to cooperate with us closely—exchange some students and professors—use us as a social laboratory in the Deep South, etc. When Brown men were here for a week making a survey of us they wrote a report in which they did not speak very highly of the faculty. So—if Dr. Beittel could be dismissed so casually—perhaps the rest of us can also. And, as I said before, the contracts have been held up—presumably because Dr. Beittel was waiting to hear from the Ford Foundation, hoping he could offer raises. I'm beginning to think there may have been other complications that caused him to be unable to make the contracts.

Sunday, May 3, 1964

This last week my main project was with Cleveland Page, a Negro member of Tougaloo's faculty who teaches organ and piano. He is without a doubt one of the finest young men you could find—and what's more he looks the part—which makes him an ideal person to bridge the gap in human relations. He wants to go to the University of the Pacific to begin work on his doctorate. The university asked him to send a tape recording of his playing on the organ. Tougaloo has no pipe organ so I got the bright idea of approaching Dr. Cunningham of Galloway [Methodist Church] and asking permission for Cle to use the church organ.

Galloway is in the news so much—especially at General Conference discussions because of its refusal to allow visiting Negro and white ministers in, let alone Negro students. Most recently, on Palm Sunday, even Dr. Savithri, an Indian on a Fulbright Scholarship, was physically forced out of the church. On Easter Sunday two bishops were turned away—one Negro and one white.

Galloway has more sane people in it than any church around here other than the Episcopalian, Unitarian, Catholic, and Jewish. Many are heartsick over the situation and seeking ways to break out of their bondage. I felt sure Dr. Cunningham's heart was in the right place even though his words are carefully weighed to maintain his position.[20] I thought this small step away from public view might be welcomed as evidence of a willingness to do something constructive.

Dr. Cunningham was agreeable to the idea of Cle's practicing one day and recording another day. He considered how best to do it. I had suggested that he might want to take it up with the Official Board. He decided against that in favor of taking the responsibility on his own shoulders. He ruled out

20. I never appreciated what pressure Dr. Cunningham was under until he published *Agony at Galloway.*

certain times suggested on the ground that people would be around. But he did call the organist and together they set a Friday and Saturday at 10:45. The organist said she would come down and show him the organ. Dr. Cunningham [thinking Cle was a student] had referred to Cle as "a boy from Tugaloo"[21] so she was surprised to find an adult faculty member who was proficient already in his skills. Mrs. [Mary Taylor] Sigman was wonderful to him—even gave up her work in the choir room to come out and turn pages for him. They found much in common in their music and past instructors.

Thursday night Cle was getting so tense about going that he wanted another person to go with us. I decided to call Mrs. Arrington who is a pillar of the church and thinks "right"; she has been out here a number of times to our [Tougaloo] events. After I explained the situation she dropped everything to come and just sit in the sanctuary. Mrs. Arrington, talking to me as we sat through the performance, said it just near broke her heart to think of this wonderful young man placing his physical safety in jeopardy merely by playing on a church organ with full permission. She was much impressed with him and oppressed by the situation.

Yesterday when we returned the church was empty so far as offices were concerned. It was Saturday of course. But at the organ was a young college student with a young man who was turning pages. When she paused, I asked her how long she would be. She said all morning at least, that her instructor was here and giving her last-minute help for the recital she was giving next day. Then the instructor came in—a Millsaps man. He readily admitted they had not made an appointment. I said we COULD come back later if we were sure the organ would be free and not already assigned to someone else. But he was very nice and said since we had made the appointment, they should be the ones to return. He and Cle talked a bit and he said he had heard that Cle was making the recording. (We wondered how and by whom the word had spread!)

Then Mrs. Sigman came. Quite a bit later Mrs. Arrington came. Before they arrived Cle was tense and apprehensive. One can think of all sorts of ugly things with the least provocation: The church was empty except for someone who possibly had been assigned to keep us from the organ. Mrs. Sigman and Mrs. Arrington who had promised to be there were not. An unknown man at one time rattled the front doors trying to get in; all we could see was his hat.

21. Whites who use this pronunciation usually are not acquainted with people from Tougaloo College or the Tougaloo community, who begin the name with "to" rather than "tug."

Afterward Mr. Page described his thoughts as he was playing: Would a Citizens Council member learn of this? Or a KKK member? A shot in the back perhaps? If so, he thought what a dramatic ending he could make with one last minor chord as he fell forward on the keys. Fortunately we can all maintain a sense of humor about these things and Dr. Sewell, faculty member and author of numerous books, wrote Mr. Page this poem:

PIECE D'OCCASION

for Cleve Page

Someone has begun to play
In the church at Galloway.
Organ music, proud and fine,
Echoes round the sacred shrine.
Who is playing? That is Cleve.
Wow! whoever gave *him* leave?
For within this hallowed spot,
Some may play and some may not—
(Axiom that would seem dippy
Anywhere but Mississippi).
In the haunts of Methodism
Cleve, defying separatism,
Adumbrates a cataclysm.

Busy with baroque arpeggi,
He is feeling slightly edgy.
That requires no understanding:
Bach's sufficiently demanding—
But, his back to aisle and pew,
Cleve has other things in view,
Thoughts to make the stoutest quiver:
Bang! a bullet in the liver.
Contemplating being shot
Makes one's playing go to pot.
Do the skimming fingers falter?
(Who's that lurking by the altar?)
Classic fugue-dom and toccata-dom
Do not normally lead to martyrdom;

Are White Citizens familiar
With the fate of Saint Cecilia?
Anyway, in Jackson town
Everything is upside down:
That the righteous cause may win,
Christians do their brothers in,

To protect with gun and knife
Mississippi's Way of Life.
Any Protestant church pillar
Could conceal a ruthless killer.
Facing premature Nirvana,
Cleve thinks Papua or Ghana
Might know more of *vox humana.*

As he's playing, Cleve, meanwhile,
Plans to die in splendid style.
If dispatched to meet the Lord,
He will strike a monstrous chord.
Seventh, maybe, and diminished
For his Symphony Unfinished?
Pathos far as it will go,
Pianissimissimo?
Tune the bellows' final wheeze,
Then fall forward on the keys?
No! if he must choose his fate,
Cleve decides to play it straight:
Surely nothing could be finer
Than expire in C Sharp Minor.
Having taken which decision,
Exorcised the grisly vision,
He concludes in deft precision.

Let the anticlimax fall:
Nothing happened after all.
We are rather glad, dear friend,
It was fugue's, not journey's end.
Remains to say, in love and rage,
May better worlds your gifts engage—
Long life and happiness, Cleve Page!

—Elizabeth Sewell

Sunday afternoon: I did go to church and joined—at last the fatal step. People were very cordial. It was interesting to answer their queries about where I was living: "I'm living on campus at Tougaloo." No one batted an eye, however. One said, "We call it Tugaloo."

I noted that the ministers did not announce the addresses or occupations of any of the four of us who joined this morning. He just told where we were from. Sometimes he goes into great detail on these points so people with common interests can get to know the new ones. In a way I should be grateful that he did not, as it might have called in the 37 men who were guarding the doors this morning [when I arrived]. Actually, I counted that many and I didn't go around to the side door. I had been told that a real demonstration was anticipated today because of General Conference being in session. To the first two groups of three men I beamed a "Good morning!" The next three were separated by a few feet from each other. One wore a large Texas-type hat and had a huge cigar in his mouth. None of the three would even look at me as I passed them. I should think if they must guard, they could ostensibly be a welcoming committee—greeters. But I suppose those three were not even church members. Inside I couldn't resist saying to the man who gave me my order of service, "I'm surprised there are any men left to perform their duties inside—I saw so many out in front."

I was determined not to join the church without being known and known for my position on life in Mississippi. Cleveland Page assured me of that achievement. Both ministers had no difficulty recognizing me this morning and calling me by name. I didn't want to have them learn of me afterward as a troublemaker. I told the assistant pastor that I believed there were many ways of working without using the direct assault method—but this didn't mean I was not in favor of church visits or that I wouldn't become involved in such again as I had in the past. However, I think the little contact which Cle made did as much or more good than a sojourn in jail for trying to attend a service where we are not welcome. All methods are needed and each must be used by those who can use them best.

I was introduced as being from Orangeburg, South Carolina—which makes me a real Southerner. Many who came up to shake my hand wanted to talk about South Carolina.

This is Parents Day. I must now go to a coffee hour. I had to skip church [on campus] this morning so was sure to go to the 2:00 convocation where all the intricacies of the college were explained to the parents.

May 9, 1964

Some of you received a letter in which I mentioned that Eli Hochstedler, a good student from the North, had applied for admission to Millsaps, the white Methodist college in Jackson. He was refused because he had attended Tougaloo for a semester. The following story of a recent experience, unfortunately typical of this area, is related by Eli. The Marion Gillon in the story is one of my freshman students.

"A friend and I were arrested for trying to use our tickets to the Holiday on Ice Show, Thursday evening, April 16, 1964. We were arrested because Marion Gillon, a Negro, and I, Eli Hochstedler, wanted to sit together at the city-owned coliseum. We had tickets for seats #1 and #2 in the same row. We were hauled away to the city jail in a paddy wagon. During the questioning, my interrogator observed that probably neither one of us would change his beliefs, and that after all we had the right to our own beliefs. (The only difference, I observed, was that I had been arrested for exercising my right.) On the following day we were photographed and fingerprinted for the criminal files. In the afternoon we were each fined $500.00 and sentenced to six months in jail on a charge of Breach of Peace. My friend and I were cufflinked together and marched to Hinds County jail to begin serving our sentence.

"Before putting me into the white cell area, the jailer ordered me to button up my collar. I later learned that the jailer had beforehand told the prisoners who I was, the nature of my 'crime,' and that I would be identified by a buttoned collar. There were six common cells with eight bunks in each. All these cells and a large bull pen were opened during the day from 6:00 a.m. to 10:00 p.m. I was directed to a bunk in the cell farthest from the entry into the cell area. When I started over to where the other prisoners were watching TV in the bull pen, one of the prisoners told me 'You had better get into your bunk if you know what is good for you.'

"Around 9:30 p.m. about a dozen prisoners came into my cell where I was trying to get to sleep. One of them said they wanted to talk to me. They insisted that I get out of my bunk to talk. They asked a lot of questions about my reasons for coming to Mississippi and attending Tougaloo College. I tried to explain that I came as a transfer student paying my own way, that I had *not* come to stir up trouble, but more so to get a more accurate picture of the South, to meet new friends, and to broaden my education by living and studying in a different environment. I tried to explain that I was young, a student, and did not claim to know all the answers. I told them if they could give me some good reasons for not doing what I had done, I would be willing to listen and learn. But all they said was that 'We are going to have to show you and any other outsiders coming down to stir up trouble, what is going to happen to them.'

"The spokesman for the group then told me to stand up and meet the first one who was going to work on me. He pointed to a huge man called 'Tiny.' As I stood up Tiny hit me near my left eye and knocked me flat on the floor. Just as I stood up he hit me and again knocked me down. After two or three blows I landed in a lower bunk bleeding from my face and nose. When they saw I was bleeding freely one said, 'That should be enough for right now.' I crawled back into my bunk. Tiny ordered me to roll up my mattress and place it on an adjoining bunk, which I did. I then lay down on the steel plate of the bunk.

"After a few minutes the prisoner who had introduced me to Tiny came over to me with a leather belt about an inch wide and three feet long. He announced that he would be the next to work on me. After lying on the steel about ten minutes, I was ordered to come down off my bunk. I hesitated but the prisoners threatened to kill me if I didn't follow orders. So I did as told. A prisoner then told me to lean over with my head down on the lower bunk. I was wearing only my underwear shirt and shorts. He then started lashing me with the belt. After eight licks he ordered me to lower my shorts, after which he continued the whipping. During this time I was repeating, 'Father, forgive them, because they really don't know what they are doing,' and 'Lord, help me to take it and forgive.' The prisoners jeered and made remarks like, 'The Lord won't help you here.' After 16 or 18 lashes I felt I couldn't take it any longer, so I screamed. (Incidentally, the TV in the bull pen had been turned up very loud.) As I yelled, I stood up. Something (I think it was Tiny's fist) then hit me near the right jaw and sprawled me out on the bottom bunk. They thought I had been knocked out. If I was out I don't remember it, but I did remain completely limp for several minutes. Tiny then came over and asked, 'Hasn't he come to yet?' He then shook my shoulder and told me to get back into my bunk. Staggering, and starry-eyed, I managed to crawl back into the bunk. They then shoved my mattress back under me and threw the covers on top of me. A prisoner, called the 'cage boss,' then came in and suggested that I had had enough for one night.

"About 10:30 on this night the cells were locked up. On most of the other nights I was there, the doors were locked before 10:00. The jailer locks up by remote control. During the beating he was nowhere near. I'm sure he knew what was going on.

"The next day my left eye was nearly swollen shut. My right jaw had swollen so much that I could scarcely open my mouth wide enough to eat. I also had difficulty in sitting down. In the morning the jailer asked me what had happened to me the night before. Because all the prisoners were nearby, I didn't want to say. I told him I had run into something. He chuckled and asked me what I had run into. One of the other prisoners said I had slipped and fallen in the shower. The jailer again asked what really had happened. I told him, 'I'd rather not say.' He laughed and walked out. He at no time offered medical assistance.

"At breakfast Saturday morning I gave most of my food away, giving my coffee to Tiny. Later on in the day Tiny and a few others talked with me. Tiny told me that he just couldn't figure me out. He said he had a soft heart and didn't want to see me get hurt but that what I had gotten last night was only a taste of what some of the guys had planned for tonight. I had expected to be released from jail on Saturday on an appeal bond. But for some reason or other the money never came. When I realized I would not be getting out of jail Saturday, because of fear and deep depression I made a statement with the pretense that I was changing my beliefs on civil rights. From then on I received no more attacks or threats while I was in jail.

"On Sunday, several people came to visit me, but the jailer would not let them in to see me although the other prisoners had visitors. Books and messages were brought to the jail, but I received none of them except one telegram on Tuesday morning. On Sunday morning, the jailer told Marion, 'You won't be seeing your buddy anymore. We killed that s.o.b. We'll get you tonight.' The jailer threatened to throw him over into the white section of the jail. Marion did not find out I was still alive until we were released on Tuesday morning."

Signed by Eli Hochstedler

Neither Eli nor Marion would have done this had they not been promised bail should they be arrested. The promise was harder met than expected. This is the reason I feel I must keep a good bank balance at all times. Eli and Marion were released on $500 bonds but adults seldom get off for less than $1000. I don't aim to get in jail as I merely present myself in company with friends at church, restaurant, or theater. When we are denied admission, we express our disappointment and leave. However, even this technique has not always kept others out of jail. I have no martyr blood in my veins and should I inadvertently get in jail, I want to be sure I can get out without waiting for some organization to collect the bail money!

I hope Dr. Silver's book will be out this month as he earlier anticipated. He is getting publicity aplenty. The legislature of Mississippi is still trying to get rid of him on one pretext or another. Of course, to fire him now (from the University of Mississippi) would merely be proof of his contention: Mississippi is a closed society. Do avail yourself of the book when it is out.

And, if any of you are interested in helping one of the rare free voices in

Mississippi to continue, I suggest you subscribe to Hazel Brannon Smith's *Northside Reporter*, 5048 North State Street, Jackson, Miss. ($5 per year). The editorials are worth the full price and will keep you informed as to what the issues are here. Mrs. Smith just won a Pulitzer prize. The money is negligible, but we hope the prestige will encourage financial help desperately needed because of the many libel suits against her.

In all your judgments of Mississippi, remember: The White Citizens Council, the KKK, the Sovereignty Commission, Eastland, [U.S. Senator John C.] Stennis, nor Barnett speak for all the people. They seem bigger than they are because they represent the power structure which is as real as it is invisible in these parts.

Sunday, May 10, 1964

As I sat munching my wheat-bread-wafers with peanut-sesame spread and Tupelo honey (courtesy of Dr. Calhoun), I thought "what a Mother's Day celebration this is!" And then I realized how grateful I am that I don't have to eat this way Mother's Day or any day, that I have children who would gladly share their homes with me, and that I have children who graciously allow me to go my own peculiar way. Many wouldn't, I know. In fact, the former dean of students here has never been welcome in his son's home since the son learned his father was in a "nigger" school.

The greatest news for me is that I have my contract for next year with a $500 raise. So Dr. Beittel's delay, hoping he could give a raise, paid off. All his effort to get foundation support cost him his position though. As near as we can gather the foundation wants a younger man who can stay with the program for the next ten years at least. Doing anything constructive in Mississippi has its hazards at best.[22]

Next Friday evening and Saturday I shall be in Atlanta at the meeting of the Board of Directors of the Southern Conference Educational Fund.

22. Later, the Mississippi State Sovereignty Commission reported having met in New York on April 21, 1964, with three Tougaloo trustees. The Commission representatives showed documents confirming their point "that Mississippi and Tougaloo College were on a collision course." They told the trustees that the crisis might be avoided "if Dr. Beittel were dismissed and a new president appointed who was more concerned with education than agitation. On April 25, 1964, Dr. Beittel was dismissed." George Owens, Tougaloo's business manager, became acting president September 1, 1964.

Only this week and half of next. It doesn't seem possible that the year is over so soon. It has been a good year.

[Too busy to write at the end of the 1964 school year, I quote here from my book written ten years later, *Mississippi: The View from Tougaloo* (University Press of Mississippi, 1979), pp. 199–200.

"Until the spring of 1964 foreigners, even of dark complexion, were served in Jackson restaurants. But three incidents during the week of Indian Prime Minister Jawaharlal Nehru's death [May 27, 1964] ended this tolerance for a time. Jerrodean Davis, a Tougaloo student, Dr. Savithri Chattopadhyay, a visiting Brahman Indian professor, and a white faculty member went to Morrison's downtown cafeteria where, to their great surprise, they were served. Police did nothing beyond keeping watch through the large windows. The next day when word came of Nehru's death, Dr. Savithri and Mr. Dennis Strete, also an Indian, were stricken with grief. They drove to Jackson to send a cablegram. On their way back to the college they stopped at Morrison's other cafeteria on the outskirts of the city and were refused service. Dr. Savithri demanded an explanation and was told by the manager that on the day before three women, one a white and one an Indian dressed in a sari, were served at the downtown cafeteria because no one knew for sure whether the third was a Negro or another Indian. Since then it had been learned that she was a Negro. As a result Morrison's two cafeterias had orders not to serve any Indians.

"On the following day, Dr. and Mrs. Beittel, at the request of the U.S. Department of State, met Dr. Ram Manohar Lohia and his traveling companion at the airport. Dr. Lohia was a member of the Indian parliament and head of the Socialist Party in that country. Returning from the airport, the Beittels took their guests to a Morrison's cafeteria and were stunned when they were refused service.

"Dr. Lohia was a pacifist in the tradition of Gandhi. He insisted on returning the next day for lunch, not as a representative of India but as an Indian citizen. To do less would not show concern for the treatment of local blacks, he believed. He informed the manager at Morrison's, the police, and the press of his intention. Dressed in a white robe and sandals, he walked to the door of the cafeteria. There he was met by the manager, who informed him that his business was not wanted, that he was on private property, and that he was being asked to leave.

"Dr. Lohia replied, 'I tell you with the greatest humility I am not leaving.'

Then the police arrested him and led him across the street to a paddywagon. Dr. Lohia talked with the police about the meaning of justice for some twenty minutes, after which he was released.

"Each of the three incidents was independent of the other. Mr. Strete, who took Dr. Savithri to Morrison's after sending the cable, knew nothing of the incident at the downtown Morrison's; Dr. Beittel knew nothing of either of the two previous episodes. Yet it would have been hard to convince Morrison's that the three incidents were not planned, each bringing into the act persons of greater prestige than those of the day before."]

Summer 1964

[Carnegie Tech, Seminar for Black College Professors]
Pittsburgh, Pennsylvania
June 17, 1964

I'll just pass over all the exciting events near the end of school such as our being physically pushed out of a restaurant when we had no Negro with us. I must have some things to tell you when I see you.

Jeannette King, wife of Chaplain Ed King, went with me as far as Oxford, Ohio. We made our first stop at the University of Mississippi. One of my students, Cleveland Donald, was to have enrolled that day but the enrollment was put off until the next morning. We talked to one of the sympathetic professors who said the decision was made to avoid his registering at the same hour as [James] Meredith had, and to wait until all unauthorized cars were off the campus. On a normal registration day, it is impossible to control the cars that have no business being there. We hear so little about the registration or Donald's presence that [we suppose] everything must be going smoothly. I don't know why I say that, as I know events in Mississippi are not always reported. A student with whom we ate said some of the students had formed a "We dig Donald" club to eat with him! Certainly he must be having a much better time of it than did either of [his black predecessors].

Then we stopped at Rust and were invited to stay overnight at President Smith's. The Yale team came in for the evening. Actually the team is made up of about a dozen young men and one young lady from three or four universities who volunteered as summer tutors. They were the grandest young people I have met—or so it seemed on so short an acquaintance. Jeannette was shocked at the men's dorms—and the women's too, for that matter. Two Methodists on the team were very dismayed over conditions. One of them, Grant, is a student at Garrett. I hope he voices his concern where it can do some good. However, the new science building is going up at Rust and the contracts for the two dorms are to be let in July. Encouraging.

At Western College in Oxford, Ohio, the National Council of Churches was planning an orientation session for those going into Mississippi this summer to work in the Freedom Schools. [I left Jeannette, a native Mississippian, there, as she was to be one of the leaders.] About 100 were preparing for the sessions which began this week. About 800–1000 are expected.[1] The National Council stepped in to do this in an attempt to prepare workers for the dangers, hoping to screen those who go, to eliminate the ones who "can't take it" and to educate [all] in the mores of the area. I sat in on two meetings—most impressive.

Here at Carnegie Tech we have everything done to make our stay profitable and comfortable. This is a beautiful campus—the dorm is elegant and new. I'm interested in economies that were made nevertheless. No running water in the rooms; a community bath for 44 girls on this floor. But we get maid service every day to clean our rooms—this is regular service. I'm on the 6th floor. More than I like, the course revolves around methods. Had I known that, I would not have come, but being here I'll try to get as much out of it as possible. I'm sure I can improve my methods but I do need content. The Institute is run by historians so I'll surely get some history out of it.

(Note: This letter was written in answer to one I received asking my feeling regarding some of the demands Negroes are making today. Cited were some admittedly stiff demands regarding employment at the Bank of America in California.)

Pittsburgh, Pennsylvania
June 27, 1964

Was it Mark Twain who said, "It is not what I *don't* understand about the Bible that worries me, but what I do"?

I say, "It is not the *un*reasonable demands of the Negroes that worry me but the reasonable ones."

When you and I do something to assure Negroes those rights which you say they should have—voting, education, economic opportunity, and acceptance in local churches—then and only then are we in a position to say, "Come now, you are being unreasonable."

I don't go along with all Negro leaders; neither do all Negro leaders agree

1. Mississippi's 1964 Freedom Summer was coordinated by an umbrella organization, the Council of Federated Organizations (COFO), with Aaron Henry as president 1963–65.

with each other. Substitute the word "white" for "Negro" and the statement is just as true.

I fear it is a shallow mind that falls back on cliches, but I'll risk another: "When self-discipline breaks down, law takes over." I am a Republican.[2] I suppose if there is one distinct difference between Republican and Democratic philosophy today, it is that Republicans believe we should keep as much local control as possible. I, personally, abhor fair employment laws and fair housing laws that curtail one's right to hire and rent as he pleases. If during the past 100 years—if even during the past five years when we saw this crisis coming—we had used the same criteria for hiring a Negro employee as a white or for renting to a Negro as a white, I am convinced the law would not now be dictating to us on these details.

Because we refused to rent to [black diplomat and Nobel Prize winner] Ralph Bunche, or to my colleague Mr. Page (who arrived in Ann Arbor, Michigan, two weeks before school began that he might make his usual rounds of apartments and have time to overcome the depression that always engulfs him after about the third refusal), we must now be *made* to rent to him. In the enforcement of such details there are sure to be mistakes. Perhaps some landlord will find he is forced to rent to a person whom he believes of poor character—character is difficult to judge. But if such occasions occur, don't blame the Negro; don't blame the law; blame our own stubborn refusal to rent to Negroes of good character when there was no law to make us.

You didn't say it, but I doubt you approve the public accommodations section of the Civil Rights Act. (If I have misjudged you stop right here!) Unfortunately, the Lord made us all too equal in our basic needs for food, elimination, etc. I have traveled with a Negro colleague when we could find no place to eat. Finally, we resorted to crackers, cheese, fruit and milk from the grocer and I started to turn in at a rather spacious roadside park. She, wiser in the ways of the South, stopped me. "Perhaps," she said, "we could if no one were there, but that other car might not approve." I have bought gas and been stopped when we started toward the restroom. "*You* may use it but not that other person with you." We were forced to drive miles and miles in considerable discomfort before we found a restroom which would accommodate her. Did you ever think what happens to the mind and emotions of persons thus denied recognition of their common humanity?

2. Though I cast my first Democratic vote in the fall of 1964 for President Lyndon B. Johnson.

Government has interfered with business and public accommodations before. They have been licensed (after meeting certain requirements); they have been regularly subject to certain fire and sanitary inspections. Now one more requirement is added: When a man hangs out his shingle asking for business he must accept such business as comes without regard to color.

When plans were being made for the Freedom Schools in Mississippi this summer, Mr. Aaron Henry, NAACP president of Mississippi, explained why white students were being asked to join in great numbers. "We learned at Hattiesburg when the visiting white ministers were arrested, the government took notice. If there is violence this summer and white persons are involved, we can expect federal support." Mrs. [Michael—Rita] Schwerner said on TV the most tragic thing about this whole tragic affair is that if her husband and Andy Goodman (two whites) had not been involved, James Chaney's disappearance would hardly have been noticed. This is so true. Five deaths this spring of Mississippi Negro civil rights workers. How much have you heard about them?

The Mississippi Sovereignty Commission has spent thousands of dollars to carry ads in papers outside the South, to send out speakers the nation over. The theme has been states' rights—only incidentally segregation. Nearly half the people of Mississippi have had their tax money used thusly to promote continued denial of their own rights. And the tragedy is so many Americans have fallen for the line. Believe me, when the Southerner says we want states' rights, he means, "We want the right to keep the Negro in *his place.*"

The Civil Rights Bill[3] is only the beginning. These laws were long overdue. We need laws against murdering your neighbor, though love for your neighbor is a matter of the heart. Now we must work not only for enforcement, but for good human relations which can only spring from the heart.

You, at this point, probably feel like the little boy who wanted a book on penguins. For his birthday, his grandmother sent him an exhaustive study of penguins. He dutifully wrote: Dear Grandma, Thank you for the book on penguins. It tells me more than I wanted to know about penguins.

I hope you don't mind if I send a copy of this to my family and several others who have expressed concerns similar to yours. Not that what I've said has any claim to being right in every respect, but it is an expression of how I feel based on experiences I've had and reading I've done—which is about all any of us can offer, I suppose. Thanks for writing me.

3. The Civil Rights Bill passed by Congress in 1964 required equal access to public accommodations and outlawed discrimination in employment.

June 29, 1964

Dear Dr. Silver,

We should capitalize on all the publicity you're getting—run you for President or something.

We should form a "Friends of Silver" to underwrite a secretary for you, especially since the legislature wants you to spend more time with your students. If the legislature were consistent it would pay you to stay away from classes.

Tougaloo is an exciting place! Thus far I have stayed out of jail, but I always take my toothbrush to church with me—when I am in "improper" company.

However, like you "I like it here," and hope to stay. I'm on my way to becoming a Mississippi citizen—have paid a poll tax.

I hope your publishing company will mail an announcement of your book to the enclosed people. They are expecting it as I told them I was sending their names to you. I think they are all good for a book and for spreading the word to others.

One of my freshmen would like to attend Ole Miss this summer. Any chance? He rather doubts it as he has been in jail. He is a fine person, though, and I wish he could make it. We'll see.

Tougaloo College, MS, 1964–65

September 16, 1964

Sunday passed without my getting a letter written.

We have a good-looking class of about 180 freshmen. Some have had tremendous experiences. One, for example, was in Europe all summer with a special group. One is from Jordan, another from Japan. Two are whites from the North.

Eighty-two were here this summer for a pre-freshman program. I'm told there was a high level of interest. Everyone carried a book around with him. The Harvard students had discussion groups on these books. Harvard seemed to make quite an impact.

I have 13 freshmen to advise all through their four years. Also as head of the History Department I have added duties of a tedious nature. (Being chairman of a department is not really an honor—just a job.) One good thing is that our class load in the History Department is less due to Julia Allen's help this first semester. She is here on a labor of love similar to my first year at Rust. However, she is retired, officially; she formerly was with Berea College in Kentucky. She is on the national board of the YWCA and is a real powerhouse. After she leaves in February, Joe Herzenberg, from Yale, and I will have a heavy load again even as Bob and I did last year. But I'm grateful for a little respite this semester to get my History Club going, my advisee program started, learn the department duties, and hopefully to do a better job teaching.

Dr. Pfauts from Brown University is here to further coordinate our work. So far he is very pleasant and easy to have around.

The Mississippi social climate is unbelievably different from what it was when I left in June—before civil rights laws. Two Negro students ate with three white faculty members (including me) at the Holiday Inn about three miles from here. This was beyond the realm of possibility in early June. Now—no trouble. We were even seated in the center of the dining room where all could get a good view of us. A few places are holding out. Primos, for one. The Rotisserie ("Get your d—— b—— out of here") has become a private club.

Saturday, October 3, 1964

Today I took five from my Mississippi History class to the museum at the Old Capitol building in Jackson. Four of them had parts to play as guides. They had prepared talks to explain what we were seeing. Afterward we stopped at the Holiday Inn for refreshments. Both being able to go to the museum and stopping at the Holiday Inn are achievements which have not always been possible. I noticed that the restroom signs in the building were changed. They now say "Men" and "Women" without any qualifying adjective. And the drinking fountains no longer say "For White Only" as they did the last time I was there.

Last Sunday Marvin Palmore, a fine-looking student, and I went to Galloway Church. There were not the usual "ushers"—guards—out in front. We got up the many steps and were right at the door. I thought we had made it for sure when up ran two young men—perhaps in their thirties—and stood in front of us blocking our entrance. One said, "May we help you?" I felt like saying, "Yes, you may stand aside," but didn't. I did say we would like to attend the service. He said it was against their policy to allow colored inside. They would be happy to take him, pointing to Marvin, to the colored church. I said no, we were together. I told them I was a member of the church but had been away for the summer. It was my understanding that the policy of the church had now changed. "No ma'am, it has not changed." So we went to the [restaurant at the] Sun-N-Sand motel where we were graciously received. It has come to the point where business reflects Christ better than the church.

The first papers I had my students write in class just made no sense at all. At first I was most discouraged then I realized that this was the way we started out last year—which caused Yas to say they were about like my basic junior high papers [in Pasadena]. Actually, in a way they are worse because they are trying to say more complicated things. So the next day I put a topic sentence appropriate for the lesson on the board. Then we worked out the composition in class, complete with the clincher sentence. All done orally. Then I asked them to write it for me over the weekend. Now I'll hope I can make some sense out of them. It is wonderful to feel you have a job to do! To be needed!

Tougaloo College
October 18, 1964

I cringe every time more corruption is revealed in the present administration. But I recall even Eisenhower was plagued with some—and he took quite a while in deciding to remove Sherman Adams. Nevertheless, it is disconcerting to have to choose between two candidates—neither of whom you can wholeheartedly support. (Probably people being what they are, I'm asking too much.)

I still like Ed King's button, "Part of the way with LBJ" [Democratic candidate Lyndon B. Johnson]!

Don't get me wrong. I'm not wavering. It will have to be Johnson as against a man opposed to U.N., Supreme Court decisions, civil rights, atomic test bans, etc. [Republican candidate Barry M. Goldwater]. And isn't it sad to hear all the name-calling just to be cute and get a laugh. This is more a commentary on the American people than on the candidates. It seems to be necessary, to get elected, to appeal to our worst elements. Maybe I'm in a pessimistic mood today.

Last Sunday evening we went to a new swanky motel. We were greeted with open arms—after all, 6 dinners at $2-$3 each was not to be welcomed lightly. But then Miss [Zenobia] Coleman's face became distinct. We were left standing at the entrance of the dining room for about 20 minutes. The ones in charge were busily using the phones and running here and there. Finally we were told very softly that it was against their policy to serve colored. We left and went to the Sun-N-Sand. Joe Herzenberg, my colleague in the history department, a fine young chap from Yale, wrote Burke Marshall of the Justice Department in Washington. Dorian Bowman, the tutor—lawyer—from Columbia, is writing the home office of Admiral Benbow.

Next week I expect to be in New Orleans so if you don't hear from me it will be because I'm too rushed. Ruby Berkley of Red Banks, Mississippi, near Holly Springs will go with me. You may remember I knew her in Augusta where she was the deaconess in charge of Bethlehem Center. She is now retired and [living with her two sisters in their family home]. Have much to do getting classes ready to leave with others. Am quite pleased with the classes this year. I think last summer's institute in Pittsburgh was a great help to me. Also, the students are a bit better prepared, perhaps. This is a question we argue pro and con.

Tougaloo College
January 1, 1965

This letter should have been timed to emphasize the importance of asking your Representative to delay the seating of the Mississippi Congressmen pending an investigation. The never-used section of the 14th Amendment stating that states which deny adult citizens the franchise shall have their representation cut proportionately is the basis of this action. If there is still need for nudging your

Congressman when this letter is received, I know most of you will do so—if you haven't already.

Even our chaplain, Ed King (white), was unable to vote in November. Though no reason was given—one either passes or fails—the only possible excuse was that he failed to satisfy the examiner on the literacy test—reading and explaining a portion of the Mississippi constitution. Since Ed is a graduate of Millsaps, one of the best colleges in Mississippi, and has his divinity degree from Boston University, one can only ask who is the illiterate, the applicant or the examiner? Obvious to those in the know, Ed and his wife Jeannette, both native Mississippians, have fallen into disfavor because of their participation in the civil rights movement. A carpetbagger such as I or a Negro in the movement is more easily forgiven than a native white who is nothing short of a traitor to his people and their way of life.

Last year after the ratifying of the 24th Amendment, Mississippi demanded, as a requisite for voting in the federal primary, a receipt from the county clerk—the same one who usually collects the poll tax—saying *the poll tax had not been paid*! My county—Madison—even charged a dollar for the receipt saying the poll tax had not been paid. But before the November election, the federal court ruled out the requirement of a *receipt* for not having a *receipt.*

But of course the real deterrent to voting in Mississippi is the economic threat and physical harassment—punctuated at times with the burning of a church or a death to emphasize the danger all Negroes incur when they insist on this basic federal right.

This year I haven't had so many students absent by reason of their being in jail. In fact none since Douglas MacArthur Cotton was jailed a few days before the November election for distributing Johnson-Humphrey[1] leaflets in Jackson. It takes a contortionist to be a politician in Mississippi these days. He must be a local Democrat and a national Republican. The one good thing that evolved from the November election in Mississippi was the political split. We actually elected one Republican to Congress. Though Mississippi Republicans are no better than Mississippi Democrats, if we can get a two-party system, each party hopefully will soon be bidding for every possible vote—even the Negro's.

Since the passage of the Civil Rights Act, we have been able to eat out occasionally. In Jackson we usually have success. We try not to "favor" any one

1. Hubert H. Humphrey was the Democratic vice presidential candidate.

place with a disproportionate amount of our patronage as we don't want any restaurant to get the name of being a "you know what kind" of a place.

Our History Club I hope will fill a social need as well as an academic need. I decided to use the money several of you sent me for a History Club banquet—a first time to eat at a formerly segregated place for most of the members. After making arrangements at the Caravan where we previously had been served in small groups, our reservations were suddenly canceled. "We appreciate your business but we don't want it." I then made reservations over the phone at the Holiday Inn. The manager did not ask the composition of the party and I didn't volunteer it. The day of the affair I weakened and decided I better learn the score before all 27 of us converged on the Inn as the parents of some of the students might have jobs that would be in jeopardy if their off-spring were involved in a controversy over restaurant service. Thus I took one of the students with me in the afternoon to decorate, thinking his very presence would be an indication of what was to come.

The two waitresses on duty received us well, even finding extra candles for us. For placecards we had historical names. Each student was to be given a slip with a description of one of the names. He was, of course, to find his place by matching his slip with the place-name. As I was putting the names out I said to the waitress standing by, "Aren't we having a distinguished group tonight?—Here's Socrates, Plato, Cicero." She followed me around and when I put down "Martin L. King" she left, returning soon with the other waitress. They both looked at the card—"Martin L. King." Then one asked, "Is 'Martin L. King' 'Martin LUTHER King'?" I assured her it was. "THE Martin Luther King?" "Yes," I answered gleefully, "and Socrates is THE Socrates; Hannibal is THE Hannibal." "Really," she asked with obvious concern now, "Is MARTIN LUTHER KING coming HERE, TONIGHT?"

Then it dawned on me that of all the names, the only one that meant anything to either of them was that of Martin L. King. I said, "I'm sorry. I didn't mean to lead you on. All these are historical names—most of them are dead and gone, but a few such as Martin Luther King are still making history."

The banquet was a success. Only a few slightly sour notes such as when the manager became aware of who we were. He insisted I had told him I was entertaining some of my women friends with a Christmas party—which I suppose would be the natural assumption when a woman makes reservations for 25 persons in socially conscious Jackson.

In November Miss Altamese Rutledge, president of the History Club, went with Joe Herzenberg (white), history instructor, and me to the Southern

Historical Association meeting at Little Rock. A lengthy but important faculty meeting delayed our start so that it was 12:30 midnight when we stopped at the Travel Inn in Indianola (birthplace of the White Citizens Council). Though we did not parade Miss Rutledge before the two men on duty at that hour, we thought they recognized her in the car. But the next morning all faces froze when we entered the restaurant and we were quickly ushered out by the owner who was aghast that we had stayed there overnight. After talking with him about ten minutes we continued to the Holiday Inn in Greenville, Hodding Carter's[2] town, usually considered as enlightened as any area in Mississippi. Holiday Inn has served us in several states including Mississippi at Jackson so we anticipated no trouble. But a young woman approached us at our table and with an ingratiating smile announced, "We are not serving you." When Joe asked to see the manager she said he was out and she was the acting manager. Joe said, "You are aware that you are violating the Civil Rights Act of 1964?" She turned on her heel and left us.

In my rush the evening before I hadn't eaten dinner and about then was feeling a bit starved. I solved that problem by drinking the cream and eating the peach jam on the table. As we left I offered to pay for what I had devoured but was told, "That won't be necessary."

From there we went to the Downtowner—another fine new structure. As we walked in, the hostess stopped statue-like with her coffee pot held at arm's length in front of her. By the time she recovered we had seated ourselves. She conferred with the manager and then coming to us said, "We will serve HER," indicating Miss Rutledge, "but we will not serve YOU," indicating Joe and me. Joe went to the desk and asked the manager for an explanation. He was told it was against their policy to serve mixed groups. We discussed our problem among ourselves and decided to separate—to THREE different tables. I was served first. When I was about half finished with my breakfast, Joe was served. When I was entirely finished, Miss Rutledge was served. Eventually after a few more expressions from personnel indicating lack of sympathy for us, we were on our way to Little Rock. Oddly enough, through all this the other patrons of the restaurant showed little if any concern for our presence.

Returning three days later we stopped at Vicksburg for food at 9:00 p.m. The owner was obviously upset over his predicament. For 25 minutes (by Joe's

2. Hodding Carter, Jr., editor and publisher of Greenville's *Delta Democrat-Times* beginning in 1938, had received a Pulitzer Prize in 1945 for his editorials against racial segregation in the South.

watch) we attempted to persuade him to serve us. He asked that we give him just a little more time. I said, "Time? *We* Mississippians have had 100 years! How much more time do you want? A week? Two weeks?" Of course he wasn't thinking in terms of weeks but eventually he said, "O.K. Give me just two more weeks." I said, "If we come back it would be on a Sunday when you'd have many other customers. To make the special trip worth our while we'd bring a larger group." Joe interrupted to add, "Yes, we have 500 students from which to draw."

At one point the owner said, "Any minute someone may come in who's had too much to drink and I can't be responsible for what he'd do." I said, "Now look, wouldn't it make better sense for you to refuse service to the drinking person? Here we are tee-totallers: Miss Rutledge, a fine young Christian woman; Mr. Herzenberg, a dignified (he's very young and looks younger) college professor; and I'm just a sweet little grandmother. Surely you'd do better to serve us than someone who has had too many drinks!" Several times we reminded him that if he had served us when we first arrived we'd be gone by then. Eventually he said, "If I give you coffee, will you leave?" We agreed and to Miss Rutledge who didn't want coffee he brought milk. While we were drinking he said, "You ought to be a diplomat. I'd like to know your name." He even told us his name, which indicates what a fine person he is, as usually we are asked our names but no one will give us his. When I tried to pay he said, "No, this is on the house." As we left, Joe said to the three other customers who had watched the whole proceeding, "Thanks for not walking out."

These little adventures may sound insignificant but they do hold some importance. If no one claims these rights specifically confirmed under the Civil Rights Act, the restaurants will soon forget we have them. This already is the case in small towns as our experience on the Little Rock trip pointed up. An administrator at Ole Miss was amazed to learn that we are served in Jackson[3] restaurants. This indicated to me a need for some of us to move out weekends into outlying areas to eat.

Students do not have money for meals out—in fact, faculty members with family responsibilities don't either. Thus I may channel more of the money sent me by generous friends to the payment of dinners for those who can make our little Sunday dinners integrated.

One great difference now over last school year is that the law is on our side instead of against us. Whenever we are refused service the FBI comes out

3. The University of Mississippi is in Oxford, a *small* town.

and takes statements from us. The [Admiral] Benbow Inn, the first place to refuse us in Jackson, is now open. I tried to congratulate the FBI men on their success, but they disclaimed any credit though they had conferred with the local management.[4]

I'm pleased that so many of you have subscribed to Hazel Brannon Smith's paper, *The Northside Reporter*. Her editorials not only make YOU aware of the real concern some white Mississippians have for justice, but also help HER to keep these weekly papers rolling off the press. Earlier in the school year her Jackson office was bombed. The opposition continually tries to "get her" one way or another.

For you who are interested in keeping abreast of the activities in the entire South, the *Southern Patriot* edited by Anne and Carl Braden is excellent. I am a board member of the Southern Conference Educational Fund which sponsors this monthly paper—not as a house organ but as an interpretive news service covering racial problems and advances in the South. SCEF pioneered in civil rights in the South long before it was the popular issue it has become today. As a result the organization has been the target of many smear campaigns. But it continues to do an outstanding work, quietly without fanfare.

January 3, 1965

Mr. W. Bryant Ridgway
President of the Official Board
Galloway Methodist Church
Jackson, Mississippi

Dear Mr. Ridgway:

Several days ago I invited two friends to go to Galloway with me today. This morning I learned that three other friends, one of whom is Negro, wanted to attend church in Jackson since we have no service on campus during vacation.

Remembering how another Negro friend, whom I invited to church last September when I first returned after the summer, was refused admittance at

4. Before the three civil rights workers were murdered in June 1964, the FBI was as dangerous to us as the KKK. After that event, President Johnson sent 51 new FBI men to Mississippi. Some of us soon believed we could trust them.

Galloway, I suggested that we go today to an Episcopalian church where we could be assured a welcome.

This policy of selectivity among our worshippers is not only inconvenient, but—more important—it is a matter of Christian concern to many of our members. This leads me to ask: Who has the power to make such a policy binding on every member of our church?

I have talked with several members who seem as unhappy as I in this matter. One Official Board member tells me the board voted unanimously two years ago to exclude persons of color. Another board member says he is physically and mentally ill over the church's policy of exclusion. Was he absent when the board made the unanimous decision? Or has the "closed society" permeated our Official Board to the extent that a member dare not vote his conscience? Was the board's action taken on a show of hands or a secret ballot?

Finally, in view of the great amount of thought that has been given this question throughout our Southland during the past few years, might we do well to reconsider Galloway's policy?

Sunday, January 17, 1965

We just returned from a day's trip—an attempt to show Julia Allen a bit of the Delta before she leaves. Julia is the graduate of Holyoke who has been dean of women at Berea College in Kentucky (mountain white school).

We saw the LeRoy Percy State Park—a good place to go if you are white—the Mississippi River and levee.

We toured the grounds of the Mississippi Valley [State] College whose band went to the Rose Parade [in Pasadena, last New Year's Day]. Beautiful new buildings and grounds.

We ate in one of the places that formerly turned us down—the Holiday Inn at Greenville. Had a snack in Jackson where we had not been allowed to have the banquet. Had breakfast in Yazoo [City]. The Negro faculty member of the party was not as dark as usual. She was recognized by the owners or managers but maybe they thought others wouldn't notice. We had conversations about two restrooms which were for "White Only."

When Dr. Pfauts of Brown said we needed a foundation grant to pay our expenses at restaurants to secure our rights, I thought that was a nice facetious remark—but I received a letter yesterday from Helen Barnes (Delta Kappa

Gamma)[5] with $50 in response to that letter saying "if you have the guts to go I guess I can send the wherewithal." Last week I received $25 from a Negro member of DKG [Wathea Jones]. She had mimeographed 200 copies of my May letter. Another $25 from Jane Hood.

Sunday evening 8:30, February 21, 1965

Another weekend gone without a letter and unprepared for school. Friday and Saturday I spent several hours each at the civil rights hearings. I do hope some of you were able to get part of them on TV. That commission did a tremendous job. First it had testimony from those who had been beaten, bombed, burned out, etc. for trying to vote. All our iniquities were laid out for us and the world to see. Then the Commission tried pulling out the little points of improvement and asking questions of the community leaders, sheriffs, lawyers, mayors, etc. "Does this indicate the way improvement can be made? Governor Johnson has said, 'Tell the nation to get off our backs and at our sides.' If we get at your sides what will it be for?"

Wish I had never joined Galloway Methodist. I can't bring myself not to go if the pastor appreciates my being there, and he does seem to. He says something each Sunday on the race problem now. I know he sweats over how to bring it in, but I'm afraid it is just enough to lose those who oppose him and not enough to bring people of any real conviction to his side. This morning I asked the two policemen if the church had requested their services. They were noncommittal saying something about being sent. Then I asked one of the "bouncing committee." He said no but he was mighty glad they were there. "Why so?" I asked. "Well, I can remember not too many Sundays ago when we had demonstrations right there on these steps." I said, "Are demonstrations so bad? And are you sure they were demonstrations rather than honest desires to attend church?"

Tonight we had an art show of the works of Clinton King. And we had a large attendance. For the first time the local newspaper carried an announcement of an event at Tougaloo. Some of our new-found white friends made the announcement possible.

5. DKG is a national honorary society for teachers. The Beta Eta chapter in the Los Angeles area, to which I belonged, pioneered the first racially integrated chapter in California. Its members never forgot me when I started teaching in the South.

Also today we have had two open houses—one at the dean's home and one at Judson-Cross where the men live. I went to the Sunday School class this morning since Dr. [Robert] Bergmark, Millsaps professor, is giving this special course using as a text Georgia Harkness's book, *Understanding Our Christian Faith.*

Last evening the faculty had a buffet supper at the president's house. Of course we don't have a president living there. But it was a very nice evening. Good supper and everyone, practically, came, all in good spirits. The artist and his wife were there. Also Hazel Brannon Smith and her husband. And a Mr. Gloster from Hampton Institute. I pressed him so hard about why he was here that he finally had to break down and admit he was looking the place over as a potential candidate for the office of president. It was gratifying to know we have not been utterly forgotten. We really need a president.

Tougaloo College
April 24, 1965

Where but in Mississippi could we have from one to five police cars protecting us for 60 miles?

Four students, two of them mine and two high school seniors, all intending to go to Ole Miss next fall, and I started for Oxford at the start of spring vacation. We stopped at Grenada for dinner. At first we were absolutely ignored except for the usual curious stares. Then after about 15 minutes the manager who had been sent for came in beaming a big welcome. He gave us menus and said, "It won't be long now." After dinner I asked for two rooms. "We're out of rooms," was the too-ready answer. I asked to see the manager again. He came and assured me of his deep regret that they were "pretty well" out of rooms. I asked what "pretty well" out meant. Would he mind just looking at the register to see if he could find two rooms. We looked at the record together. All 67 rooms were neatly filled—though there were few cars outside.

We drove to the only other decent-looking place we had seen in town. This time I drove in, parked, and went alone to the office. The clerk was very friendly. I paid the bill with a check, got the keys, and drove back to our rooms. As we were getting the suitcases out, the clerk called asking me to come to the office. I asked the students to go with me this time. The clerk handed me the check and demanded the keys saying I should have told him I had colored. I should have parked my car where he could see it. I told him I wasn't in the habit of describing my party and that he evidently wasn't in the habit of insisting on persons parking in any certain place or he would have done so this time as a matter of routine. I asked for the manager. Whereas the clerk was rude, acting the part of a professional hater, the manager was very civil. In the course of the conversation—the exact order of which I cannot now recall—I said, "I'll bet your rooms are often occupied by drunks; I'll even bet you have to clean up vomit after some of them. But here you have a party of as fine young people as you could ask for under any color." He said, "I'm sure that is true. But I have to depend on Mississippi for business and the motel would be ruined if it accepted your group."

I reminded him that much of his business was out of state, that the whole United States government was behind him. He could say "I have to do this because of the Civil Rights Act of '64." I told him other motels in the state had opened up—this he couldn't believe. "Perhaps," I continued, "one of the reasons we Mississippians are always at the bottom of the states in per capita income is that we refuse to do business with almost half the state." He said, "I'm sure it is." "Why should you lose business from these people? No automobile dealer would return a check because of a person's color. Department stores don't turn down business" (not entirely true, as they do if it involves trying on a dress).

When he said this was all very hard on him, I said I was sure it was. "You can't even look me in the eye." He said he was powerless. He was only the manager. The owner was in Memphis. I suggested he call the owner—even offered to pay for the call. He didn't know where the owner was staying—"there are so many motels in Memphis." "Yes," I said, "and I have stayed at several of them with my friends. Memphis is not living in the past. It is moving ahead with the times taking its business where it finds it."

I told him we were not demonstrating or testing; we really were in need of a room. However, I would not hesitate to report a refusal of accommodations. He might find it easier just to let us have the rooms. He said, "You mean I might be served with an injunction?"

As the students and I returned to the car I noticed a car filled with young men—some mere boys—waiting and watching us.[6] A police car drove up. I walked over to it and said, "With so much attention focused on us, I feel the

6. I later learned through the Freedom of Information office of the U.S. Justice Department that they described the gathering as "white trash, troublemakers, and known bootleggers, some of whom had done time in the state penitentiary."

need for police protection." The clerk called out, "You had the courage to come here so I reckon you can find the courage to go on." But the policeman said, "I agree you need protection. I wish though you had come to us before you got yourself in this mess." I said it would never occur to me to seek out a policeman before getting a room. He said it should as I certainly knew I was in a segregated state. "Not exactly. I'm from Jackson and the motels there are open to all." He called headquarters saying a "white woman with four Nigras" wanted protection. The city prosecutor came out. I asked his name.[7] "What difference does it make?" "None," I answered. "My name is Campbell and I'm really glad you came." We talked a bit about the route. He went to his car, then sauntered back to me and said, "Ma'am, I don't mind your knowing my name. It's Dye."[8]

It was a dark, rainy night. The [new] interstate highway took us through miles of swampland with no buildings and not a soul in sight. It would have been the easiest thing in the world for a car of hoodlums to push us off the side of the road into the swamps. And who would believe that we hadn't just skidded into our watery grave? But we were not alone. From two to five police cars followed us the entire 60 miles to Oxford. At an ingress a new highway patrol car would await us. As we passed it would swing into line behind us, and I suppose a car at the end would drop out. Leaving the interstate for Oxford we found the last few miles of road torn up. It was still raining. I slowed down to maneuver the detours. None of the cars behind me were close enough to be endangered by my reduced speed.

Entering Oxford, we couldn't shake our protectors. We wanted to get in touch with our two Ole Miss Negro students but didn't want to lead all those police cars to their door. Finally we stopped at a gas station to phone. All five police cars drew up behind us. I walked back to the first and said, "Where but in Mississippi could one have such protection as this?" "Protection?" the patrolman growled. "I don't know anything about that, but I do know you are the worst driver I've ever seen. Don't you know you're not to slow down to less than 30 miles on a highway?" I said, "It was difficult for me to know where I was to go. It was because I didn't know these roads that we tried to get motel rooms at Grenada." Not to be sidetracked he continued, "You had a whole string of cars behind you that you were holding up." I looked at all five lined up and said, "It seems that a number of them were police cars." Asking for my

7. The FBI had asked us to get names whenever possible.
8. Brad Dye, later Lieutenant Governor of Mississippi.

driver's license, he seemed surprised to find I was actually able to get a Mississippi license. He said, "I'm going to follow you and if you don't drive better, I'm giving you a ticket." (While in Oxford a student drove thereafter.) The police remained with us for about 30–45 minutes. Finally I called a minister acquaintance[9] who lives in Oxford. He called the university officials to alert them to our difficulty, thinking it better for them to learn of it from us than from the press or the police. Then he came down. Just before he arrived, the police left, but as soon as we started toward the campus two police cars appeared again behind us. Our friend stopped and walked back to speak to the police. They said they weren't following us; they were merely cruising the area. But they left us then, though within a block two campus security cars picked up our trail. We never lost our campus security cars that night nor the next morning. They followed us to the Lyceum Building where we were to keep an appointment with the dean. Just as we were stopping they swung around in front of us. The officers jumped out and ran into the building ahead of us—cop and robber fashion. We walked in sedately and as we reached the door of the dean's office, they were just coming out. The university officials were very nice to us. We had a most satisfactory interview concerning the students' plans for next year.

We tried to eat at the school cafeteria but were met by two security officers and the accountant, who refused us entrance saying it was against the policy of the Board of Trustees to serve outsiders. The Ole Miss student, now with us, could eat but no others. I asked if this policy were directed only at Negro outsiders, adding that a friend and I had recently eaten there without being questioned.

With the police still following, we drove to the new Downtowner Motel. We were accepted for lunch and couldn't resist the temptation to stay overnight. It was still raining and we had no heart for starting home with police following us. (Considering that a group of our [Tougaloo] students had their car practically wrecked at Ole Miss two days ago by rioting students—you have by now read of it—we may well consider ourselves fortunate to have had the police "protection.")

The next morning we drove home by way of the Natchez Trace—a trail with a bloody history in pioneer days but on that Sunday morning it was quiet and highly scenic. As we neared Canton, our county seat, we decided to stop at Wardell's restaurant. We were ignored. I asked if we might have two tables

9. Rev. Duncan Gray, Jr., later an Episcopal bishop.

put together. "We are not serving you—AT ALL," the man shouted. "Why?" "It's against our policy."

"You realize you are violating the Civil Rights Act of 1964?" I asked. "I know it is the law of the land and this is the land of the law," he raved, "but I continue with the policy I've followed for 35 years." I asked his name. "My name is Wardell Thomas and I want you to get it straight. I'm going to give it to you in writing." He pawed through a stack of papers and came up with a letterhead.

Later I learned that COFO and SNCC had tested all the restaurants in Canton (a dangerous area) the day before. Mr. Thomas had threatened to shoot the next colored person who came in his restaurant—and we entered as fools do where angels know enough to fear.

Rumor had it that Galloway Methodist would be open by Easter. It was not. But at least the two police and the 15–20 men on guard in front of the church did not arrest us. The two students and I had an interesting conversation with three different men on the steps and I have since sent letters to several key men in the church as well as talked with one on the phone. It is usually agreed that opening is only a matter of time. I wish the church role could be one of leadership rather than "followership." Mississippians are very conscious just now of the state's image. (Economic groups such as the Chambers of Commerce are making significant moves ahead, largely for this reason.) I have thought of suggesting to you a postcard shower using this statement which I found in the Chollas View (San Diego) bulletin: *Segregated worship services suggest that too much of our religion is only skin deep.* If you think well of the idea you might address your postcard to Galloway Methodist Church, Jackson, Miss.[10]

Thanks to all of you who have sent money to me for a "Dining Out Fund" and other miscellaneous items. I never expected such a response as I know each of you receiving my letters give generously in your own area to a multiplicity of causes. However, there is something to be said for "cross-fertilization" in reform movements.

The following projects were done with your help—in your name:

Jan. 17	Trip to Greenville, 5 faculty members, 2 meals out—one at the Holiday Inn which had previously refused us	15.00

10. The doors were opened to black worshippers January 10, 1966, by Official Board vote of 65–40.

Jan. 20	Shorts, shirts, p.j.'s, etc. for a student going on Xchange to a Northern school for the semester	35.00
Jan. 22	Morrison's cafeteria—3 faculty members	6.00
Jan. 24	Refreshments for History Club reception honoring an instructor from Berea	10.00
Jan. 25	Students and faculty at Holiday Inn on Highway 80—4 of us	10.00
Jan. 27	Morrison's—faculty and student—3 persons	6.00
Jan. 27	*Northside Reporter* to send sample copies to my friends	10.00
Jan. 29	SCEF contribution to send sample copies of *Southern Patriot*	25.00
Jan. 29	To student who typed 250 names to send *Reporter* and *Patriot*	6.00
Feb. 4	Morrison's—3 faculty members	4.50
Feb. 7	Piney Woods School for dinner after having been turned away from the Revolving [Tables] Restaurant at Mendenhall—7 faculty and students	10.00
Feb. 13	Wardell Restaurant in Canton—accepted to our surprise but later events proved our Negro member too light for a true test	7.50
Feb. 16	Admiral Benbow (where we were once turned away)—4 faculty members	8.00
Feb. 20	Morrison's after Civil Rights Commission hearings—one of our party had never eaten in a "white" place—he had given testimony at the hearing on bombing of his store—4 of us	6.50
Feb. 21	9 of us after taking in some of the Pilgrimage—History Club members	18.00
Feb. 27	3 students and myself at Morrison's	5.50
Mar. 21	Faculty group at Morrison's (we were turned away at Primos)	15.00
Mar. 24	Contribution to students going to Selma-to-Montgomery March	15.00

Mar. 12	Caravan Restaurant—a "consolation lunch" after being turned away from the Governor's Mansion where we had an appointment—the Mansion is a point on the Pilgrimage Tour	6.00
Apr. 2	Ole Miss trip—as described in letter	49.00
	Coming up—History banquet	45.00
	with awards for scholarship and essay contest	45.00

You will conclude we have been living high on your bounty—but few have had more than one meal off you. Several, including our new Tougaloo College president, had their first experience in a "white" restaurant with us. And so again, our thanks to you for helping us to secure—make fast—these newly confirmed rights which have for so long been forgotten.

It would sound from my letters as though I spend all my time and thoughts on these extra activities. Not so. Most of my hours and energy are used in teaching. I am a firm believer in the necessity of upgrading the educational program if civil rights are to be effective.

Thanks to those of you who have subscribed to the *Northside Reporter.* Remember, it is the editorial page that is of value. With it and the *Southern Patriot* you will keep well informed of the important happenings and interpretations by the liberal Southern element. (*I* do not attempt anything beyond my own personal involvements.)

[The next important events for me were a six-week tour with a peace organization, Promoting Enduring Peace, of Russia and Eastern European countries, followed by three weeks in Western Europe.

[Though I wrote only postcards, Hazel Brannon Smith published an extensive account of my new experiences and insights.

[In September of 1965, I enrolled at Ole Miss. After four wonderful years of study, I had earned my Ph.D. in history. I then returned to Rust, my first love, and remained until I retired.]

Epilogue

During a difficult period at one of the Southern black colleges at which I taught, a visitor asked, "What can be expected of these students?" To my surprise, a top administrator answered, "Very little."

What could one expect from students whose early education had been minimal because of state laws, and who still had poor food and housing, a shortage of teachers, and a maximum of racial handicaps? Looking at those students today, one learns that many have achieved a great deal for themselves and contributed significantly to society.

Just from my tenures have come elected officials, lawyers, judges, teachers, principals, college presidents, ministers, doctors, nurses, engineers and researchers. In business, some are successful enough to send sizeable contributions to their alma maters. There are artists and musicians—even the founder/director of the famous Harlem Boys Choir. And undergirding all are homes and businesses of integrity.

The stories of these colleges are success stories. All three were severely tested at one or more times when survival itself was in question.

The professors and administrators, those who staffed the kitchens and sanitation facilities, and citizens who gave sacrificially to the colleges can feel that their resources and confidence were well invested in the young people who passed through—more likely, worked their way through—Rust, Claflin, and Tougaloo colleges.

They all deserve a big hand and our continued support.

Index